The Big Business Reader

Other Books by Mark Green

With Justice for Some (1971, edited with Bruce Wasserstein)

The Closed Enterprise System (1972, with Beverly C. Moore, Jr. and Bruce Wasserstein)

The Monopoly Makers (1973, editor)

Corporate Power in America (1973, edited with Ralph Nader)

The Other Government: The Unseen Power of Washington Lawyers (1975)

Verdicts on Lawyers (1976, edited with Ralph Nader)

Taming the Giant Corporation (1976, with Ralph Nader and Joel Seligman)

Who Runs Congress? (3rd edition, 1980)

The Big Business Reader

edited by Mark Green and
Robert Massie Jr.

The Pilgrim Press
New York

Copyright © 1980 The Pilgrim Press
All rights reserved

No part of this publication may be reproduced, stored in a retrieval system, or transmitted in any form or by any means, electronic, mechanical, photocopying, recording, or otherwise (brief quotations used in magazines or newspaper reviews excepted), without the prior permission of the publisher.

The Pilgrim Press, 132 W. 31st Street, New York, New York 10001

Acknowledgments

Many individuals contributed to the assembly and editing of this book and we are grateful to them all. Michael Jacobson, Alice Tepper Marlin, David Salomon, Jean Highland and Victor Kamber provided valuable advice from the beginning. Mary Ellen Iskenderian and Sheila Teimourian assisted with the research. The staffs of Public Citizen's Congress Watch and Big Business Day-1980 offered their help at important moments.

To the authors of the articles contained in this volume, who unanimously donated their works so that Americans might learn more about corporate power and irresponsibility, and to the Rev. David Burgess, who made this book possible, we express a very special thanks.

Mark Green
Robert Massie, Jr.

"Food Monopoly: Who's Who in the Thanksgiving Business," by Jim Hightower. © *The Texas Observer*, November 17, 1978. Reprinted by permission.

"The Case Against the Oil Companies" by Robert Sherrill, October 14, 1979 Magazine © 1979 by *The New York Times Company*. Reprinted by permission.

"How Moral Men Make Immoral Decisions," by J. Patrick Wright. © 1979 by J. Patrick Wright. Reprinted from *On A Clear Day You Can See General Motors—John Z. De Lorean's Look Inside The Automobile Giant* with permission of Wright Enterprises.

"The Southern Textile War," by Ed McConville, © 1976 *The Nation Magazine*, Nation Associates, Inc. Reprinted by permission.

"The Devastating Impact of Plant Relocations," by Don Stillman © 1978 *Working Papers For A New Society*. Reprinted by permission.

"From Brass Knuckles to Briefcases: The Modern Art of Union Busting." Testimony by Robert A. Georgine, President of Building and Construction Trade Department, AFL-CIO, before the subcommittee on Labor-Management Relations of the House Committee on Education and Labor, October 17, 1979.

"Democratizing the Workplace: A Case Study," © 1978 by Daniel Zwerdling. Reprinted by permission. © 1980 Harper & Row.

"Nutrition and the Politics of Food," by Michael Jacobson. © the author. Used by permission.

"The Drugging Industry," by Amanda Spake. Reprinted by permission from *The Progressive*, 408 West Gorham Street, Madison, Wisconsin 53703. © 1976, The Progressive, Inc.

"Manslaughter in a Coal Mine," by Harry M. Caudill. © 1977 *The Nation Magazine*, Nation Associates, Inc. Reprinted by permission.

"The Asbestos 'Pentagon Papers'," by Samuel S. Epstein, M.D. Reprinted from *The Politics of Cancer*, ©, 1978 by S. S. Epstein, M.D. by permission of Sierra Club Books.

"And Filthy Flows the Calumet," by Edward Greer. Reprinted by permission from *The Progressive*, 408 West Gorham Street, Madison, Wisconsin 53703. © 1976, The Progressive, Inc.

"Love Canal and the Poisoning of America," by Michael H. Brown. © 1979 by the author. All rights reserved. Used by permission.

"The Corporation and the Community," by Mark Green. © 1971 Corporate Power in America.

"Hucksters in the Classroom: A Review of Industry Propaganda in Schools," by Sheila Harty. © Public Citizen.

"Corporations and State Taxes: The Big Ones Get Away," by James Rosapepe. Reprinted with permission from *The Washington Monthly*, January 1975. © 1975 by The Washington Monthly Co., 1611 Connecticut Ave., N.W., Washington, DC 20009.

"Redline Fever: How the People are Beating the Banks," by Jack Newfield. Reprinted by permission of The Village Voice. © The Village Voice, Inc., 1978.

"Business Lobbying: Threat to the Consumer Interest." © 1979 by Consumers Union of United States, Inc., Mt. Vernon, N.Y. 10550. Reprinted by permission from *Consumer Reports*, September, 1978.

"Labor Law Reform and its Enemies," by Ferguson & Rogers. © 1979 *The Nation Magazine*, Nation Associates, Inc. Reprinted by permission.

"Regulation that Works," by Steven Kelman. Reprinted by permission of *The New Republic*, © 1978 The New Republic, Inc.

"Free Speech Within the Corporation," from *Freedom Inside the Organization*. © 1977 by David W. Ewing. Reprinted by permisison of E. P. Dutton.

"The Corporate Climber Has to Find His Heart" by Michael Maccoby, from *The Gamesman*, Simon & Schuster, © Michael Maccoby, 1977. Reprinted by permission.

"Another Day, Another $3,000: Executive Salaries in America," by Paul Blumberg. © 1978 *Dissent*. Reprinted by permission.

"Nuclear Power," by Ralph Nader. Reprinted with permission from *Mechanical Engineering*. © 1976 American Society of Mechanical Engineers.

"The Promise and Perils of Petrochemicals," by Barry Commoner, September 25, 1977 Magazine © 1979 by *The New York Times Company*. Reprinted by permission.

"Who Owns the Sun?" by Richard Munson. Reprinted by permission from *The Progressive*, 408 West Gorham Street, Madison, Wisconsin 53703. © 1979, The Progressive, Inc.

"A Democratic Technology," by Martin Carnoy & Derek Shearer. From *Economic Democracy: The Challenge of the 1980's*, by Martin Cornoy and Derek Shearer. © 1980 by M. E. Sharpe, Inc., White Plains, NY. Reprinted by permission of the publisher.

"The Global Shopping Center," from *Global Reach* by Richard Barnet & Ronald Muller. © 1974, by Richard L. Barnet and Ronald E. Muller. Reprinted by permission of Simon & Schuster, a division of Gulf & Western Corporation.

"How American Banks Keep the Chilean Junta Going," by Isabel Letelier and Michael Moffitt. © *Business & Society Review*. 870 7th Ave. NYC 10019. Reprinted by permission.

"U.S. Investment in South Africa: An Overview," by George Riley. Reprinted with permission of *The Multinational Monitor* © 1979.

"Babies, Bottles, and Breast Milk: The Nestles Syndrome," by Leah Margulies. © *Business & Society Review*. 870 7th Ave. NYC 10019. Reprinted by permission.

"The Dumping of Hazardous Products on Foreign Markets," by *Mother Jones*. Reprinted with permission from *Mother Jones Magazine* © 1979.

"The Myth of Shareholder Democracy," by Ralph Nader, and Joel Seligman. From *Taming the Giant Corporation*, © 1976, Norton.

"The Interlock of Corporate Power," by Markley Roberts. © The *Federationist*. Reprinted by permission of *The AFL-CIO American Federationalist*, official monthly magazine of the AFL-CIO.

"Prying Open the Clam: On Proxies and Disclosure," © Alice Tepper Marlin and Susan Young. © 1980 Council On Economic Priorities. Used by permission. All rights reserved.

"The Uses of an Economic System—and of Economics," by John Kenneth Galbraith. From *Economics and the Public Purpose*, by John Kenneth Galbraith. Copyright © 1973 by John Kenneth Galbraith. Reprinted by permission of Houghton Mifflin Company and the author.

"What's Wrong with Conglomerate Mergers?" by Michael Pertschuk & Kenneth M. Davidson. Reprinted by permission from the *Fordham Law Review*.

"The Road to Monopoly," from *Taming The Giant Corporation*, by Green, Nader, and Seligman. © 1976, Norton.

"Inflationary Capitalism," by Robert L. Heilbroner. © 1979 by the author. Used by permission. Adapted from materials which first appeared in *The New Yorker*.

"Switching to Public Ownership," by Richard Morgan, Tom Riesenberg, and Michael Troutman. From *Taking Charge: A New Look at Public Power* © 1976 by The Environmental Action Foundation. Reprinted by permission. All rights reserved.

"The Case for a Public Energy Company," © Karl Frieden, 1980. Used by permission. All rights reserved.

"Pension Funds and the Economy," © Randy Barber and Jeremy Rifkin, 1980. Used by permission. All rights reserved.

"How to Investigate Your Local Big Business," © Thalia A. Zepatos, 1980. Used by permission. All rights reserved.

"On the Importance of Small Business," by The Committee on Small Business, House of Representatives.

Index of groups in Appendix adapted from *Minding the Corporate Conscience*, Council on Economic Priorities.

Contributors

—Gar Alperovitz and Jeff Faux are Co-Directors of the National Center for Economic Alternatives and founders of COIN (Consumers Opposed to Inflation in the Necessities).
—Randy Barber and Jeremy Rifkin are the Co-directors of the Peoples Business Commission and co-authors of *The North Will Rise Again: Politics and Power in the 1980s.*
—Richard J. Barnet, Senior Fellow at the Institute for Policy Studies, is the author of *Roots of War* and *The Lean Years: Politics in the Age of Scarcity,* to be published Spring 1980.
—Jules Bernstein is a labor lawyer in Washington, D.C.
—Paul Blumberg teaches Sociology at Queens College, CUNY. He is the author of *Industrial Democracy: The Sociology of Participation* and *The Future of Inequality in an Age of Decline,* forthcoming later in 1980.
—Michael H. Brown is a freelance writer interested in the environment whose book, *Laying Waste: Love Canal and the Poisoning of America* is being published by Pantheon in May.
—Martin Carnoy is a Professor of Economics and Education at Stanford University and was formerly a resident economist at the Brookings Institute.
—Harry M. Caudill is an attorney who has worked in Whitesburg, Kentucky, for 28 years. Author of six books, he is currently Professor of Appalachian history at the University of Kentucky.
—Barry Commoner is the Director of the Center for Biology of Natural Systems, and the author of *The Politics of Energy, The Poverty of Power* and *The Closing Circle.*
—The Consumers Union prepared the article "Business Lobbying" that appeared in *Consumer Reports.*
—"The Corporate Crime of the Century" was researched and compiled by the *Mother Jones* investigating team.
—John Z. DeLorean ran General Motors Pontiac Division, then Chevrolet. He quit in 1973. He wrote *On A Clear Day You Can See General Motors* with J. Patrick Wright, a reporter for Business Week.
—Mark Dowie is an investigative reporter who has served as publisher of *Mother Jones* since 1978.

- The Environmental Action Foundation's article was prepared by Richard Morgan, Tom Riesenberg, and Michael Troutman. EAF maintains a Utility Clearinghouse for those interested in public power.
- Samuel S. Epstein, M.D. is Professor of Occupational and Environmental Medicine at the School of Public Health of the University of Illinois, and the author of *The Politics of Cancer*.
- David Ewing is a faculty member of the Harvard Business School, Executive Editor of the Harvard Business Review and author of *Freedom Inside the Organization*.
- Thomas Ferguson and Joel Rogers are members of the political science departments at the Massachusetts Institute of Technology and Princeton University, respectively. Their column, "The Political Economy," appears regularly in *The Nation*.
- Karl Frieden is a staff member of the National Center for Economic Alternatives.
- Dr. John Kenneth Galbraith is Professor Emeritus of Economics at Harvard University. He has authored numerous articles and books including *The Affluent Society* and *The New Industrial State*.
- Robert A. Georgine is the President of the Building and Construction Trades Department of the AFL-CIO and a leading advocate of employees rights, corporate responsibility, and occupational safety and health legislation, for workers.
- Edward Greer is an Associate Professor of Law at Northeastern University in Boston.
- Sheila Harty has taught high school and college, written scripts for children's educational films, and worked as an educational specialist for Ralph Nader's Center for Study of Responsive Law.
- Dr. Robert L. Heilbroner is currently Norman Thomas Professor of Economics at the Graduate Faculty of The New School for Social Research. His two main fields of interest are classical political economy and contemporary trends in capitalism. He has authored numerous articles and books including *The Worldly Philosophers*.
- Jim Hightower is the author of *Eat Your Heart Out* and *Hard Tomatoes, Hard Times*. He recently resigned as editor of the *Texas Observer* to run for a seat on the Texas Railroad Commission.
- Michael Jacobson is Executive Director of the Center for Science in the Public Interest in Washington, D.C. He is the author of *Nutrition Scoreboard*, the co-editor of *Food for People Not for Profit*, and has written extensively on nutrition, politics, and health.
- Victor Kamber is a labor consultant, previously with the Building Trades Department.
- Steven Kelman is the Assistant Professor of Public Policy at the Harvard University Kennedy School of Government. Cur-

rently he is on leave to head the planning office at the FTC Bureau of Consumer Protection. His study of occupational health and safety regulation will be published in Fall 1980.
—Isabel Letelier and Michael Moffitt are fellows of the Institute for Policy Studies, a research and educational organization in Washington.
—Ed McConville covers labor relations in the south for *The Washington Post, The Nation,* and other publications.
—Michael Maccoby is the author of *The Gamesman* and the Director of the Harvard program on Technology, Public Policy and Human Development.
—Leah Margulies has been the Director of the Inter-faith Center on Corporate Responsibility's Infant Formula Program since it was formed in 1975.
—Alice Tepper Marlin is the founder and Executive Director of the Council on Economic Priorities, which has researched and published more than 70 studies and reports on corporate social performance.
—*Mosiac* is a publication of The National Science Foundation.
—Ronald Müller is Professor of Economics and International Finance at American University and author of *Critical Juncture: The Econopolitics of Stagflation* forthcoming in Fall 1980.
—Richard Munson is Coordinator for Solar Lobby and the Center for Renewable Resources. Formerly co-director of the Sun Day Organization, he has authored many articles on solar energy, nuclear energy and materials conservation.
—Ralph Nader, the consumer advocate, has authored numerous books, studies and articles on corporations and their role in society.
—Jack Newfield is a Senior Editor of the Village Voice and co-author of the *Abuse of Power,* ånd the *Populist Manifesto.*
—Michael Pertschuk is the Chairman of the Federal Trade Commission and former Chief Counsel of the Senate Commerce Committee. Kenneth Davidson is an attorney with the Bureau of Competition of the FTC.
—George Riley is the former editor of the *Multinational Monitor* and is currently at Harvard Law School.
—Markley Roberts is an economist at the AFL-CIO and has been a union member for 27 years.
—Mitch Rofsky, an attorney at Public Citizen's Congress Watch, was the original Secretary of the National Consumer Cooperative Bank in late 1979-1980.
—James C. Rosapepe is a partner in the Washington based consulting firm of Rosapepe, Fuchs Associates. A former legislative assistant for Senate Finance Committee member Fred Harris (D-Ok), he has worked on tax policy issues for the Small Business Administration, Multistate Tax Commission, and the Service Employees International.
—Joel Seligman is a Professor of Law at Northeastern School

and the author of *The High Citadel*. He is completing a book on the Securities and Exchange Commission.
—Derek Shearer is a Professor at the UCLA School of Architecture and Urban Planning and a member of the Board of Directors of the National Consumer Cooperative Bank.
—Robert Sherrill is the White House Correspondent for *The Nation*.
—Amanda Spake is a writer interested in environmental, consumer, and women's issues. She has served on the Editorial Board of *Mother Jones* since 1977.
—Joe Sims was the deputy assistant attorney general in charge of antitrust from 1977-1979. He is now in private practice in Washington, D.C., where he regularly writes for *Legal Times*.
—Don Stillman is Editor of *Solidarity*, the magazine of the United Auto Workers, and is press secretary to UAW President Douglas Fraser.
—David Thompson is a writer and organizer of consumer cooperatives.
—Susan Young is a free lance writer living in New York.
—Thalia Zepatos is an investigative researcher who has helped state-wide groups in Maryland and Virginia fighting utility rate increases and worked with local groups in Massachusetts to uncover arson for profit.
—Daniel Zwerdling is presently an associate of the Public Resource Center in Washington, D.C. He is the author of *Democracy at Work*, and has written numerous articles on workplace issues.

About the Editors

Mark Green is a lawyer and the director of Public Citizen's Congress Watch in Washington, D.C. He is the author or editor of several books on government, business and law.

Robert Massie, Jr. is a 1978 graduate of Princeton University and the director of research for "Big Business Day—1980."

CONTENTS

NADER INTRODUCTION ... 1

THE CORPORATION AND THE CONSUMER ... 7
  Food Monopoly
    by Jim Hightower ... 9
  The Case Against the Oil Companies
    by Robert Sherrill ... 19
  How Moral Men Make Immoral Decisions—
  A Look Inside GM
    by John Z. De Lorean with J. Patrick Wright ... 36
  The Prosecution of Price-Fixing
    by Joe Sims ... 50

THE CORPORATION AND LABOR ... 57
  The Southern Textile War
    by Ed McConville ... 59
  The Devastating Impact of Plant Relocations
    by Don Stillman ... 72
  From Brass Knuckles to Briefcases:
  The Modern Art of Union Busting
    by Robert Georgine ... 91
  Democratizing the Workplace: A Case Study
    by Daniel Zwerdling ... 111

THE CORPORATION AND HEALTH ... 129
  Nutrition and the Politics of Food
    by Michael Jacobson ... 131
  The Drugging Industry
    by Amanda Spake ... 139
  Unsafe in Any Mine—The Story of
  Big Black Mountain
    by Harry M. Caudill ... 148
  The Asbestos "Pentagon Papers"
    by Samuel S. Epstein ... 162

THE CORPORATION AND NATURAL RESOURCES — 175

And Filthy Flows the Calumet
  by Edward Greer — 177
Acid from the Sky
  by *Mosiac* — 188
Love Canal and the Poisoning of America
  by Michael H. Brown — 199

THE CORPORATION AND THE COMMUNITY — 219

Big Business as Neighbor
  by Mark Green — 221
Hucksters in the Classroom:
A Review of Industry Propaganda in Schools
  by Sheila Harty — 240
Corporations and State Taxes:
The Big Ones Get Away
  by James Rosapepe — 247
Redline Fever
  by Jack Newfield — 254

THE CORPORATION AND POLITICS — 263

The Rise of Business Lobbying
  by the Consumers Union — 265
Labor Law Reform and Its Enemies
  by Thomas Ferguson and Joel Rogers — 279
Regulation that Works
  by Steven Kelman — 288

THE CULTURE OF THE CORPORATION — 299

Free Speech Within the Corporation
  by David Ewing — 301
The Corporate Climber Has to Find His Heart
  by Michael Maccoby — 318
Another Day, Another $3,000:
Executive Salaries in America
  by Paul Blumberg — 330

THE CORPORATION AND TECHNOLOGY — 347

Nuclear Power
  by Ralph Nader — 349
The Promise and Perils of Petrochemicals
  by Barry Commoner — 360
Who Owns the Sun?
  by Richard Munson — 374

A Democratic Technology
   by Martin Carnoy and Derek Shearer   382

THE IMPACT OF MULTINATIONALS   393
The Global Shopping Center
   by Richard J. Barnet and Ronald Müller   395
How American Banks Keep the Chilean Junta Going
   by Isabel Letelier and Michael Moffitt   413
U.S. Investment in South Africa: An Overview
   by George Riley   427
Babies, Bottles, and Breast Milk:
The Nestles Syndrome
   by Leah Margulies   432
The Dumping of Hazardous Products
on Foreign Markets
   by Mark Dowie and *Mother Jones*   444

CORPORATE GOVERNANCE   459
The Myth of Shareholder Democracy
   by Ralph Nader and Joel Seligman   461
The Interlock of Corporate Power
   by Markley Roberts   472
Prying Open the Clam: On Proxies and Disclosure
   by Alice Tepper Marlin and Susan Young   481

THE CORPORATION AND MARKETS   489
The Uses of an Economic System—and of Economics
   by John Kenneth Galbraith   491
What's Wrong with Conglomerate Mergers?
   by Michael Pertschuk and Kenneth M. Davidson   498
The Road to Monopoly
   by Mark Green   512
Inflationary Capitalism
   by Robert L. Heilbroner   525
How to Beat Corporate Inflation
   by Gar Alperovitz and Jeff Faux   542

ALTERNATIVES TO BUSINESS AS USUAL   549
Cooperatives Deserve Credit
   by Mitch Rofsky and David Thompson   551
Switching to Public Ownership
   by Richard Morgan, Tom Riesenberg and
   Michael Troutman   564
The Case For a Public Energy Company
   by Karl Frieden   584

Pension Funds and the Economy
  by Randy Barber and Jeremy Rifkin 592
On the Importance of Small Business
  by Committee on Small Business,
  House of Representatives 600
Conceptual Draft of Corporate Democracy Act
  by Jules Bernstein, Mark Green, Victor Kamber
  and Alice Tepper Marlin 606
How to Investigate Your Local Big Business
  by Thalia A. Zepatos 621

APPENDIX
Index of groups interested in corporate accountability—adapted from *Minding the Corporate Conscience*, from the Council on Economic Priorities 631

INTRODUCTION

Ralph Nader

Writing in the late Fifties, William Gossett, the vice president of Ford Motor Company, described the corporation as the dominant institution of American society. His candor troubled some of his business colleagues who liked to diminish the impression that corporations have the power to control or condition so much behavior in this country. What Mr. Gossett said over twenty years ago is even more accurate today.

The mercantile values of the modern giant corporations shape more than market forces in their image. They pervade government politics, law, taxation, environment, education, communications, foundations, athletics, and even institutions formerly believed to be outside their influence, such as the family or organized religion. The calculated penetration of children's minds by exploitive advertisements on children's television illustrates how the mercantile thrust can undermine parental authority, as well as a proper diet. Indeed, both in space and time, the large corporation is expanding its impact, as multinational activity and chemical and other technological burdens on future generations increase. Many multinational corporation's general revenues today dwarf the GNPs of dozens of foreign nations. General Motors, Exxon and IT&T together took in more dollars last year than the Pentagon—the largest military budget in the world.

A corporate economy, a corporate society, a corporate state were not always part of the American ethos. Jefferson viewed the new representative government as curbing the excesses of "the monied interests." The pre-Civil War period reflected an established belief in the merits of a decentralized economy based on farmers and small businessmen, which culminated in the Homestead Act under President Lincoln's administration. There was suspicion widespread during the first half of the 19th century about letting "legal fictions" called corporations, with limited liability to their investors, engage in production without legal constraints. Advocate Daniel Webster could thunder in court about a corporation having "no soul." Legislatures were very restrictive in their chartering of corporations.

The post-Civil War period of that century witnessed what some historians describe as a major and dramatic change in the economy and in the prevailing ethos. The industrial revolution was underway with large corporate capital gobbling up small competitors. The oil, steel, tobacco, sugar and other "Trusts" ushered the first wave of corporate concentration. The Horatio Alger ideology with its mercantile definition of success insinuated itself deeply in the psychology of the culture. At the same time, the restrictions on corporate chartering loosened. State legislatures delegated the functions to state agencies and they in turn delegated more discretion about what economic pursuits corporations could follow to company officers and boards of directors. Late in the 19th century, states, led by New Jersey, began to turn corporate chartering into a competitive race for state revenues by enacting more permissive chartering laws. This "race to the bottom," in Professor William Cary's words, was won by Delaware in the early 1900s, which remains the domicile of many of the world's largest corporations.

The Delaware corporation syndrome, which pulled other states toward a lower common denominator for chartering, represented a major victory for corporate power in America. No longer would corporate charters constitute even a pretense of being a corporate governance mechanism providing accountability to shareholders and other affected corporate constituencies. Instead, the state-granted charters devolved with each succeeding weakening of the Delaware corporate law over the next eight decades. By conscious lobbying, corporations turned restrictive charter laws into instruments for further concentration of power in the hands of management. A constitutional structure for accountability rights by people inside as well as outside the corporate structure passed into history.

By contrast, the growth of various forms of corporate management power over shareholders, workers, consumers, community residents, taxpayers and governments proceeded apace—through the "Robber Barons" period into World War I (wars always promote a lasting kind of corporate entrenchment), the "Business of America is business" Twenties, the "New Deal" Thirties, World War II and the massive acceleration of influence and impact during the past generation. Greater aggregations of natural resources, capital, labor and technology under more centralized management also daunted the ability of entrepreneurs, inventors and small businesses to challenge this megacorporate hegemony. Small business instead survived increasingly by becoming an appendage, a franchisee to corporate headquarters, economically and politically.

Yet monopolies, oligopolies and giant business generally did not expand without challenge. A series of these challenges began in the Eighteen-eighties with the farmers revolt out of Texas and Oklahoma so well chronicled by Lawrence Goodwyn's "Democratic Promise: The Populist Moment." The banks and railroads were the focus of this fundamental power struggle which, in weakened form, led to the populist progressive movement a few years later. The first regulatory agencies, price supports, public enterprises (grain elevators), producer cooperatives and direct democracy instruments (initiative, referendum and recall) emerged from this agrarian political and economic mobilization. This reform movement was probably the most basic and deeply rooted in our country's history. For all its continuing legacies, however, it failed to stem the tide of Big Business. Four other challenges during this century have had some intermittent success in curbing some of the more egregious excesses of these large industrial and financial companies—the labor, consumer, civil rights and environmental movements.

In understanding the subject of this volume, it is important to pay as much attention to the manner in which corporations have responded to outside pressures as it is to the abuses and struggles so well described in the following chapters. There is a uniquely consistent pattern to the strategy of response by companies once they decide that they cannot totally defeat the reform drive. Where regulations or standards are issued by an agency for health and safety, a deliberate process of delay, attrition and political influence is initiated. That is why statutes read more promising than the regulations and the latter read more promising than the reality in the marketplace, workplace and environment. Wherever the political government is empowered to protect the interests of labor, consumer or other constituencies, the corporate government increases its financing of political elections. Where the law requires a redirection of investment to reduce the costs of pollution or consumer injury, companies find ways to transfer these costs to the victims themselves, through tax preferences or administered pricing; they often avoid internalizing these proper costs to compete against other internal cost decisions (safety vs. style in cars). And because of the inordinate secrecy permitted these multinational companies, management can wildly exaggerate the costs of compliance to prod public resistance to health and safety standards while at the same time keeping secret the evidence of hazards (chemical waste dumps, automobile defects, food contamination and drug side effects).

Presently, industrial and commercial corporations are increasingly demanding that local communities provide them with tax exemptions or abatements as the price of establishing or expanding their business there. Furthermore, some industries, such as nuclear power, have succeeded in passing laws limiting their corporations' liabilities vis a vis claimants. These trends illustrate the extraordinary special privileges which corporations are entrenching in our legal structure.

There is always a lag between the actual adverse impacts of large corporations and public knowledge about them. This is true of almost every industry exposed during the past thirty years, from pesticides to nuclear power to occupational diseases. There is also a great lag from corporate diagnosis to public prescription. The public consequences of these dual lags for people, nation and world are becoming more ominous with the advent of highly perilous technology in the hands of country-hopping multinational corporations. Fifty years ago an imperious utility might have cost consumers a few exorbitant dollars a year on their electric bill. Today that same utility is building or operating a nuclear plant in their community. Fifty years ago, the petro-chemical industry was in its infancy; today it is flooding the human environment with carcinogens and a wide variety of other toxic chemicals. Love Canal-type dumps are being discovered all over America the Poisoned. Wherever Love Canals are revealed there are no conservatives and there are no liberals; there are only victims becoming angrier.

The approach of this book is decisively empirical. The articles deal in facts so compellingly that they self-evidently etch fairly basic value conclusions. The contemporary challenge to giant business is quite modest compared to historical movements in our past. There is little by way of demanding basic ownership changes. The furthest the contemporary critique goes is to offer alternatives such as greater self-reliance, more consumer cooperatives and a little public enterprise involving, for example, energy on federal lands, to compete with the big companies. The principal call is almost primeval in nature. It is a call for corporations to stop stealing, stop deceiving, stop corrupting politicians with money, stop monopolizing, stop poisoning the earth, air and water, stop selling dangerous products, stop exposing workers to cruel hazards, stop tyrannizing people of conscience within the company and start respecting long range survival needs and rights of present and future generations.

It is not sufficient to rely on external forces and standards to humanize corporate decisions. The internal governance of these institutions must be addressed as they are in this volume. Because these articles show how corporate misdeeds touch people so intimately, readers should see how important it is for them to have the ability to respond. Thus, the final two chapters provide some concrete suggestions and references which will help citizens develop the civic strategies for greater initiatives and participation in major multinational, national, regional and local decisions which now are so primarily shaped by a handful of giant corporations.

The purpose of Big Business Day on April 17, 1980, timed to the publication of this volume, is to publicize such alternatives and the abuses that make them necessary. The Day—in the tradition of Earth, Food and Sun Days—will stimulate hundreds of communities and thousands of citizens to consider how corporations govern them, and how they in turn should govern corporations. It will be a day of education and action. And it will be not a culmination but an ignition for a new era of corporate reform. If the 1950s focused on the role of "big labor" in America and the 1970s on "big government"—the 1980s should scrutinize the role and reach of big business over America.

February 1, 1980

THE CORPORATION AND THE CONSUMER

From the moment we are born to the time we die, we consume the products corporations sell us. We have come to depend on them for the food we eat, the air we breathe, the clothes we wear, the houses we live in, the vehicles we travel in, the entertainment and education we enjoy.

Theoretically, consumers have their hands on the tiller of the marketplace, steering it in desired directions. Thousands of sellers supposedly scramble over each other to appeal for our dollars, rapidly altering their products to meet our changing needs and desires. Every time we purchase something, presumably, we decide on the basis of the most complete and truthful information.

But over the past few years—after the problems of Red Dye #2, nitrates, cyclamates, corporate pay-offs, the chemical TRIS, the DC-10, and many others—it has become apparent that, in Professor Galbraith's phrase, producer sovreignty has replaced consumer sovreignty. Instead of thousands of sellers, we now see huge oligopolies and conglomerates dividing up the market in very non-competitive ways. Instead of full and honest information, we have been flooded with advertising that stresses the least important characteristics of the product while often deliberately obscuring the things we most need to know. Instead of corporate responsibility, there is often corporate crime.

The articles in this section look at the different ways corporations affect our lives as consumers. Jim Hightower outlines how giant food conglomerates can carve up the consumer. Robert Sherrill, in a study of corporate *deja vu*, recounts a half century of oil industry claims of energy shortages. John DeLorean's piece, written with J. Patrick Wright, is an insider's view of corporate machinations. De-

Lorean details GM's sale of unsafe cars, its petty bureaucracies, and false promotions. Finally, Joe Sims describes the prevalence, cost and under-prosecution of antitrust crime.

Food Monopoly

Jim Hightower

Americans have come a long way since the first Thanksgiving meal was brought to some New England colonists by local Indians, in a spirit of sharing, 367 years ago. Maybe we've come too far. At least those Pilgrims knew where their meal came from—it was the bounty of nature, delivered by Indian people, and presumed to be the blessing of God.

No longer is that the case. These days, nature has less and less to do with our meals, which are not even put on the table by farmers, much less Indians; and if modern food is God-ordained, as Earl Butz once suggested, then the religious fundamentals are right—we've ticked off the Lord something awful. His revenge is a Brave New Thanksgiving that, unbeknownst to most Americans, is the product of monopolized markets, conglomerate bookkeeping, genetic engineering, integrated factory systems, centralized procurement, national advertising, chemical artifice, standardized taste, and The Bottom Line. It's not especially good, or good for you, and it's very expensive, but you can be thankful for one thing: there's plenty of it.

It's easy to forget that food remains America's largest business—larger than oil, chemicals, steel or automobiles. Last year, U.S. eaters spent $223 billion on this most basic consumer item. To offer some perspective, the entire commercial music industry (records, concerts, clubs, etc.) had $3 billion in sales last year, while just the sale of potato chips, popcorn, pretzels and other snack foods totaled more than that—$3.8 billion.

No longer are farmers in charge of this industry. Indeed, dramatic as their presence is, the new wave of industrial "farmers" poses the least problem in our food economy at the moment. Of far greater significance are the processing and retailing empires amassed in a very short period by a handful of food manufacturing conglomerates, national supermarket chains, and fast-food franchisers. This middle sector between farmers and consumers takes 60 cents of every food dollar spent today. It is here that the chances for big profits lie in the food industry, and here is where the monopolists have concentrated.

Pop into any grocery store and you will be faced by a phantasmagoria of products, giving the impression of robust competition among thousands of companies. It's a false impression—there are more than 30,000 food processing companies in the U.S., but precious few of them are represented on the shelves of your supermarket. Instead, less than 1 percent of them own practically every brand you see, and just 50 national processors corner about 90 percent of the industry's profits.

These 50 are consumer product conglomerates that purvey hundreds of brands of highly processed, highly advertised food items and monopolize the marketplace. The two largest are not even U.S. firms—they are Unilever, a British-Dutch conglomerate (owning such brands as Lipton tea, Imperial margarine, Lucky Whip topping, Mrs. Butterworth syrup, Wish Bone salad dressings, Knox gelatine, and Good Humor ice cream) and Nestlé, the huge Swiss corporation (holding such U.S. brands as Nestea, Libby McNeil & Libby canned goods, Stouffer frozen foods and restaurants, Jerlsberg cheese, and Taster's Choice coffee). The largest U.S. food conglomerate bears a name you've probably never heard of—Beatrice Foods Company, a Chicago firm that made $6.4 billion in sales last year on more than a hundred brands, including Dannon Yogurt, LaChoy Chinese foods, Sunbeam bread, Meadow Gold milk, Martha White flour, Rosarita Mexican foods, Eckrich sausages, Louis Sherry ice cream, Rainbo pickles, and Butter Krust bread.

Even the old-time food firms like Kraft, Heinz, General Mills, Carnation and Borden are now holding companies that have bought up dozens of brands and are far removed from their original trade in milk, tomato products, and cereals. They join a few other conglomerates—including such little-known giants as Consolidated Foods, Heublein, American Brands, CPC International, Anderson Clayton, Standard Brands, American Home Products, and International Multifoods—in controlling the majority of grocery items.

Don't be fooled by the package—even if it's got a

smiling granny or a down-home name on it, chances are it is in conglomerate hands.

Such conglomerates are operated by financial managers who are much less concerned with food than with corporate growth. They have not established their positions of market dominance by innovation, superior efficiency, or any of the other grubby aspects of true free enterprise; rather, they have bought their positions, swallowing up regional brands that have already been established by independent entrepreneurs. Beatrice Foods, which has made nearly 400 such acquisitions in the last 25 years, says that it looks for companies manufacturing products with regional brand identification, strong market share, longterm growth potential, and higher-than-average profit margins. Beatrice managers refer to its 400 or so subsidiaries as "profit centers." *Business Week* magazine reported last month that a couple of conglomerates "are building small snack-food empires from scratch." How? "By buying out smaller, regional companies." One of the empire builders cited by *Business Week* was Acton Corporation, which started "from scratch" recently by buying Morton Foods, Inc., the long established Dallas potato chip maker.

The merger activity of these giant firms is the biggest news in the food industry, yet there has been practically no press attention to it. Far from abating, the movement is escalating, with national companies now becoming takeover targets. Del Monte, the largest processor of fruits and vegetables, has just been bought by R. J. Reynolds. The big canner's chief rival, Green Giant, is now a subsidiary of Pillsbury. Seven-Up was bought this summer by Philip Morris. Tropicana has merged into Beatrice Foods. Pet, which itself is a billion-dollar-a-year conglomerate built by mergers, was picked off this year by IC Industries, the parent firm of the Illinois Central Railroad. It's hard to keep up, it's happening so fast.

All this brand-name concentration means that there is far less competition than meets the eye in the supermarket. It is not that there is one big monopoly over food, as there is over automobiles, but that there is a series of shared monopolies in the food industry, with four or fewer firms controlling a majority of sales of a certain product. As *Fortune* magazine explained the market-share game in its September issue ". . . food-company managers look at the marketplace not as a whole, but by product category. A product category, in the consumer-goods sense, defines a distinct, self-contained market, the battle-ground upon which all the direct competitors of a product are to be found. What's important to the marketer is not what people are doing with food, but what they're doing with frozen lima beans or single-layer cake mixes."

Within these categories, there are fewer and fewer competitors. In fact, the food industry already has become more concentrated than most other industries, with the majority of sales in the average product category being controlled by four or fewer firms. Such oligopolies (or, shared monopolies) are reaching into every food line; in its July issue *Progressive Grocer*, a trade publication, reported the following astounding levels of market control by just the top three brands in various categories:

Product	Share of market held by top three brands
Table salt	91.7%
Flour	80.4%
Catsup	86.1%
Mustard	76.2%
Peanut butter	78.6%
Salad & Cooking oil	85.5%
Vinegar	84.1%
Gelatin desserts	98.4%
Whipped toppings	85.6%
Canned evaporated milk	82.3%
Marshmallows	98.2%
Instant puddings	96.0%
Shortening	81.0%
Jams & jellies	75.2%
Nuts	80.7%
Honey	82.2%
Frozen potato products	82.2%
Frostings	97.7%
Spaghetti sauce	85.9%
Pickle relish	79.2%
Instant tea	86.0%
Frozen dinners	92.8%
Corn & tortilla chips	86.7%
Canned spaghetti & noodles	94.0%

Ready-to-serve dips	81.5%
Non-dairy cream substitutes	86.1%
Pretzels	85.6%
Dry milk	80.1%
Add-meat dinner mixes	90.7%
Canned stews	83.6%
Instant potatoes	83.9%
Pizza mix	86.6%
Instant breakfast mixes	90.8%

Consumers pay dearly for this kind of market control. Once a few firms gain a monopoly position in a product category, the market for that category is considered to be "mature," again using Wall Street's patois, and the companies are able to "harvest" it, meaning that they can push up prices. Taking one product at a time, such artificial inflation doesn't make a dramatic impression on shoppers—a few cents more on shortening, a little extra for the pizza mix. But when the whole market basket is pushed to the cash register, consumers have been nickel-and-dimed to death. These shared monopolies are *the major cause* of inflation in the food economy, which is one of the major causes of inflation in the whole economy.

In an extremely important but little-noted study, two highly regarded economists, one from the Federal Trade Commission and the other from the Department of Agriculture, have teamed up to calculate the extra price that consumers pay for food because of these monopolies. Russell Parker and John Connor figured the overcharge conservatively, using 1975 data and three different and independent methodological approaches. They concluded in their recent paper that "[c]onsumer loss due to monopoly in U.S. food manufacturing industries in 1975 was at least $12 billion."

That's $55 a year given away to food conglomerates by every man, woman and child in America. For a poverty-level family of four, it means 10 percent of their total food budget is being misappropriated by monopolists. The industry's structure has become more concentrated since 1975, so the problem is only growing worse—Parker and Connor estimate that "consumer loss for 1978 would be at least one to two billion dollars greater than the estimate for 1975."

A big chunk of this monopoly price-tag ends up in the coffers of the monopolists as excess profits—Parker and Connor calculate that $3 billion of the 1975 over-charge went for profits that the firms would not have enjoyed in a competitive world. Here are a few of the profiteers:

- $173 million in excess profits to the bread and cake purveyors, the top four of which are ITT, American Brands, Campbell Taggart and Interstate Brands
- $186 million to the breakfast cereal makers, the top four of which are General Foods, General Mills, Kellogg and Quaker Oats
- $333 million to the fluid milk marketers, the top four of which are Borden, Kraftco, Beatrice and Carnation
- $104 million to the canned specialties manufacturers, the top four of which are H.J. Heinz, Campbell Soup, American Home Products and Gerber
- $29 million to the frozen specialities firms, the top three of which are Campbell, RCA and Consolidated Foods
- $108 million to the coffee roasters, the top four of which are Procter & Gamble, General Foods, Nestlé and Standard Brands
- $344 million to the brewers, the top four of which are Anheuser-Busch, Philip Morris, Schlitz and Pabst
- $343 million to the soft drink purveyors, the top four of which are Coca-Cola, PepsiCo, Royal Crown and Philip Morris
- $111 million to the shortening and cooking oil makers, the top four of which are Kraftco, Norton-Simon, Procter & Gamble and Esmark.

Being this big and powerful may enrich the monopolists, but it does nothing for their efficiency. As Adam Smith long ago noted, monopoly is the enemy of good management, since it destroys incentive to control corporate expenses and maintain maximum production. In addition to excess profits, the $12 billion overcharge in 1975 was the result of wasteful advertising and promotional expenses by the monopolists, conglomerate inefficiencies, managerial waste, collusive pricing decisions, and excess capacity.

Unfortunately for consumers, the manufacturers do not form the only monopoly in the food economy. In most U.S. cities, supermarkets themselves are monopolistic, with four or fewer chains controlling a majority of local grocery sales, putting them in a position to set local prices. A report released recently by Congress's Joint Economic Committee calculated that these food retailing monopolies had cost U.S. consumers another $662 million more than they would have paid if local market structures had been competitive.

Safeway is the biggest grocery chain in the world—if it were listed among *Fortune*'s top 500 industrial firms, its $11 billion in sales last year would rank it as the 13th largest, ahead of such giants as Shell Oil and U.S. Steel. It has more than 2,400 stores that in 1977 pulled $2.3 billion in gross profits from local neighborhoods into its Oakland, California, headquarters.

That's enough, but, alas, it's not the end of it. Today, the fastest growing and most profitable segment of the food industry is the chain restaurant business, a fact that has not escaped the notice of many of the same firms already mentioned.

From 1972 to 1976, the number of meals eaten away from home doubled as restaurants became production units in a business with sales of over $50 billion a year. What has traditionally been a mom-and-pop industry and a major channel of upward mobility in American society is fast falling to chain operators who use factory techniques and are backed by huge advertising budgets. Already, more than a fourth of American restaurants are chains, and a third of the total eating-out business is in the hands of the fast-food artists.

Just as in other segments of the food industry, competition in the restaurant business is shrinking. McDonald's alone holds 20 percent of the national fast-food market and shares more than half of it with the next nine largest chains. But even that understates their reach—people generally do not travel beyond the city limits in search of a place to eat, and in the country's most heavily populated local markets, the national chains have a much tighter grip.

"Who cares?" you might ask. "McDonald's will fill you up cheaper than any hamburger joint in town!" Wrong. A "Big Mac" is selling here in Austin for 90 cents. At a whopping four ounces (including bun and napkin), that's hamburger at $3.60 a pound. There are at least two small local hamburger chains here that sell a bigger hamburger at half that cost, and just for the hell of it, they throw in flavor and nutrition.

Greyhound, the bus company that owns Armour meats and is one of the largest turkey producers in the country, sent a press release this month to food editors, trying to promote consumption of the traditional Thanksgiving feast: "Today's meaty, broad-breasted turkey is a far cry from the tough, wiry bird the Pilgrims knew," boasted the release. Indeed it is, but not just because it's bigger; today's turkey (most specimens of which are produced nowadays by Greyhound, Cargill, Esmark and Ralston Purina) leads a crowded, caged, nasty and short assembly-line existence. The creature passes from the hatchery to intense formula-feeding to slaughter to dressing to the freezer—but not before fat, sodium, sugar, artificial flavor, artificial color, emulsifiers, preservatives, antioxidants and water are added to it. One brand even sticks an internal "thermometer" in its frozen bird.

Today's thanksgiving is a highly processed meal, and there is much more of the same in your future. Our "food" is becoming little more than a low-quality medium to which food manufacturers add coloring and flavoring to give the stuff minimal consumer appeal, a dozen or so basic vitamins to give it "nutrition," several chemicals to hold it together, preservatives to give it a shelf-life probably greater than your own allotted years, sugar to cover up any mistakes, and a package to make it "convenient."

Every major food company is pushing more processing with a vengeance; even meat packers are launching a shift from simple cuts of meat to such advanced preparations as already-seasoned meats, gourmet cuts, sausages, and cook-in-the-pouch servings. Why? Because basic foodstuffs are low-profit, slow-growth products that hold no fascination for the money machines now dominating the industry. By doing as much as possible to the food, they can puff the price far beyond the genuine value of the commodity, adding a profit for themselves at each stage of processing.

Fortune magazine has approvingly described the trend in these terms: "The efforts of a company like General Foods, which styles itself a 'processor of packaged convenience foods,' have been directed at extending the convenience spectrum upward, attracting the consumer to its progressively higher reaches with new products and improvements in existing brands. Not coincidentally, in this direction usually lie an increase in the value added, higher [profit] margins and less dependence upon agricultural commodities." What sort of new and improved products are they talking about? *Fortune* cites as "genuine innovations" General Mills' Breakfast Squares and General Foods' Stove Top Stuffing (which, the magazine notes, "makes it possible to serve stuffing without a bird"). Thanks a million.

The indispensable extra ingredient that makes these decoctions palatable to the public is advertising, big-time advertising. Check the Thursday food ads in your newspaper and see what's being promoted, complete with ten-cents-off coupons. It's not basic foods they're trying to get you to eat; rather, it is their branded, instant, pre-cooked, cheese-kissed, ready-to-eat, frozen mug-o-lunch, which comes with a packet of spices and disposable spoon in each box.

Better yet, spend a Saturday morning in front of the television set and get a load of what the big firms are selling to kids. For starters, if it doesn't have sugar on it, you won't find it advertised on what's come to be known as "kiddie-vision." The Federal Trade Commission finally cracked down on the use of a kid-show host to push the sponsors' creations, but the animated cartoon characters simply stepped in to do the shilling. A recent industry survey found that while most Americans can't name their U.S. senator, more than 90 percent of the country's three-year-olds know who Fred Flintstone is.

It takes a lot of ad dollars to impress a product's name on even a three-year-old mind, and it is not surprising that half of the top 25 national advertisers are big food companies: Procter & Gamble, General Foods, Philip Morris, American Home Products, R.J. Reynolds, General Mills, Unilever, Norton-Simon, PepsiCo, Beatrice Foods, McDonald's, and Colgate-Palmolive. Last year, just these dozen firms spent $2.2 billion to tout their wares.

Not only do consumers pay for this needless cost directly in the form of higher prices, but they also pay in the form of reduced competition in the marketplace. Advertising—especially television advertising—has become a potent weapon wielded with greatest effect against local, mom-and-pop businesses. Again quoting *Fortune*: "What the entry of the big companies into a product category usually means is a substantial increase in marketing expenditures by everyone who can afford the raised ante." Very few homegrown enterprises can ante up and survive. McDonald's, for example, targets $15,000' worth of advertising each year *per store*.

Can anything be done? Yes. The shifting balance of power in the food economy is not an economic phenomenon, it is a political phenomenon. The monopolistic trend is ordained neither by God nor by the inevitable march of some economic dialectic; rather, the problem is that we have not paid much attention to the changes taking place and by default have allowed a few firms to gain too much power. Plenty of methods and resources are at hand to redress the balance. If we had the political will, we might at least put state and federal governments to work for consumers, competitive businesses, and family farmers, using such means as cooperative banks, government procurement budgets, argicultural research and extension programs, direct marketing between farmers and consumers, hard-nosed antitrust enforcement, graduated corporate income taxes, limits on the tax deduction for advertising expenditures, and so on.

As overwhelming as the facts of monopoly power seem to be, they ought not have a depressing effect. The corporate takeover of Thanksgiving is not complete. There still are healthy competitive elements—mon-and-pop restaurants, a fledgling cooperative movement, independent processors, a struggling family-farm system—and if consumers can be enlisted, the drift can be halted. People cannot fight back until they know what they are fighting. Consider this the clarion call.

The Case Against The Oil Companies

by Robert Sherrill

Quite frankly, the oil industry has developed the reputation over the years of being a robber, cheating and despoiling the environment.
—Frank Ikard, President of American Petroleum Institute, 1971.

Ever since Jimmy Carter arrived in Washington, he has been trying to convince the American people that the periodic oil and natural-gas shortages are not contrived deceptions used by the industry to squeeze more profits from consumers. In his first major speeches to the nation in 1977, when he put on a sweater and declared moral war on the energy problem, he said, "I realize that many of you have not believed that we really have an energy problem." He seemed sympathetic. But then, there he was again, during the great gasoline shortage of 1979, back on television, giving his fifth energy speech, still with the same theme. This time he had obviously lost patience. "The energy crisis is *real*," he said, going up half an octave. "It is worldwide. It is a clear and present danger to our nation. These are the facts—and we simply must face them."

The address was probably the most impassioned of his political life. Yet neither that plea nor the gas shortage itself seemed to have much effect on public perception. After the speech, 65 percent of the public still thought the current energy shortage was a hoax, according to a New York Times/CBS poll.

It's not hard to understand why the majority of Americans feel the way they do. Over the years, they have been told by many knowledgeable politicians and lay experts that the oil companies are quite capable of duplicity. George P. Shultz, a Secretary of Labor in Richard M.

Nixon's Cabinet, who headed a Cabinet Task Force on Oil Import Control, found that "the industry is capable of behaving irrationally . . . and even of contriving an apparent disaster" and of "downward manipulation" of reserve statistics to squeeze more money out of consumers. In 1973, the Federal Trade Commission charged eight of the largest oil companies with conspiring to destroy competition and with conspiring to cheat the public out of billions of dollars by price fixing. The oil companies' lawyers are still in court fighting those charges, but in its sweeping accusations—and in its futility—the case stands as the nagging question of this energy decade. It has been a decade in which headlines such as "Oil Giants Exploited Energy Shortages, Probers Charge" —a vintage piece from The Washington Star —have appeared almost as regularly as Mobil's ads proclaiming the industry's innocence.

Above all, this has been a decade of *déjà vu*. Opening his famous "obscene profits" investigation in 1974, Senator Henry Jackson delivered a Whitman-esque outburst:

"The American people want to know why the prices of home heating oil and gasoline have doubled when the companies report high inventories of these stocks. . . .

The American people want to know whether major oil companies are sitting on shut-in wells and hoarding production in hidden tanks and at abandoned service stations. . . ."

The American people want to know why the oil companies are making soaring profits. . . ."

It was an outburst that still seems perfectly contemporary, for the rumors, manipulation and suspicions of 1979—scarcity in the midst of plenty, tankers waiting to unload, charges of hoarding by the companies, hidden supplies, blame on the Middle East—have not changed. It is the *déjà vu* more than anything else that makes Americans now so hard to convince. For more than 50 years, Americans have been confronted with periodic energy "crises," and they have noticed that the only thing certain is that the crisis or prediction of crisis has been accompanied by increased oil prices, concessions from the Government to the major oil companies, expanded oil-company holdings or some combination of these. What follows is an account that might be called Six Crises.

1920: *A Taste of the Future*

The United States was producing about 65 percent of the world's oil in those days. The Standard Oil companies dominated, but they had few overseas sources. This made them unhappy and restless. Standard wanted to share in the oil of Iraq, then the most productive country in the Middle East. But Iraq was under British control, and the British would not let Standard in.

A propaganda war was called for, and suddenly the American people were plunged into a crisis. On Jan. 1, 1920, the U.S. Geological Survey—drawing its information, as always, from the oil companies—told The New York Times that "the position of the United States in regard to oil can best be characterized as precarious." Dr. George Otis Smith, director of the U.S.G.S., then warned that within the near future "Americans will have to depend on foreign sources or use less oil, or perhaps both." Within weeks, another U.S.G.S. official predicted that "unless our consumption is checked, we shall by 1925 be dependent on foreign oilfields to the extent of . . . possibly as much as 200 million barrels of crude each year, except insofar as the situation may . . . be helped to a slight extent by shale oil. . . . Within perhaps three years, our domestic production will begin to fall off with increasing rapidity, due to the exhaustion of our reserves." Oil industrialists began telling the press that, when America's oil reserves were gone, it would be at the mercy of the British, an ungrateful lot who had been saved by United States oil in World War I and now only waited for a chance to gouge us.

The people were soon given a taste of that merciless future. In some parts of the country, gasoline was sold only in one-or two-gallon lots. In some places, the price more than doubled—to 35 cents, equivalent to more than $1 in today's currency. The magazine Automotive Industries reported rumors of refineries shipping gasoline away from urban centers until the prices went up. There was talk of having to make synthetic gasoline from Kansas wheat. There was even some loose talk of going to war with Britain, if necessary, to get "our" share of the oil supply.

The strategy worked. Seeing the State Department and the Congress militantly carrying the oil companies' flag, and seeing the American public exercised, the British gave in and agreed to join hands with the Americans in Iraq. With that, the crisis ended, almost as suddenly as it had begun.

This was not by any means the first time the oil industry had declared that it was running dry, but it was such a dramatically successful use of the technique as to inspire two British writers, E. H. Davenport and Sidney Russell Cooke, to observe in their book "The Oil Trusts and Anglo-American Relations," published in 1924: "There is this strange habit peculiar to the American oil industry which one should observe in passing. Although it doubles its output roughly every 10 years, it declares every other year that its peak of production has been passed and that its oilfields are well-nigh exhausted. . . . One cannot doubt that the lugubrious prophecies of American oil men are in some way related to the wish for higher prices."

1929–31: *'Perfect Pattern' of Monopoly*

This time, the crisis was created in the name of "conservation." In 1929, the Federal Oil Conservation Board warned that the United States was "exhausting its petroleum reserves at a dangerous rate." It advised bringing in all the foreign oil possible, particularly from South America, and to cut back on production in the United States. The most important foreign source in this hemisphere was in Venezuela, where the dominant American producers were Standard and Gulf—the latter company being controlled, interestingly, by the family of Andrew Mellon, who was then Treasury Secretary and the most influential aide to President Hoover. Gulf and the other international companies wanted a good patriotic excuse for bringing their cheaper oil into this country. Thus the big push to "conserve" our resources.

But then, in 1930, independent oil operators began bringing in the fabulous East Texas field. Here came the legendary Spindletop and subsequent discoveries, some with wells gushing 10,000 barrels daily. The major oil companies had had little to do with the discovery of the East Texas fields. So, the majors, pretending to be horrified at the wildcatters' wasteful production methods, demanded that the government of Texas force the small companies to "conserve" —i.e., sell only as much as the big companies said they should sell. When the small companies refused to knuckle under, the majors gave them a rugged dose of competition by slashing the price they would pay for crude—from nearly $1 a barrel to 10 cents. The resulting economic devastation forced the Texas legislature in 1933 to pass a "market demand" law. Production of oil would thereafter be "prorationed," held down to what the "market" (that is, the major oil-company buyers) desired, and, since Texas was the dominant oil state, the price paid for oil in Texas would pretty well determine the national price. Thereafter, when the majors wanted to create enough scarcity to bolster prices, they simply placed smaller orders and the state prorationing commission ordered lower production. Senate investigators later concluded that the system had been set up not for conservation but rather as part of "a perfect pattern of monopolistic control over oil production . . . and ultimately the price [was] paid by the public."

1947: 'An Honest Man is Rare'

During World War II, Interior Secretary Harold Ickes persuaded President Roosevelt to establish a Government corporation (the Petroleum Reserves Corporation) to buy out the American oil partners—Standard Oil of California and Texaco—in Saudi Arabia. Ickes, who had seen enough profiteering to conclude that "an honest and scrupulous man in the oil business is so rare as to rank as a museum piece," wanted the public to have more control over supplies. The oil companies were powerful enough to kill Ickes's proposal in the cradle; they had ideas of their own for further strengthening their Middle Eastern cartel.

Standard Oil of California and Texaco had controlled the concession in Saudi Arabia since before World War II, but their marketing outlets were not adequate to handle Arabia's bountiful output, so they brought in the great Standard Oil of New Jersey and Mobil as partners. This is the Arabian American Oil Company (Aramco) we know so well today. A domestic arrangement like that would clearly be a violation of America's anti-trust laws, and could be expected to encounter fierce public resistance. Again, it was time for an emergency and a storm of gloom.

In 1947, the chief of the Department of State's Petroleum Division flatly stated that "sufficient oil cannot be found in the United States." Two years later, Julius Krug, the Secretary of Interior, said that the "end of the United States oil supply is almost in sight." Giving credence to the gloom, the oil companies claimed shortages and raised prices. But the true character of the "shortages" did not go unnoticed. In 1949, the Senate's Special Small Business Committee observed that "during the year and a half the committee has been investigating the oil industry, there never has been a real overall shortage. . . . At the time that consumers were feeling the greatest pinch, in January and February 1947, there were 220 million barrels of crude oil in storage, mainly controlled by the larger units, which could have been distributed among independent refiners who were running under capacity."

1959: *Putting the Lid on Foreign Imports.*

By now the major companies were making enormous discoveries overseas, but so were some of the more aggressive independent oil men—fellows like J. Paul Getty and William Keck and the Hunts, father and sons. The world, by the mid-50's, was awash with oil, and the development of a freewheeling, truly free-enterprise market suddenly seemed to be a dreaded possibility. The majors had long ago perfected the art of global price fixing by controlling supply. They were not about to send so much cheap foreign oil to the United States—still the world's largest market—that prices would be forced down. But the independent men felt no such restraint. They were wild hares, and the majors feared—rightly—that there were so many independents roaming the globe with their drilling rigs that they couldn't possibly be controlled.

The majors rose to the occasion by proclaiming, and having their friends in Congress and in the Eisenhower Administration also proclaim, the imminence of a national-security crisis. Americans, it seems, were in danger of being subverted by cheap foreign oil. Most of it must be blocked at our shore. The argument went like this: Middle East oil could be produced for one-tenth the cost of domestic oil. So naturally it could be bought for much less. If it were allowed to undercut domestic prices, our oil men couldn't afford to go out and find new oil in American fields, and if they didn't find new oil at home we would increasingly become dependent on foreign oil, and if we became dependent on foreign oil, we would be terribly vulnerable in case of war.

With that patriotic reasoning, Congress inserted a provision into the 1958 Trade Agreement Act to give the President power to set mandatory controls over oil imports. President Eisenhower, whose closest adviser in such matters was Treasury Secretary Robert Anderson, a Texas oil man, lost no time in imposing the controls. Foreign-oil imports were held down to about 12 percent of domestic production, and only the companies with refineries—for the most part, the large companies—were allowed to import. The larger companies made millions, bringing oil in at a price between $1.25 and $1.50 less per barrel than domestic oil.

Did the import-quota program make the nation more secure in its oil supply? Hardly. One effect was that the independent oil industry began a long slow decline. Another was that it gave the major international companies the excuse they wanted to take most of that wonderfully cheap Middle East oil and develop new markets in Europe. That's where they began building their refineries—*not* in America. They were doing it, moreover, with indirect subsidies from the American taxpayers.

Opposition to the program became intense in the 60's. Prof. M. A. Adelman, an oil expert at the Massachusetts Institute of Technology, argued, along with others, that keeping foreign oil out was costing American consumers at least $4 billion a year. And Pentagon officials proclaimed that, as far as they were concerned, the oil-import program had not had the slightest thing to do with national security. In 1974, when the program was dead and candor could be indulged in, Z. D. Bonner, president of Gulf Oil Corporation, acknowledged that "oil import controls were used as a price-control mechanism."

1973: 'All the Sheiks' Horses'

By the mid-1960's, there was so much Middle East oil available that Professor Adelman was predicting that a Middle East oil price "as low as $1 a barrel, though not imminent, has a 50-50 chance of occurring in, say, five years." *A dollar a barrel.* In February 1969, Fortune magazine writer Gilbert Burck predicted that "barring a great international cartel that will tie up the world of oil as no international organization has ever tied up anything before, everyone in the oil business faces a long series of adjustments. . . . All the sheiks' horses and all the sheiks' men will never put the comfortable old price structure together again. Consumers everywhere should rejoice."

Fortune was not giving the oil industry sufficient credit for ingenuity. A "great international cartel" capable of tying up oil as never before already existed. The Organization of Petroleum Exporting Countries (OPEC) had been formed in 1960. So far it had been dormant. But with a little luck, and the right emergency, perhaps enough lightning could be directed through this monster's body to make it rise and do the major companies some profitable service.

In the early 1970's, the right crisis seemed at hand. The Middle East was in a froth. Arabs and Jews were at each others' throats. Israel's Middle East enemies were talking about using oil as a weapon—and if they did, the major oil companies would be ready to exploit the showdown.

But first the consuming public was softened up with a series of smaller, preparatory crises. Although, in fact, the majors were holding the highest inventory of gasoline they had ever had, they managed to produce a "gasoline shortage" in the spring of 1973 even before the Arab embargo. By June they were warning of a likely shortage of home heating oil the next winter, although, as David Bird wrote in The Times, "the warnings are surprising some people, because the stocks on hand seem to be larger than they were at this time last year."

The shortage, contrived or not, gave the majors an excuse to cut off gasoline supplies to independent wholesalers and discount dealers; about 3,000 went out of business in 1973. Meanwhile, the majors were forcing the price of gasoline up 39 percent, and their profits shot up 63 percent in the first nine months of 1973—with the embargo still to come. When it did come, the majors were ready.

On Oct. 6, 1973, Egypt and Syria invaded Israel. Two days later, the major companies met with representatives of OPEC to begin talking about a new price structure. Bearing in mind that up to this moment OPEC had never in its life shown anything remotely resembling courage, one may justifiably conclude that its new aggressiveness was somehow the result of collaboration with the companies. (As one oil-company executive earlier told Newsweek, "In the Middle East, we carry the enemy flag.") On Oct. 16, OPEC announced a stunning 70 percent increase in prices and the next day declared that the Arab members of OPEC would cut production 5 percent each month "until Israeli withdrawal is completed from the whole Arab territories occupied in June 1967 and the legal rights of the Palestinian people are restored." It also declared that, because of the United States' and the Netherlands' friendship with Israel, those two countries would be cut off completely.

Enterprising reporters, however, found abundant evidence that the Arab embargo did not, in fact, cause any shortages. Libya did not shut off its supplies. Neither did Iraq. Nor Iran. If the Netherlands was being boycotted, what were all those tankers doing out there in the harbor waiting for a berth? Jack Bax, a press aide for the city of Rotterdam, told reporters in January 1974, "Personally, I think the whole thing is a hoax." And if there was a shortage in this country, why were fuel-oil barges backed up along the Ohio River? So much oil was available in the United States that some crafty merchants were buying low-sulfur oil on the Gulf Coast for 21 cents a gallon and shipping it to Europe to resell for 34 cents.

Nevertheless, the market operated as though there were a scarcity, and profits went through the ceiling. Occidental Petroleum Company announced that 1973 earnings were 665 percent higher than those of 1972. Other big companies were not burdened with quite such embarrassingly large *percentage* increases, but they were doing all right. On Jan. 1, 1974, OPEC raised the price to $11.65 a barrel—five times the price it had been only three years earlier. By the end of 1974, Exxon Corporation, the world's largest oil company, moved to the top of the Fortune 500 list—easily unseating General Motors, which for 40 years had held the premier position. Four other oil companies—Texaco, Mobil, Standard Oil of California and Gulf—joined Exxon in the top seven rankings.

Two weeks ago in The Times, reporter Jeff Gerth shed more light on how the giant Exxon, for example, was able to make the most of the moment. Reporting on a previously unpublized civil trial in Canada—a Nova Scotia public utility successfully blocked Exxon price increases—Gerth said that "during 1973 and 1974, Exxon documents show, the company disguised increases in its profit margins by backdating them to blend in with price increases tied to OPEC increases. These concealed profit increases appear to contradict broad assurances that Exxon submitted in writing in early 1974 to the Senate Finance Committee that its price increases since 1973 had 'essentially only' covered increased costs."

On its own, OPEC might have remained a motley assembly of whiners, but with the patient instruction of the majors, it had become the industry's friend supreme in raising prices. It had also become the great dramatist, writing the panic script that made oil at any price acceptable to the consumer nations. A few years later, when a reporter at The Washington Star asked James Lee, president of Gulf Oil, if he thought OPEC was a "good thing," he admitted that it had "done us a favor by forcing the price of oil as it did." Carmichael C. Pocock, chairman of Royal Dutch Shell, also conceded that, since OPEC took over the pricing of oil at the production level, "our role is much happier."

Some expert observers believe that OPEC's economic terrorism could have been permanently ended in 1975 if the major companies and our Government had made the effort to do so. The inevitable glut of oil developed by the end of 1974 because the higher prices had curtailed use. As 1975 opened, world oil prices were beginning to sag. OPEC looked shaky. A group of energy specialists brought together by the Brookings Institution predicted in January 1975 that OPEC would likely be crushed by falling prices by 1978.

At that point, the oil companies apparently cut back

production. John Blair, former chief economist for the Senate Antitrust and Monopoly Subcommittee, states, in his book "The Control of Oil," that "had it not been for the cutbacks, the market would have been flooded with 'distressed' oil, OPEC would indeed have broken down, and oil prices would have fallen sharply." But if the major oil companies betrayed the consumers, so did our Government officials: most of the top policy makers in the Ford Administration publicly denounced all efforts to drive down world oil prices.

1977: *Gas to Burn*

When the Federal Power Commission was ordered in 1938 to set the interstate price of natural gas, there was some disagreement as to whether this meant controlling the price of the gas only after it reached the interstate pipelines or at the well. In 1954, the Federal courts finally ruled that controlling prices in the pipeline would be meaningless unless prices were also controlled from the very beginning, at the wellhead. It ordered the F.P.C. to do so.

Industry, the independent companies as well as the majors, fought back. First, they tried to get Congress—with the encouragement of a stunning outpouring of campaign contributions—to pass a law removing natural gas from all Federal controls. When this failed, industry lawyers tried the Supreme Court, arguing that the lower prices imposed by the F.P.C. were keeping explorers from looking for new gas supplies.

But the industry lost. In 1968 the Supreme Court ruled that the market regulation was fair: there was no evidence that the proconsumer prices were hurting gas exploration. The Court noted that every year, according to industry's own records, more gas was found and added to the reserves than was burned by customers.

It was a striking coincidence, to say the least, that industry reported an increase in its reserves every year until the Supreme Court's adverse decision and a decline every year since then. Now, for the first time in its history, the natural-gas industry began planting dire stories about shortages. To give these warnings substance, some companies fudged on their mandatory reports to the Government.

James T. Halverson, director of the Federal Trade Commission's Bureau of Competition, said gas reserves in some areas were underreported by 1,000 percent. Congressional investigators said they found hundreds of wells capped in the Gulf of Mexico. Explorations for new gas plummeted. Beginning in 1971, the industry warned that "next winter" there would be shortages—enough shortages to close some factories and chill some homeowners. There were indeed shortages of a sort, created, as was later discovered, by some companies' hoarding supplies or transferring them from markets where they were desperately needed to markets where they weren't.

Through it all, as Homer Bigart reported in The New York Times, there were still some energy experts who believed the shortage was "a hoax perpetrated by the industry to force the Federal Power Commission to increase the price of natural gas sold in interstate commerce." For whatever reason, the F.P.C. did indeed heap new riches on the natural-gas peddlers; between 1972 and 1976, the price of new gas in interstate commerce was permitted to rise by more than 300 percent.

But the industry wasn't content. It wanted freedom from price regulation altogether, and it thought it saw its big opportunity in the energy package President Carter sent to Congress in 1977. To be sure, Carter took the position at first that he wanted to continue natural-gas price regulation, but it was plain that most of all he wanted to pass an energy bill—in almost any form—and that he would probably accept deregulation if he had to. Industry read the President right. When its friends in Congress, after months of debate, finished butchering the President's program, a bill arrived at the White House that would deregulate new natural gas, after regular annual increases, as of 1985. Carter signed it.

Suddenly there was once again an abundance of natural gas. Virtually overnight it became a surplus commodity. But the crisis had resulted in a slight difference. The price of gas of the average homeowner was now nearly 50 percent higher.

How could so many of these "crises" that turned out not to be crises have been allowed to happen? The most obvious answer is that there was virtually no resistance from the Government. No industry has been so pampered, so indulged in its waywardness, as the oil and gas industry. Every Administration supplies its own example of slavishness. In Nixon's days, the spirit was nicely caught by Interior Secretary Rogers C. B. Morton, assuring a group of oil executives at a White House briefing that they had nothing to fear from the Office of Oil and Gas because "our mission is to serve you, not regulate you. We try to avoid it. . . . I pledge to you that the department is at your service." And in the Carter Administration one could hear the soft symbiotic graciousness in former Energy Secretary James Schlesinger's promise to American Petroleum Institute conventioneers that with Carter's help they would see over "the next 20 years, a Golden Age for the industry that will rival, in many respects, the romance of oil of the past."

But there is another crucial reason: the oil industry controls the books. It controls the statistics. No other industry of comparable importance gets to operate with such secrecy. If the Government wants to know how many cars G.M. has in inventory, the Government need only send an agent around to storage lots and count them. But, if it wants to know how much oil and gas Exxon, and Mobil, for example, are sitting on, it must ask Exxon and Mobil. Whether or not the statistics it receives are accurate is anybody's guess. (And it may not receive the data it wants, at all; frequently, when the D.O.E. seeks sensitive details that would be really useful, the oil men take the bureaucrats to court and fight for their secrecy—it's a tough way to get the full picture.)

The only experts in how much oil and gas exists in the world, and where, are those who actually sink holes to find out. The U.S. Geological Survey which, from time to time, estimates present and future oil and gas reserves, doesn't do this. Neither does the Department of Energy. These agencies get their information from the industry. Obviously, those in the oil and gas business do drill wells, and they have a great deal of data. But they prefer to keep most of it secret. Rawleigh Warner Jr., chariman of the Mobil Corporation, was quite correct when he wrote in a recent letter to the editors of The Times that this is "a time when facts, and not villains, are badly needed." The reason the public, and many members of Congress, are so willing to make villains of the oil companies is that the oil companies have made it so difficult for anyone to get those facts.

For years, Senator Jackson had been considered one of Congress's half-dozen best-informed members in energy matters. But even he admitted, during his Senate investigation in 1974, that he didn't have the slightest idea what was going on. "We meet here this morning," he said, "in an effort to get the facts about the energy crisis. The facts are—we do not have the facts." For the next four days, he and other members of that sub-committee grilled the oil men, and came away virtually as ignorant as when they started. Senator Jackson ended with the confession that "the one point that this hearing has brought home clearly is our lack of timely, reliable, complete and credible information about the energy industry."

Then he ticked off a stunning list of blind spots: "We do not have reliable current data on primary crude-oil and product stocks, and there is no usable information at all on secondary stocks. Import statistics are covered with confusion and doubt. The wholesale-price statistics of the Federal Government regarding gasoline and fuel oil are not believable or usable. We know almost nothing about the international pricing and investment policies of the companies and the tax benefits they enjoy. . . . We are struggling here. It is the most ludicrous operation in the world when the United States of America simply does not have the facts to deal with a problem of this magnitude."

That's the chairman of the Senate Energy Committee talking. If he felt ludicrously ignorant, what senator didn't?

In 1977, when the White House was trying to move Congress to vote on the natural-gas bill, Senator John Durkin said the information he was getting from industry and the bureaucracy left him totally baffled as to whether we "are running out of natural gas, or swimming in it. . . . We sit here today like map makers of centuries ago, attempting to chart unseen lands by relying on secondhand information."

He had cause to complain. One official at the Energy Research and Development Administration had just finished a study showing that there would be plenty of affordable natural gas for at least the next 40 years. But since this conflicted with the gloomy forecast currently pushed by industry, the study was killed. The runaround, and the complaints about it, are constant. Representative Bob Eckhardt of Texas, chairman of the House Commerce Subcommittee on Investigations, says, "The Department of Energy relies solely on information it pumps from the companies, and that's one hard pumping job. The information D.O.E. gets is always at least two or three months old. Congress goddamn well isn't going to make sensible decisions concerning problems it's facing right now on information that old. . . . And the preliminary figures may be as much as 10 percent at variance with the facts."

Last August, the Department of Energy cleared the oil industry of charges of hoarding during the summer's gasoline shortage. As investigations go, however, the D.O.E.'s wasn't much, for—once again—it had relied solely on data supplied by the industry and had, moreover, been unable to obtain information relating to industry activities later than May, although the worst shortages occurred in June and July.

The upshot of all this is that when Congress is confronted with such questions as whether to deregulate natural gas or whether to permit the President to decontrol the price of oil, it must base its judgment on only such information as the target industry will release. It gets little help from the U.S. Geological Survey, whose predictions have fluctuated wildly over the years and have often seemed suspiciously like propaganda aimed at supporting the industry's latest crisis. In general, Government officials have racked up an almost perfect record of inaccurate predictions. In 1970, for example, the President's Cabinet group studying imports concluded that if the import-quota system were phased out rapidly, the U.S. and Canadian oil industry (it was fair to think of them as a unit since about 75 percent of Canada's oil was controlled by United States companies) would be so productive that in 1980 it would be able to supply 92 percent of those two nations' needs without rationing and more than 100 percent of their needs with rationing—*even if they were cut off from all, yes, all, Middle Eastern and Latin American imports*. Today, still one year short of the time when that forecast was supposed to apply, the oil industrialists claim America faces a future of dependency and that they are helpless to meet America's demands without importing nearly half its oil from abroad. One might say that the two positions were a bit at variance; indeed, it seems obvious that neither the 1970 statistics nor those of 1979 have much usefulness.

So right at this moment the only genuine crisis we're certain of is a crisis of ignorance. The nation is chronically short of reliable energy data. Should it base its energy policy on, say, the pessimism of a James Schlesinger, who believes we will run out of oil and gas "in 30 or 40 years," or on the optimism of a Russell Long, himself an independent oil man and privy to the innermost councils of the industry, who says "it should be apparent to all that, as long as we have oil producers in this country, we will have oil. The only essential for the next 1,000 years is the oil producer"?

The question of who's right can't be answered so long as industry holds an information monopoly. This is not a hopeless problems. It could be solved most easily by following the suggestion of the A.F.L.-C.I.O. to nationalize the oil and gas industry, thereby coming into the possession of all the industry's secrets in one swoop. A less drastic way to break the monopoly on information would be for the Federal Government to begin financing exploration parties of its own—to get out and drill holes in the ground and find out what is down there, at least in a few key areas.

Although Senator Long hates the idea of the Government's doing such a thing as exploring for oil, he nevertheless admits the soundness of the principle. Borrowed statistics won't get the job done; geological hypotheses based on past experience may be useful but they are still guesswork. Truth lies in the drill bit. As Senator Long once put it, "Until one has explored, there is no reason on earth to assume one acre of land is any better than any other acre of land anywhere on earth."

Most of the unexplored land in the United States is in the Federal domain, so the Government's oil explorers wouldn't have trouble getting permission. And 98 percent of the Federal land has never been explored. A dozen Spindletops may be out there waiting to be found. Or perhaps the nation is truly running dry. We will never know for sure until we find out independently of the oil companies.

A leap in that direction has been proposed by several members of Congress in a variety of bills that would set up a Federal oil and gas corporation either to buy oil directly from other producing nations or explore for (and produce) oil and gas at home, or both. Getting the Government directly into the oil and gas business as a way to escape the stupidity of borrowed data and the market variables imposed by industry is not exactly a new idea. It was proposed in the Senate at least as early as 1920 and it has been cropping up periodically ever since in both houses of Congress.

Enthusiasm for the notion has so far been slight. But sooner or later, having grown sufficiently fed up with whatever crises lie ahead, Congress may decide to create an energy policy based on the substitute for villainy Rawleigh Warner was talking about. To do that Congress will have to send its own buyers into the marketplace and its own roughnecks into the fields.

How Moral Men Make Immoral Decisions — A Look Inside GM

by John Z. De Lorean with J. Patrick Wright

"We feel that 1972 can be one of Chevrolet's great years. . . . Most of the improvements this year are engine and chassis components aimed at giving a customer a better car for the money. . . . I want to reiterate our pledge, the 1972 Chevrolets will be the best in history. . . ."

The words seemed to fall out of my mouth like stones from an open hand. Effortlessly. Almost meaninglessly. It was August 1971. I was powergliding through the National Press Preview of 1972 Chevrolet cars and trucks at Raleigh House, a mock-Tudor restaurant in suburban Detroit. The audience was filled with reporters from all over the country along with a plentiful sprinkling of Chevrolet managers. The presentation and question-answer went smoothly. I was stepping down from the podium and receiving the usual handshakes and compliments when a strange feeling hit me:

"My God! I've been through all this before."

Somehow I felt detached from it all, looking down on myself in the banquet hall surrounded by executives, newsmen and glittering Chevrolets and questioning why I was there and what I was doing. The answers were not satisfactory.

"This whole show is nothing but a replay of last year's show, and the year before that and the year before that," I thought. "The speech I just gave was the same speech I gave last year, written by the same guy in public relations about the same superficial product improvements. And the same questions were being asked by the same newsmen. Almost nothing has changed."

I looked around the room for a moment searching for anything that could show me that there was real meaning in the exercises we were going through, that the national press conference and the tens of similar dealer product announcements I conducted across the country were something more than just hypes. But I found nothing.

Instead, I got the empty feeling that what I was doing there might be nothing more than perpetuating a gigantic fraud. A fraud on the American consumer by promising him something new but giving him only surface alterations—"tortured sheet metal" as former chairman Frederic G. Donner used to say—or a couple of extra horsepower and an annual price increase. A fraud on the American economy, because I always had a vague suspicion that the annual model change might be good for the auto business in the short term but not good for the economy and the country.

And a fraud on our own company. When General Motors began to grow, on the principle of annual model changes and the promotion of something new and different, cars were almost all alike, with the same basic color—black. There was room for cosmetic changes as well as substantial advancement in technology with new and better engines, more sophisticated transmissions, improved performance and comfort characteristics. But by now there was nothing new and revolutionary in car development and there hadn't been for years. As a company, we were kidding ourselves that these slight annual alterations were innovative. They were not. We were living off the gullibility of the consumer combined with the fantastic growth of the American economy in the 1960s—salting away billions of dollars of profits in the process and telling ourselves we were great managers. This bubble was surely to break, I thought. The consumer is going to get wise to us, and when he does we will have to fight for a long time to get back into his favor.

Those feelings during the preview led me to tell newsmen during lunch that I would probably leave the auto industry when I was age 55 or so, to get involved in helping find answers to America's problems. There was skepticism and disbelief in their voices as we talked.

The Fourteenth Floor, the executive stronghold of GM's world headquarters in midtown Detroit, went through the ceiling when the stories appeared the next day saying I was going to forsake GM in eight or nine years. It looked to them as if I was trying to force their hand by saying: "Make me president by then or I'll quit."

To anyone in the corporation who asked, I explained that my luncheon comments, though not irrevocable, were sincere and that I was having some internal conflicts about my job. My doubts about the worth of the annual model change were just a part of a growing concern I had about the general level of morality practiced in GM in particular and parts of American business in general.

It seemed to me then, and still does now, that the system of American business often produces wrong, immoral, and irresponsible decisions, even though the personal morality of the people running the businesses is often above reproach. The system has a different morality as a group than the people do as individuals, which permits it willfully to produce ineffective or dangerous products, deal dictatorially and often unfairly with suppliers, pay bribes for business, abrogate the rights of employees by demanding blind loyalty to management, or tamper with the democratic process of government through illegal political contributions.

I am not a psychologist, so I can't offer a professional opinion on what happens to the freedom of individual minds when they are blended into the group management thought-process of business. But my private analysis is this:

Morality has to do with people. If an action is viewed primarily from the perspective of its effect on people, it is put into the moral realm. Business in America, however, is impersonal. This is particularly true of large American multinational corporations. They are viewed by their employees and publics as faceless. The ultimate measure of the success and failure of these businesses is not their effect on people, but their earnings per share of stock. The first question to greet any business proposal is, how will it affect profits? *People* do not enter the equation of a business decision except to the extent that their reaction will hurt or enhance earnings per share.

In such a completely impersonal context, business decisions of questionable personal morality are easily justified. A person who shoots and kills another is sentenced to life in prison. A businessman who makes a defective product which kills people may get a nominal fine or a slap on the hands, if he is ever brought to trial at all.

The impersonal process of business decision-making is reinforced by a sort of mob psychology that results from group management. Watergate certainly proved what can happen when blind devotion to a system or a process of thought moves unchecked. Members of the Nixon administration never raised any real questions about the morality of the break-in and cover-up. Their only concern was to save the system. So too in business. Too often the only questions asked are: What is the expedient thing to do? How can we increase profits per share?

Never once while I was in GM's management did I hear substantial concern raised about the impact of our business on America, its consumers, or the economy. When we should have been planning switches to smaller, more fuel-efficient, lighter cars in the late 1960s, in response to a growing demand in the marketplace, GM refused because "we make more money on big cars." It mattered not that customers wanted the smaller cars, or that a national balance-of-payments deficit was being built, in large part because of the burgeoning sales of foreign cars in the American market.

Refusal to enter the small car market when the profits were better on bigger cars, despite the needs of the public and the national economy, was not an isolated case of corporate insensitivity. It was typical. And what disturbed me is that it was indicative of fundamental problems with the system.

GM certainly was no more irresponsible than many American businesses. But the fact that the "prototype" of the well-run business engaged in questionable practices and delivered decisions which I felt were sometimes illegal, immoral, or irresponsible is an indictment of the American business system.

Earlier in my career, I accepted these decisions at GM without question. But as I was exposed to more facets of the business, I came to a realization of the responsibilities we had in managing a giant corporation and making a product which substantially affected people and national commerce. It bothered me how cavalierly these responsibilities were often regarded.

The Corvair case is a first-class example of a basically

irresponsible and immoral business decision which was made by men of generally high personal moral standards.

The Corvair was unsafe as it was originally designed. It was conceived along the lines of the Porsche. These cars were powered by engines placed in the rear and supported by an independent, swing-axle suspension system. In the Corvair's case, the engine was all-aluminum and air-cooled (compared to the standard water-cooled iron engines). This, plus the rear placement of the engine, made the car new and somewhat different in the American market.

However, there are several bad engineering characteristics inherent in rear-engine cars which use a swing-axle suspension. In turns at high speeds they tend to become directionally unstable and therefore difficult to control. The rear of the car lifts or "jacks," and the rear wheels tend to tuck under the car, which encourages the car to flip over. In the high-performance Corvair, the car conveyed a false sense of control to the driver when in fact he might have been very close to losing control of the vehicle. The result could be fatal.

These problems with the Corvair were well documented inside GM's engineering staff long before the Corvair was offered for sale. Frank Winchell, now vice-president of engineering but then an engineer at Chevy, flipped one of the first prototypes on the GM test track in Milford, Michigan. Others had the same experience.

The questionable safety of the car caused a massive internal fight among GM's engineers over whether the car should be built with another form of suspension. On one side of the argument was Chevrolet's then general manager, Ed Cole, an engineer and product innovator. He and some of his engineering colleagues were enthralled with the idea of building the first modern, rear-engine American car. I am convinced they felt the safety risks of the swing-axle suspension were minimal. On the other side was a wide assortment of top-flight engineers, including Charles Chayne, then vice-president of engineering, Von D. Polhemus, engineer in charge of chassis development, and others.

These men collectively and individually made vigorous attempts inside GM to keep the Corvair, as designed, out of production or to change the suspension system to make the car safer. One top corporate engineer told me that he showed his test results to Cole but by then, he said, "Cole's mind was made up."

Albert Roller, who worked for me in Pontiac's advanced engineering section, tested the car and pleaded with me not to use it at Pontiac. Roller had been an engineer with Mercedes-Benz before joining GM, and he said that Mercedes had tested similarly designed rear-engine, swing-axle cars and had found them far too unsafe to build.

At the very least, then, within GM in the late 1950s, serious questions were raised about the Corvair's safety. At the very most, there was a mountain of documented evidence that the car should not be built as it was then designed.

But Cole, who later became GM's president, was a strong voice in company affairs. In addition, the car as he proposed it would cost less to build than the same car with a conventional rear suspension. Management not only went along with Cole, it also told the dissenters in effect to "stop these objections. Get on the team, or you can find someplace else to work." The ill-fated Corvair was launched in the fall of 1959.

The results were disastrous. I don't think any one car before or since produced as gruesome a record on the highway as the Corvair. It was designed and promoted to appeal to the spirit and flair of young people, and sold in part as a sports car. Young Corvair owners, therefore, were trying to bend their cars around curves at high speeds and were killing themselves in alarming numbers.

It was only a couple of years or so before GM's legal department was inundated with lawsuits over the car. And the fatal swath that this car cut through the automobile industry ironically touched the lives of many GM executives, employees, and dealers themselves.

The son of Cal Werner, general manager of the Cadillac Division, was killed in a Corvair. Werner was absolutely convinced that the design defect in the car was responsible. He said so many times. The son of Cy Osborne, an executive vice-president in the 1960s, was critically injured in a Corvair and suffered irreparable brain damage. Bunkie Knudsen's niece was brutally injured in a Corvair. And the son of an Indianapolis Chevrolet dealer also was killed in the car. Ernie Kovacs, my favorite comedian, was killed in a Corvair.

While the car was being developed at Chevrolet, we at Pontiac were spending $1.3 million on a project to adapt the Corvair to our division. The corporation had given us the go-ahead to work with the car to give it a Pontiac flavor. Our target for introduction was the fall of 1960, a year after Chevy introduced the car.

As we worked on the project, I became absolutely convinced by Chayne, Polhemus and Roller that the car was unsafe. So I conducted a three-month campaign, with Knudsen's support, to keep the car out of the Pontiac lineup. Fortunately, Buick and Oldsmobile at the time were tooling up their own compact cars, the Special and the F-85, which featured conventional front-engine designs.

We talked the corporation into letting Pontiac switch from a Corvair derivative to a version of the Buick-Oldsmobile car. We called it the Tempest and introduced it in the fall of 1960 with a four-cylinder engine as standard equipment and a V-8 engine as an option.

When Knudsen took over the reins of Chevrolet in 1961, he insisted that he be given corporate authorization to install a stabilizing bar in the rear to counteract the natural tendency of the Corvair to flip off the road. The cost of the change would be about $15 a car. But his request was refused by The Fourteenth Floor as "too expensive."

Bunkie was livid. As I understand it, he went to the Executive Committee and told the top officers of the corporation that if they didn't give him permission to make the Corvair safe, he was going to resign from GM. The fear of the bad publicity that surely would result from Knudsen's resignation forced management's hand. They relented, and Bunkie put the stabilizing bar on the Corvair in the 1964 models. The next year a completely new and safer independent suspension designed by Frank Winchell was put on the Corvair. It became one of the safest cars on the road.

But the damage done to the car's reputation by then was irreparable. Corvair sales began to decline precipitously after the waves of unfavorable publicity following Ralph Nader's book and the many lawsuits being filed across the country. Production of the Corvair was halted in 1969, four years after it was made a safe and viable car.

There wasn't a man in top GM management who had anything to do with the Corvair who would purposely build a car that he knew would hurt or kill people. But, as part of a management team pushing for increased sales and profits, each gave his approval to decisions which produced the car in the face of the serious doubts that were raised about its safety.

The corporation became almost paranoid about the leaking of inside information on the car. In April 1971, 19 boxes of microfilmed Corvair owner complaints, which had been ordered destroyed by upper management, turned up in the possession of two suburban Detroit junk dealers. When The Fourteenth Floor found this out, it went into panic. We at Chevrolet were ordered to buy the microfilm back and have it destroyed.

I refused, saying that a public company had no right to destroy documents of its business and that GM's furtive purchase would surely surface. Besides, the $20,000 asking price was outright blackmail.

When some consumer groups showed an interest in getting the film, the customer relations department was ordered to buy the film, which it did. To prevent similar slip-ups in the future, the corporation tightened its scrapping procedures.

Chevrolet products were involved in the largest product recall in automotive history when, in 1971, the corporation called back 6.7 million 1965-69 cars to repair defective motor mounts. The rubber mounts, which anchor the engine to the car, were breaking apart and causing the engine to lunge out of place; this often locked the accelerator open at about 25 miles per hour. Cars were smashing up all across the country when panicky drivers couldn't stop them or jumped out in fright.

The defect need never have been. At Pontiac, when I was chief engineer, we developed a safety-interlock motor mount which we put on our 1965 car line. It was developed because we discovered that the mounts we were using were defective. We made our findings and the design of the new motor mounts available to the rest of the car divisions. None of them opted to use it.

However, reports started drifting in from the field in 1966 that the Chevrolet mounts were breaking apart after extensive use. Chevrolet did nothing. Dealers replaced the mounts—and charged the customers for parts and labor.

When I got to Chevrolet in 1969, the reports about motor mount failures were reaching crisis proportions. When a motor mount failure was blamed for a fatal accident involving an elderly woman in Florida, I asked Roger Kyes, my boss, to let me quietly recall the cars with these problems and repair them at GM's expense. He refused, on the grounds that it would cost too much. By 1971, however, the trouble was becoming widely known outside of the corporation because owners were complaining to local newspapers, the National Highway Traffic Safety Administration, and several consumer groups.

The pressure began to build on General Motors to recall the cars. GM started to repair these cars at company expense, but it refused to recall them, preferring to wait until the mounts broke in use before doing anything. Bob Irvin, of the Detroit *News,* who was receiving huge numbers of complaints, wrote stories almost daily about GM's steadfast refusal to recall all the cars.

The fires of discontent were further fanned when Ed Cole, who was opposing the recall internally, was asked by a reporter why GM continued to refuse to recall the cars. He replied that anyone who "can't manage a car at 25 miles per hour shouldn't be driving." It was an unfortunately callous remark, for which I am sure Cole was later sorry. But he became more rigid in his stance against a recall campaign. So I wrote a memo to my immediate boss, Tom Murphy, which said in part:

> "At this point in time, it seems to me that we have no alternative (but to recall the Chevrolets). Certainly if GM can spend over $200 million a year in advertising, the $30 or $40 million this would cost is not a valid reason for delaying. Certainly, it would be worth the cost to stop the negative publicity, even if management cannot agree to recall these cars on moral grounds."

Murphy received the memo and returned it to me, refusing to accept it.

Finally, about a month or so later, under the weight of government, consumer group and newspaper pressure, GM recalled the 6.7 million cars with defective engine mounts. The price was about $40 million to recall the cars and wire the engines to the car so they wouldn't slip out of place when the mounts broke.

But the cost was much greater in the incredibly bad publicity GM received because of its own unwillingness to admit its responsibility for the defect and to repair the cars on its own. It was a case of the corporation taking an attitude of "the owners be damned." The motor mount affair reflected GM's corporate attitude toward the consumer movement, an attitude shared in a variety of ways in a wide variety of industries.

GM's consumer image also suffered from a dearth of product innovations. This produced an unquenchable thirst at GM for information on what the competition was doing. This led the company into areas which I felt were of questionable legality. So concerned was management with the plans of the competition, especially Ford, that the final okay on product programs was often delayed until we received the latest intelligence report on Ford's product programs.

I was told by Lou Bauer, once Chevrolet's comptroller, that when Bunkie Knudsen took over Chevrolet in 1961, he was shocked to find on the payroll two men who worked for Ford. They worked in Ford's product planning area and passed on new product information to Chevrolet. Knudsen, I was told, fired the spies the day he confirmed their existence. But GM continued to keep Ford under close—and questionable—surveillance.

This habit reached a height of sorts when several of us walked into a meeting of the Administration Committee sometime after 1971, and found the top corporate officers poring over a very confidential "spread sheet." This report gave the definitive breakdown, product-by-product, of what it cost Ford to build and sell its cars. It was the kind of information which, for our products, never got off The Fourteenth Floor. GM top management wouldn't even let its own divisional management in on all the corporate costs. But somehow top management had gotten this information about Ford, and they were studying it with deep concentration. Corporate counsel Ross Malone was incensed. He snapped, "Goddamnit! You guys shouldn't be doing this."

His voice was angry and pleading. It was obvious to me that Malone thought what was taking place had serious legal overtones.

After he spoke, someone scooped up the Ford cost report and hustled it off to one of the front offices. None of us at the divisional level ever heard about the report again. Now, I am sure that the men studying these confidential cost sheets would be outraged at the suggestion of similar conduct in their personal lives. Like most Americans, they were probably angered by the disclosures in the wake of Watergate that the CIA, U.S. Army, FBI, and other government agencies spied on unsuspecting citizens. And yet, at GM, they were justifying the very same sort of conduct on the grounds that "this is business."

GM also took its place in the line with scores of other American businesses in promoting what I think are, at the very least, improper political campaign contributions from its top executives. The system was complicated and far more secretive than the outright corporate political gifts for which a number of major corporations have paid fines.

The contributions program was operated, as I understood it, by the financial side of the business with assistance from some people on the public relations staff. The finance staff apparently collected the money and a few PR people distributed it with guidance from The Fourteenth Floor.

There were two tiers to the system. Middle level managers were generally allowed to contribute a sum of money to the party of their choice. However, once an executive reached upper managment levels, it was decided for him how much he would contribute and to whom it would go.

When I was a general manager, the divisional controller once walked into my office with a sheet of paper that apparently had been given to him by the corporate finance staff. On the sheet was written my name and the amount I was to donate to that year's election campaigns—national, state, or local. I was told to make a check out to "cash" for the amount assigned to me and give it to the controller. Once the check was made out, an executive did not know to whom or for whom the political contribution was made, nor the manner in which it was made: whether it was an anonymous cash contribution, one that was made in his name or a corporate gift. All the executive knew was that he wrote a check to "cash" for the predetermined amount.

The sums were big. For a GM vice president, it might be as much as $3,000 in a presidential campaign, less for an off-year congressional election, and so on down to a few hundred dollars for a city election.

I participated in the system several times at Pontiac. I cannot recall whether I made the donations myself or wrote a check to "cash." But finally, I just couldn't accept the practice, and I refused to participate. The thing seemed wholly improper. My franchise to vote and donate as I saw fit was too important to me as a citizen to delegate it to management or some guy on one of the corporation has no right to tell any executive how to vote, or to know how he votes.

After I refused to participate in the contribution program at GM on several different occasions, top management hit the roof. As in the past, the chore of trying to bring me into line fell to Kyes. He was ready for battle.

"John, you'd better damn well play this game," he said. "If you don't, you are telling us you aren't on the team. We don't think highly of guys who aren't on the team at GM."

Then he sought to reduce the doubts in my mind to money, the common rationalization in business.

"We take care of you at bonus time. When you make this contribution, you get it back as part of your bonus. And if you don't make the contribution, then you aren't going to get that much bonus."

The meeting ended angrily, as usual, with neither of us giving an inch. I continued to boycott the political contribution system at GM, and instead made personal donations to candidates I thought were worthy. And I must admit I never noticed an inexplicable drop in the bonus I received for my work at GM thereafter.

While these business practices involved questionable ethics exercised for the good of the business, sometimes upper management executives used their positions of power and knowledge to profit *personally* in corporate business. These were by no means widespread and perhaps confined to a few individuals.

When I was directing Pontiac, several GM dealers were purchasing the troubled National Car Rental Company for almost nothing—less than $4 million. The price, as I remember, was two or three dollars per share.

While they were doing this, they also worked a deal with upper corporate management for GM to provide $22 million in advertising assistance, because National was going to emphasize GM cars in its business and promotion. The confirmation of this arrangement was known only to a few people. But once it became public the stock of the company would surely jump in value. One day one of the participants in the purchase of National came to me and said, "You've got to get some of this stock." I said, "That's an obvious conflict of interest. I can't do it."

He said, "Hell, I'll buy it for you and keep it in my name. Tell me how much you want." I refused his second offer because it was wrong, and what's more, once you let a guy do something like that, he owns you forever. You're his puppet. He was irritated by my refusal and said, "Hell, we're doing it for ———" and he named a high-ranking GM official. It was quite a surprise.

I never personally verified whether the guy this dealer named was in on the deal or not, which is why I am not disclosing the names involved. But I do know that the word was rife through the corporation that officers were making bundles from insider information on National stock. So wide-spread was this rumor that management conducted an investigation and demanded to examine National's stockholder list to see if any GM executives were on it. There were none. But then there wouldn't be—if the stock were held in someone else's name.

On another occasion when I was at Chevrolet, word got around that company and divisional executives were speculating on land around the Lordstown assembly plant in Ohio. Since these people were privy to our plans for the Lordstown area, they could buy the land and sell when its value rose.

Again the corporation conducted an investigation and apparently fingered several people, including one of our Chevy managers. Word was that the culprits would be fired. One day, the Chevy executive in question walked into my office obviously nervous and excited, and snapped: "If you guys make something out of this, I'm going to blow the lid off this goddamn thing."

"What the hell do you mean?" I asked.

He replied by telling me the name of a real estate man in the Lordstown area who he said was acting as the agent in these land transactions, and who was willing to implicate top corporate managers. Some of the executives were the same ones trying to have him fired in the brewing scandal. I told the guy I knew nothing about the matter and was not part of the firing action. But he must have put the same threat to his prosecutors in the corporation—because it wasn't too long before this executive who was on the verge of being fired was plucked from Chevy management, promoted to a corporate job, and given a $5,000 raise.

The Prosecution Of Price-Fixing

by Joe Sims

In early 1978, there was an article in the *New York Times* titled "How to Make Crime Pay." The author, attorney Steven Gillers, had several rather common sense suggestions for those on the wrong side of the law interested in minimizing their risks: (1) steal from large numbers of people as indirectly as possible, since there is less emotional reaction to an impersonal offense; (2) commit a federal crime rather than a state crime, because "federal judges are more worldly and less likely to send you to jail or for as long . . . [and] federal prisons are nicer places to stay;" (3) commit a crime the judge can relate to, such as "tax offenses, securities violations, antitrust violations, international bribery and falsifying certain kinds of documents;" (4) look prosperous and have many influenttial friends who can vouch for your character; and (5) start a lawyer fund, since "hundreds if not thousands of people in jail today would not be if they had saved up money for a good lawyer."

A number of these suggestions in fact are characteristics that would commonly apply to a typical antitrust criminal defendant. They go a long way toward explaining why so few antitrust criminal defendants have in fact received anything which could objectively be described as severe punishment.

Of course, many individual antitrust defendants would argue (some accurately) that they became involved in the conduct for which they were prosecuted as the result of somewhat different influences than your average run-of-the-mill criminal. Many would quite honestly argue that their actions were not undertaken with a specific design to line their pockets with someone else's money, nor were they intended to harm any other individual. Rather, what they did was done because they were under pressure to get their profits up, or because the competition forced them to it.

Whatever the rationale for what is a *per se* crime, *there is no doubt that price-fixing is a common, everyday occurrence in the United States, and it cannot be doubted that the result is significant additions to the costs of goods and services in our economy.* The true costs of price-fixing and similar violations, of course, can never be measured. The cost in terms of inflationary impact, of loss of innovation, of the inability of honest small businessmen and women to keep their businesses alive because of artificialities in the market created or strengthened by collusion among established firms—these are all unquantifiable, largely unknown, and very real. For although the Justice Department's Antitrust Division has in fact been uncovering and prosecuting more price-fixing violations, we have seen no indication of diminishing returns for our efforts. In fact, we see only increased signs of more and more price-fixing activity.

It is clear that the Division has so far failed to eliminate price-fixing. In fact, there is no reason to believe that it has done anything but scratch the surface. But that failure does not rest entirely or even primarily on the shoulders of the Antitrust Division. In my view, the federal courts must accept a substantial portion of the blame, for they have been unwilling to hand down the kinds of sentences that are clearly necessary if meager prosecutorial efforts are ever to have anything more than *de minimis* impact.

For example, let's look at the period between the time the felony statute was passed (December 21, 1974) and the time that individual sentences were handed down in the *Folding Cartons* case (November of 1976). This is a good period to examine for comparative purposes, since it was a time when the Division was not really publicly campaigning for stiffer sentences, and there was a typical mixture of cases.

During this period, ninety-eight individual defendants were sentenced. Of those, seven, or just over seven percent, received actual jail sentences. The total sentences meted out to those seven individuals were 285 days, an average of just under 41 days each. Total jail sentences, divided by total defendants sentenced, averaged just under three days per defendant.

Typical sentences included one year unsupervised probation (following a trial and guilty verdict), and six months suspended sentence (following a guilty plea). When the likelihood of being discovered and prosecuted is small to begin with, and the likelihood of receiving a jail sentence if discovered and successfully prosecuted is only seven out of one hundred, is it at all surprising that there is no evidence of any significant deterrent effect from this level of sentences?

The *Folding Cartons* case was the beginning of a significant effort by the Antitrust Division to raise the visibility of the problem. Donald Baker, who was then the Assistant Attorney General in charge of the Division, appeared before Judge James Parsons in 1976 to personally argue for the appropriateness of significant jail sentences in that case. The judge, however, meted out minimal, suspended sentences.

Nevertheless, although the division was not successful in that case, it did mark the beginning of an effort that has been very successful since. As an interesting comparison, in misdemeanor cases since the *Folding Cartons* sentences to date, there have been seventy-six individual defendants sentenced, of whom seventeen have been sentenced to serve actual jail sentences. Thus, the percentage of those sentenced in misdemeanor cases *actually* going to jail rose to twenty-two percent, a three-fold increase over the period immediately prior to *Folding Cartons*. The total time sentenced to be served by those seventeen individuals was 1,215 days, an average of just over 71 days each. This compares favorably to the average of about 41 days each in the period immediately preceding the *Folding Cartons* case. Even more impressively, the average jail time for all individual defendants sentenced was right at 16 days—five times greater than the comparable figure in the period prior to *Folding Cartons*.

Still, even this improvement has not been sufficient to keep up with Antitrust Division hopes, or even rhetoric. One is reminded of the old Chinese proverb: "Much noise on stairs; nothing coming down." Fortunately, although we have much less experience with felony cases, what experience we do have shows a truly dramatic change. For example, 294 corporate defendants have been sentenced in misdemeanor cases since the passage of the felony statute.

The total fines imposed against those 294 entities amounted to $6,812,500—an average of $23,171.77. By comparison, 41 corporate defendants have been sentenced in felony cases by March, 1978, with total fines of $5,516,000—an average of $134,536.59. So, on these numbers, the price of a corporate criminal conviction has gone up about six times.

On the individual side, the numbers are even more dramatic. Twenty-one individual defendants have been sentenced in felony cases to date, and fifteen—almost 75 percent—have been sentenced to jail. You will recall that pre-*Folding Cartons*, only seven percent of all individual defendants sentenced went to jail. Total jail sentences imposed in felony cases have been 96 months—2,880 days—an average of 192 days each. The average sentence imposed, calculated on the basis of all individual defendants sentenced, is 137 days, 45 times greater than the average pre-*Folding Cartons*.

For an even more stark comparison, let me point out that from 1890 to 1970 only 19 individuals actually went to jail for pure antitrust violations for a *total* of 28 months. In the last year alone, 1977, and only counting the felony cases, the Division has obtained 3-1/2 times the total amount of jail time obtained in the first 80 years of the Sherman Act.

Obviously, a good part of the explanation for this progress lies in the 1974 congressional action making violation of the Sherman Act a felony. Upon conviction, an individual antitrust violator can now receive a three-year prison sentence and a $100,000 fine. A convicted corporation can receive a $1 million fine. This congressional message has clearly been heard by sentencing judges, though with some difficulty.

To help amplify this message, the Anitrust Division has adopted internal guidelines for sentencing recommendations in felony cases. In summary, these guidelines require prosecuting attorneys to apply several aggravating and mitigating factors to a recommended base sentence of 18 months. Of course, under current parole provisions, an 18-month sentence would most often lead to an actual period of incarceration of something just short of 6 months.

The aggravating factors that we considered in determining each sentencing recommendation include: (1) the amount of commerce involved; (2) the position of the individual; (3) the existence and degree of predatory conduct; (4) the length of participation in the violation; and (5) the possibility of a previous conviction. As mitigating factors, we consider cooperation with the government and unusual personal, family, or business hardship.

This belief in some uniform approach to antitrust sentencing reflects the almost universal criticism of unchecked, unreviewable judicial sentencing discretion. Few today would accept the notion that it is rational public policy to determine the penalty society chooses to mete out for a particular crime on the basis of the luck of the draw of one particular judge or another.

Still, some critics might ask, why jail? Most theories of sentencing have four goals: (1) to protect the public from further crimes of the defendant; (2) to provide rehabilitation; (3) to reflect the gravity of the defendant's conduct; and (4) to deter others from commiting the offense.

In antitrust cases, the first two—incapacitation and rehabilitation—normally are not substantial factors in the analysis. The type of offense we are dealing with—a business crime committed by people otherwise engaged in normal business activity—means that we are unlikely to see recidivists, although it does occasionally happen. But the other two factors make incarceration an appropriate sanction.

Deterrence is a—perhaps the—fundamental goal of sentencing recommendations. Rational economic behavior would seem to be a common characteristic of price-fixers. Criminal antitrust violations involve rational choice—conduct engaged in only as long as, or to the extent that, the offender calculates it to be worth it. In the face of law enforcement efforts, the price-fixer must balance the increased revenues generated by price-fixing against the probability of getting caught and the severity of the punishment. To make the law enforcement deterrent credible and effective, given our limited resources, there must be the likelihood of substantial punishment. Antitrust crimes are particularly difficult to detect, the crime is usually concealed, and the victim is often not in a position to perceive the violation. We can only discover some small percentage of offenses; given that fact, only sufficiently costly punishment will lead to significant levels of general deterrence. Indeed, even with a maximum law enforcement effort creating a significant risk of discovery, a potential violator will not be deterred unless the price of being caught is substantial. Thus, even if the resource limitations of the Antitrust Division disappeared overnight (don't hold your breath), certainty of detection would not be a sufficient deterrent unless the likely punishment was severe.

There is, of course, some good anecdotal evidence indicating that prison is a particularly effective deterrent for some people and some offenses. In World War II, for example, price control regulations were found to be considerably more effective in those judicial districts where prison rather than probation was the normal punishment. Scandinavian countries have, through harsh sentences for violations, significantly reduced instances of drunken driving. Finally, our own experience indicates the deterrent effect of what are viewed as harsh sentences. Several investigations discovered a number of price-fixing conspiracies which abruptly terminated after the dramatic and well publicized prison sentences in the *Electrical Equipment* conspiracy case.

And of course, there is always the Ethiopian pepper market saga, which is distinguishable but still relevant if only by analogy. There, not too long ago, several merchants were found to have withheld some commodities from the market, inducing artificial scarcity and rising prices. Here, we would call that attempt to monopolize. There, the merchants involved—seven in all—were summarily executed. Prices fell 60 percent in three weeks. Now, admittedly there are certain significant differences between the economic and legal systems of Ethiopia and the United States. But there are obviously at least two similarities: (1) some people are greedy, and want more success than their honest efforts will bring them; and (2) people won't risk their necks (no pun intended) for a little economic gain. The language is different, but the message can be translated.

This degree of certainty in criminal antitrust law also make the notion of "alternative sentencing," as practiced in several recent cases, quite disturbing. In one of those cases, the *Paper Labels* case, Judge Charles Renfrew [now

Deputy Attorney General] required each defendant, as a condition of probation, to make twelve speeches concerning his participation in the conspiracy. This novel approach was adopted even though the Judge had characterized the conduct involved as a "classic" violation of the antitrust laws—and so it was. Members of the industry had expanded social meetings at trade association gatherings to include the exchange of very explicit information about pricing decisions and policies. These exchanges eventually developed into bid-rigging, a division of markets and allocation of customers through pricing agreements. The conspiracy collapsed when a disgruntled former employee spilled the beans.

In these speeches, as could have been expected, the defendants portrayed themselves as unwary victims, but this would only emphasize the fact that many in business need stronger indications from the courts that "classic violations" of antitrust laws really amount to criminal conduct.

THE CORPORATION AND LABOR

Workers built America. Too often we forget that the buildings, the streets, the railroads, and all the material objects that we use daily are the result of the arduous labor of millions of men and women throughout generations of American history. Far more impressive than our mechanical might, our huge cities, our vast geography, or our capital stock is the human stock who made it all possible.

Yet despite this role in generating the wealth of America, working men and women have had a long and combative history to achieve what most now consider to be the most basic rights—health, safety, equal pay for equal work, and job security. And, as Ed McConville makes clear in his article on the decade-long battle between Southern textile workers and the J.P. Stevens Co., this struggle is in no way over.

Even those workers who seem to have achieved recognition of their rights, have had to guard against other threatening forms of corporate behavior. Inspired by the lure of union-free, cheap labor, companies can, as Don Stillman tells us, simply close factories in one area and relocate thousands of miles away. Or, as Robert Georgine outlines in his article, they can enlist the services on the new union-busters, who have replaced physical violence with psychological intimidation as the tool of their trade.

Do things have to be this way? In an excerpt from Daniel Zwerdling's *Democracy at Work*, we are provided with a case study of what can happen when men and women have a greater voice and sense of participation in the decisions that affect them in the workplace. His article describes how workers can and should be involved citizens of the corporation, how a Samuel Gompers of today would answer not only "more" but "better" in response to the classic question, "What does labor want?"

The Southern Textile War

by Ed McConville

As our newspapers have portentously informed us, 1976 is a big year for labor negotiations. Yet the year's most important negotiations were already more than a year old when the Bicentennial began, and in all likelihood they will still be dragging on when the last official Bicentennial T-shirt has been taken down from store shelves.

Major contracts covering millions of workers will expire this year, but the most significant talks will directly affect only 3,600 workers in seven plants. The union representing these workers, though it faces the country's most intransigent employer, has decided its members will not strike this year, come hell or high water.

"Pattern-setting agreements" have been or will be reached in basic industries like auto, trucking, rubber, meatpacking and electrical products. Economists will argue that these settlements are primarily to blame for our continuing inflation, but the contract struggle with the most lasting effect does not really concern money. It concerns a union's right to exist. And, more important, an American worker's right to join a union.

The town involved is Roanoke Rapids, N.C. The company which owns the seven plants is J.P. Stevens and Co., the world's second-largest textile manufacturer—and the most determinedly anti-union of all major companies in the United States. The union is the newly merged Amalgamated Clothing and Textile Workers Union (ACTWU), with a combined membership of 500,000.

It is commonly supposed that the American labor movement has everywhere become just another stodgy sector of the Establishment. Wilfrid Sheed gave expression to this conventional wisdom in 1973 when he wrote in the *Atlantic Monthly* that "in 1935, after much bloody skirmishing with management, the Wagner Act was passed, defining the right to organize, strike, and close a shop, all the prerogatives that now seem prehistoric."

In sober fact, unions hold none of these prehistoric prerogatives in the South. Strikes there are virtually futile, since judges routinely hand down anti-picketing injunctions and local and state police escort strikebreakers safely into and out of struck plants. Under "right to work" laws authorized by the Taft-Hartley Act in 1947, the closed shop is illegal in all but one Southern state. As for the Wagner Act's forty-year-old guarantee of workers' "Right to organize"—"It ain't worth the paper it's printed on south of the Mason-Dixon," snapped an old union organizer recently. He was perhaps trying a little too hard to be vivid, but he is essentially right.

The Southern Textile industry is America's last major unorganized manufacturing industry, with fewer than 10 percent of the region's 589,000 textile workers belonging to a union. Today, sixty years after they began moving down from New England to take advantage of cheap labor, Southern mills employ nearly three-quarters of the nation's textile work force. Textiles is far and away the Southeast's leading industrial employer; mill hands are the bedrock of the South's economy, religion and politics.

They are also the lowest-paid industrial workers in the South and the nation, with an average hourly wage of $3.46 in November 1975. This compares with $6.43 in the automobile industry and $6.73 in the basic steel industry. Organized labor's failure to make inroads in the South is often ascribed to the inherent conservatism of the region's working people, but closer examination uncovers a history of suppressed militance. A wave of textile strikes, some Communist-led, swept through North Carolina and Tennessee in 1929. Cotton mill workers from every Southern state formed the overwhelming majority of the 376,000 workers who participated in the nationwide textile strike in 1934. The Textile Workers Organizing Committee's campaigns were considered among the best planned and executed of the CIO organizing drives of the 1930s.

Each of these attempts failed, not because Southern mill workers made a clear, uncoerced choice against unionism but because Southern employers were able to bring a panoply of pressures to bear upon them in the small, isolated towns where most mills are located. They denied their employees any allies by mobilizing the rest of their communities against them; local police, press and preachers made common cause with the Ku Klux Klan and other practitioners of mob violence.

In 1963 the labor movement decided to renew its efforts to organize Southern textiles. Acknowledging that the small, weak Textile Workers Union of America (TWUA) could not take the industry on by itself, the AFL-CIO's Industrial Union Department (IUD) contributed money and manpower to a drive to organize J. P. Stevens. With annual sales of more than $1 billion, Stevens today employs 44,000 people in some eighty plants.

The company employed a policy of economic terrorism to defeat the TWUA-IUD organizers in every union representation election held during the 1960s and early 1970s. "Hell," said one organizer, "why go to the trouble of beating someone up when you can fire him? It's not as risky and it lasts longer."

The National Labor Relations Board (NLRB) has found Stevens guilty of illegally firing 289 employees for union activity. Many times that number were afraid to be seen talking to organizers or even to accept the leaflets they offered at plant gates. Union meetings consisted of small, secret gatherings in workers' homes; public meetings attracted embarrassingly sparse attendance. Stevens paid the union $50,000 in damages for wiretapping an organizer's motel room in 1973.

Firing tactics are the chief component of a systematic strategy of pre-election harassment and intimidation known to organizers as "a Blakeney campaign." Whiteford S. Blakeney is a Charlotte, N.C. attorney who specializes in advising Southern companies, including Stevens, how they can best avoid unionization. "I can tell whether Blakeney represents a plant the first week I go in there to organize," says TWUA organizer Clyde Bush. "If people start getting fired right off, I know who I'm up against."

The National Labor Relations Act allows the NLRB to impose only two innocuous penalties for such firings: it can order the company involved to rehire the employees and to reimburse them for the wages they would have earned had they not been fired. These sanctions are even lighter than they appear. If a discharged worker finds other employment before he is rehired—as he must do if he and his family are to survive during the two and a half years it normally takes to settle firing cases—his earnings during this interim period are subtracted from the amount the company must pay him. These back-pay awards are also tax-deductible as a legitimate business expense. In addition, the total costs of these awards ($1.3 million in Stevens's case) are relatively small when compared to the much higher costs of a union contract. (Board statistics indicate that an increasing number of employers are coming to this realization. NLRB regional offices awarded $11.3 million in back pay in fiscal 1975 to 7,405 workers "discharged for union activity." These figures have been rising steadily for several years.)

For all the softness and slowness of the penalties allowed it by federal labor law, the NLRB over the years has managed to weave a legal web around J.P. Stevens which has partially limited the company's freedom of illegal movement. The board has found Stevens guilty of unfair labor practices in fifteen separate cases since the company was targeted by the IUD in 1963.

Technically, the NLRB has no enforcement powers of its own. "An order of the board does not have the force of law," wrote Charles Fahy, the board's first chief executive officer, "until it becomes the order of a circuit court of appeals." Board lawyers, although resigned to the fact that the wheels of justice grind exceedingly slow, have doggedly sought appeals court citations against Stevens. The company was held in contempt in 1972 for refusing to comply with a U.S. circuit court's decree prohibiting further unfair labor practices; three additional contempt proceedings are pending before the courts.

Federal appeals courts can order stiffer penalties for companies held in contempt, including heavy fines and what lawyers euphemistically refer to as "bodily attachment" of company officers. ("That means they throw your fanny in jail," explains Harold McIver, the veteran organizer who directs the IUD's campaign against Stevens.)

When the contempt charges began to accumulate, J.P. Stevens stopped firing. And, after more than a decade of defeat, the union won its first election over the company in August 1974, in Roanoke Rapids, a drab mill town of 15,000.

Unions had been to Roanoke Rapids before, only to be destroyed on different occasions during the 1930s, 1940s and 1950s. In 1965 the TWUA-IUD forces tried their hand there and lost a tense election. "We couldn't get open participation in that campaign because twenty-three workers were fired," recalls Scott Hoyman, now TWUA's Southern regional director. "But, as a result of all the contempt proceedings, they've stopped firing right before the election like they usually do, and people are not afraid to come out for the union anymore. We had workers handing out leaflets at the gates for the first time in Roanoke Rapids in 1974."

The victory pumped much needed adrenalin into the hard-pressed Southern labor movement. North Carolina AFL-CIO President Wilbur Hobby proclaimed "a new day in Dixie—first, J.P. Stevens, then the textile industry, and then the whole South."

It is hard to overestimate the significance of Roanoke Rapids—though, as will be described in a moment, a battle was won but the fighting continues. Unionization, with its potential for a moderate redistribution of the South's new affluence, represents nothing less than the economic consolidation and extension of the limited legal and political gains won by the civil rights movement in the 1960s. By alleviating the poverty of both blacks and poor whites, unions can allay the economic enmity which lies at the roots of so much of the South's racial tension. The labor movement's self-interest lies in aggressively promoting integration in the region. Organizers must appeal to all racial and religious groups in a work place if they are to gather the all-important "50 per cent plus one" of the votes cast in a representation election. And no union can hope to win a strike or get a good contract unless virtually all employees support its walkout.

Roanoke Rapids is a beachhead, not only of unionism but also of racial cooperation among Southern working-class people. Organizers concede they had never before been able to keep the races together as they did in the seven plants there.

"I had never been with blacks socially," says Danny Blackwell, who dyes towels in one of Stevens's Roanoke Rapids mills. "Then George [former organizer George Strawn] started taking us fishing together. He'd take a couple of whites and a couple of blacks on weekends and we really got along good. That's where I first got my feeling about blacks and whites being together in the union. They've all got pretty much the same problems and a lot of the same ideas about what to do about them. It's just a question of getting them together so they can find that out."

The unionization of the textile industry also has profound political implications. "I'd lose my job if I voted for most of the bills you want me to support," one Southern Senator told Harold McIver after his Roanoke Rapids triumph. "But if you ever get this industry organized, come back to see me and we'll talk business." By moving Southern industrial workers in a generally more progressive direction, unions could well break up the coalition of conservative Southern Democrats and Northern Republicans that has defeated reform legislation in the Senate for so many years.

Roanoke Rapids is indistinguishable from other mill towns across the South. Mill workers there are shut off from the rest of the community by the long six-day work week that is standard in the Southern textile industry. They are also isolated by a sense of shame: invidious distinctions between "cotton mill trash" and the rest of the town persist, even in the minds of the mill hands themselves. A recent study showed that 16.5 percent of the country's citizens have drinking problems, compared with 5 per cent nationally. The county's mental health director has called alcoholism Roanoke Rapids' worst medical and social problem.

He might also have mentioned byssinosis, or "brown lung" disease, a debilitating respiratory ailment caused by breathing in cotton dust. An estimated 100,000 American textile workers suffer from this occupational illness. The textile industry, which for years denied the disease's existence, today takes the position that it cannot afford to lower the dust to the levels recommended by the government's National Institute for Occupational Safety and Health (NIOSH). Noise levels in the mills are also dangerously high. Constant exposure to the clatter of the looms produces many cases of deafness and "nerve tear-up," a malady whose victims resemble the shell-shocked veterans who returned home from World War II and the Korean War.

The mill workers' extra day of scheduled overtime has not solved their money problems. A familiar sight after the shifts change in Roanoke Rapids, as in other mill towns, is the long line outside the small finance company office across the street from the mill. Young people in the line carefully pick clumps of cotton from their hair and clothing, to avoid the contempt accorded to "lint heads." Older workers, seemingly resigned to their status, often leave the cotton clinging to themselves.

"We've been trapped in the mills every generation because we can't earn enough to send our kids to college," says Danny Blackwell. "I don't worry about myself anymore," continued this resigned 20-year-old. "I want the union so my daughter can make it out."

TV cameras and reporters from most major newspapers have descended on Roanoke Rapids since the union's victory there. Gloria Steinem came down from New York to shoot a television special on the life of a woman working in the mills there.

But much of the promise and hope of Roanoke Rapids has drained away in the two years since the workers voted the union in. The company and the union have been unable to arrive at a first contract after twenty-five months of fruitless negotiations.

It is generally assumed that, once the NLRB has directed an employer to recognize and bargain with a union as the result of a representation election, management will accept the union as a fact of life and negotiate a contract with it. But J.P. Stevens, refusing to admit defeat, has resorted to a practice known in Southern labor relations circles as "bargaining a union to death." Lawyers refer to it by its proper legal name, "bargaining in bad faith."

Southern companies (several of them represented by Whiteford Blakeney) have dragged out negotiations for years, while the unions, in the words of one textile executive, "withered on the vine." Workers at some plants became so impatient that they voted to decertify the union as their bargaining agent. Even when this does not happen, a local union's lack of a contract leaves it weak and, in effect, unrecognized by the employer.

Stevens's ability to deny its Roanoke Rapids employees

a contract has effectively stalled the union's drive to organize the rest of the textile chain. "They have a union there," Stevens supervisors counsel their other employees, "and wages, benefits, and working conditions are no better today than they were before the union came in." On the other hand, says IUD's McIver, "If we get a contract there with one benefit over what they offer at their other plants, they're sort of automatically organized." So, to say that everything's riding on what happens at the bargaining table in Roanoke Rapids is merely to repeat what has become a truism among Southern union men in the last year.

Exactly what has been going on at the table? There has been little serious discussion of economic items, which the union considers "of secondary importance." While they propose to increase workers' wages and fringe benefits in the long run, TWUA officials are more concerned in these first negotiations with basic contract provisions like dues checkoff and arbitration of grievances. "You can't really talk seriously about money issues," says Hoyman "until you've established the union's ability to exist."

J.P. Stevens will not agree to checkoff and arbitration clauses, despite the fact that both are included in some 95 percent of the nation's industrial union contracts. The company's refusal to grant these items is an integral part of a detailed bargaining formula conceived by Blakeney, says Hoyman, who has dealt with it over the years in negotiations with other Southern textile companies; the "Blakeney formula" calls for company negotiators to make and stick to proposals they know the union "can't live with."

Checkoff of union dues from workers' paychecks appears to the general public as nothing more than an accounting convenience provided to unions by employers. Actually, it is a vital arrangement which determines a union's very existence. TWUA and other unions have tried to operate locals without checkoff, only to discover what the IRS could have told them all along: unless you withhold what you've got coming to you from someone's paycheck, you'll rarely ever see it. And without membership dues to pay its operating expenses, no union can long survive.

Stevens maintains that it cannot afford to make additional deductions from workers' paychecks, because lower take-home pay will encourage their employees to demand higher wages. The union points out that the company already makes a number of payroll deductions: deductions for the cost of safety equipment and tools, for U.S. Savings Bonds, for contributions to the charity of an employee's choice.

Another earmark of Blakeney's bargaining formula is to be seen in Stevens's refusal to agree to arbitration of unsettled grievances by an impartial third party. Instead, Stevens's negotiators would grant the union the right to strike to resolve all unsettled grievances, no matter how minor, as they occur during the term of a contract.

"As a practical matter," says Hoyman, "a union can't continually be on strike. We can't ask a plant full of people to sacrifice their wages for weeks at a time because one worker has a disagreement with his supervisor over one hour's pay." In effect, the union's inability to strike over all unsettled complaints would allow the company to settle these disputes exactly as it pleased.

Stevens's grievance proposal is exactly the opposite of what most companies insist on: binding arbitration as the final settlement of all unresolved disputes, coupled with a no-strike clause during the life of the contract. But then, most companies are seriously trying to negotiate a workable contract wih their unions. Blakeney's Charlotte law firm "will not represent a client who is willing to enter into a normal collective bargaining relationship," says Hoyman. "They're exclusively devoted to union-busting. When a company refuses both dues check-off and binding arbitration, then the conclusion is inescapable that the company is not trying to reach an agreement. It is trying to destroy the union."

The union also charges that the company has made unilateral changes in wages, hours and working conditions and that it has failed to provide union negotiators with informaion they need to bargain intelligently. NLRB officials often regard both actions as *prima facie* evidence of bad faith bargaining.

How does J.P. Stevens's management respond to charges that it is bargaining in bad faith? In keeping with its standard public relations policy, the company will not "comment on matters pending before the courts or governmental administrative agencies." (Which doesn't leave them a lot to comment on, as ninety-four cases involving the company's labor relations practices are pending before the NLRB.) However, Stevens's board chairman James D. Finley did give an explanation of the stalemate at his company's most recent stockholders meeting. "The union does not want a contract," he said, "unless it means everything they want. That is not bargaining in my opinion." He did not specify what "everything they want" consists of.

"The amazing thing to me," says Hoyman after twenty-five months of frustration, "is the amount of patience and determination the workers have shown under the circumstances."

"We've waited so many years to get a union," says Maurine Hedgepeth, who was fired by Stevens for union activity in 1965, "that we can wait a while longer to get a contract. Besides," says Ms. Hedgepeth, who was ordered reinstated to her weaver's job four full years after she was fired, "even without a contract, we have it better in there today than we've ever had it before. At least now we have a say-so about our jobs, and the bossman knows the union'll have something to say about it if he jumps all over our backs."

Ordinarily, of course, a union would have struck months ago to resolve such an impasse. But a strike against only one location in a giant chain like J.P. Stevens could be disastrous. The company could easily transfer the struck work to one or more of its eighty-odd unorganized plants. Stevens's negotiators have taunted the union's bargaining committee over their inability to enforce their demands with a strike. "They sit there smirking and say, 'Exercise your bargaining power,'" says one committee member.

Deprived of its strongest traditional economic weapon, the union plans to launch a massive nationwide boycott of J.P. Stevens's products. TWUA's hand was considerably strengthened when it merged with the Amalgamated Clothing Workers Union in June, thereby gaining the benefit of that union's experience in its successful boycott of Farah slacks. The AFL-CIO is expected to provide much-needed financial and logistical support to the boycott.

However, it will be difficult to mount an effective boycott against the company, as few of its products bear the

Stevens label by the time they reach the consumer. It's simple to remember not to buy Gallo or any wine "made in Modesto," but to memorize the long list of products fashioned from Stevens cloth by different companies requires a much higher level of conscious commitment. Fortunately, the remaining 30 percent of Stevens's sales comes from home furnishings (sheets, pillow cases, towels) directly marketed under the company's label.

As cynics like to point out, the poor white Southerners who stand to benefit from a Stevens boycott do not have the same chic value as the Chicanos of the Gallo and Farah boycotts. But almost one-third of the mill workers in Roanoke Rapids are black, and the attitude of many middle-class progressives toward white working people have grown more favorable in recent years.

The union has also sought the protections of the National Labor Relations Act against Stevens's delaying tactics. But, once again, federal labor law has proved entirely inadequate to the task. The Act's ponderous enforcement procedures play into the hands of employers determined to stall negotiations and alienate workers from their unions. It takes between four and four and a half years from the time bad faith bargaining charges are filed to obtain the contempt citation needed to enforce board orders.

TWUA's experience with Stevens is instructive in this context. Although the union lost an election at the company's Statesboro, Ga., plant in 1968, the board found such extensive unfair labor practices during the campaign that it overturned the election and ordered Stevens to bargain with TWUA. The company would not come to the bargaining table, and in 1971 the fifth circuit court of appeals issued a decree ordering it to bargain. In 1973 the NLRB asked the circuit court for a contempt citation, charging that the company was engaging in "surface bargaining," with no real attempt to arrive at an agreement. The court appointed a labor relations expert to investigate the charges. In June 1975 he advised the court that Stevens was clearly guilty of bad faith bargaining. But the court has yet to act on his recommendations, seven years after the company was originally ordered to bargain with the union. In the meantime, J.P. Stevens has closed the Statesboro plant down, an act Hoyman terms "the ultimate refusal to bargain." The union's charges of bad faith bargaining in Roanoke Rapids seem stuck on the same slow track. Filed in July 1975, they have barely begun their prolonged journey through the NLRB's cumbersome legal and administrative channels.

According to Daniel Pollitt, a prominent North Carolina labor lawyer, the penalty provided in the Act for refusal to bargain "would be nothing but laughable, if its consequences weren't so tragic." It consists of nothing more than a board order that an employer go back to the table and do what he has already refused to do: bargain in good faith. He can repeat the whole charade. The realistic sanction in refusal to bargain cases lies not in the board's order or its ultimate enforcement by the courts but in the economic strength of individual unions. A strong union gets bargaining from its employer; a weak one often does not.

The House Subcommittee on Labor-Management Relations has proposed several amendments to the National Labor Relations Act that would go far to replace the survival of the fittest with simple justice. One would force a firm found guilty of bad faith bargaining to agree to a "bare bones contract" incorporating the minimum standards prevailing in the organized portion of its industry in that part of the country. Such a mandated contract would include dues checkoff, arbitration, and small retroactive increases in wages and fringe benefits. As now written, the law cannot make either party to negotiations agree to any specifiic contract provision, no matter how basic.

Another proposed amendment would bar companies that engage in a pattern of "willful and flagrant" unfair labor practices from receiving government contracts for three years. (Stevens received contracts of more than $16 million from the Defense Department alone during fiscal 1975.) Procedural amendments would speed up the NLRB's handling of unfair labor practice cases.

None of these reform proposals is new; most originated in 1959 when then Sen. John F. Kennedy appointed a panel of experts to advise him on needed changes in federal labor law. For the last fifteen years, Congress has found itself too preoccupied with more trendy problems to consider unfashionable legislation protecting workers' right to organize.

But Southern labor relations remain mired in the world

of the 1930s—at least partially because they are governed by a law written in the 1930s. "Company lawyers have developed all sorts of stratagems in the last forty years for getting around the Wagner Act," says Frank McCulloch, a former NLRB chairman. "The world has changed, and it's time the Act changed with it."

There are those who would scrap the Act entirely rather than amend it. It is unquestionably true that its lengthy legalistic proceedings rob workers of their self-determination. Rather than actively participating in organizing campaigns and contract negotiations, they are reduced to waiting passively for lawyers and bureaucrats to determine their fate.

"The hell with the law," said one frustrated Roanoke Rapids worker. "Let's get out there at the plant gates with baseball bats, and we'll decide whether we get a contract or not." Such bravado would be suicidal, given the tendency of Southern governments to invoke their police powers against unions.

Most Southern labor leaders take the position that, while the Act affords them scant protection, it is better than no protection at all. As an Amalgamated Clothing Workers official told a skeptical Cesar Chavez after the victorious Farah campaign, "It's a lousy law, but without it we would have been dead."

The Devastating Impact Of Plant Relocations

by Don Stillman

Jim Farley's fellow workers at Federal Mogul Corporation's roller bearing plant on the east side of Detroit called him Big Jim—not so much because of the size of his body, they said, as because of the size of his heart.

They liked the soft-spoken yet tough manner in which he represented them as a union committeeman. And they liked his willingness to sit down over a shot and a beer at the nearby Office Lounge and listen to the problems they had with their jobs, their wives, or their bowling scores.

Jim Farley had come North in 1954 from eastern Kentucky, because mechanization of the mines and slumping demand for coal made finding work there impossible. The idea of leaving behind the mountains where he had grown up for the punch-in, punch-out factory life in a big city like Deroit didn't appeal to him much—but neither did the thought of living on relief, like so many unemployed miners in his hollow and most others in Pike County.

What he had heard about Detroit was true: they were hiring. Farley went to work as a grinder operator at the plant on Shoemaker Avenue that supplied bearings to the auto industry. The work wasn't bad and the pay was good—the plant had been organized by the United Auto Workers back in 1941 and had prospered in the years after the war.

Jim Farley prospered too. He and his wife Nancy had a son, then a daughter and another son. When he wasn't working at the plant or tending to his union duties, he would take the family to Belle Isle for a picnic, or to a Tigers game.

In the fall of 1971, Federal Mogul announced that it would be phasing out its Detroit operations by early 1974 and moving bearing production to a new plant in Alabama. Farley, say those who knew him, became a different man almost overnight—tense, moody, withdrawn. A month after the announcement he suffered a heart attack. Physically, he recovered rapidly. Mentally, things got worse. His family and friends called it "nerves."

He returned to the Shoemaker plant after his illness, but decided to begin looking for work at other companies around Detroit. With close to 20 years at Federal Mogul, the thought of starting all over again—in an unfamiliar job, with no seniority and little hope for a decent pension—was not pleasant. But Farley had little choice. Three times he found work, and three times he failed the physical because of his heart problem. The work itself posed no difficulty, but none of the companies wanted to risk high workers' compensation and health insurance premiums when there were plenty of young, strong workers looking for jobs.

As Farley's layoff date in the first week of February 1973 approached, he grew more and more apprehensive. He was 41 years old: what would happen if he couldn't find another job? His wife had gone to work at the Hall Lamp Company, so the family would have some income. But Farley's friends were being laid off, too, and most of them hadn't been able to find work yet either—a fact that worsened his outlook.

Farley was awake when Nancy left for work at 6:15 a.m. on January 29, but he decided to stay home. His nerves were so bad, he said, that he feared an accident at work. His sister-in-law Shirley stopped by late that morning and found him despondent. Shortly before noon he walked from the kitchen into his bedroom and closed the door. Shirley Farley recalls hearing a single click, the sound of a small-bore pistol. She rushed to the bedroom and pounded on the door. There was no response.

Almost 20 years to the day after Jim Farley left the hills of eastern Kentucky, his dream of a secure life for his family was dead. And so was he.

Federal Mogul's decision to close its Detroit bearing operation threw more than 2,000 men and women out of work. Many, like Jim Farley, had spent nearly their entire working lives there: average seniority was 21 years, the average age 51.

The pink slips—and the mumbled apologies that accompanied them—were not accepted graciously. One man refused to leave the plant when his last shift ended, pretending to continue operating his automatic screw machine until family members and a doctor led him crying out the door. Another hijacked a golf cart normally used by foremen to get around the shop floor and tried to run down any company officials he could spot before the guards got him.

"I spent nine years in the army medical corps, including World War II, and I never saw as many grown men cry in all that time as I did during the months Federal Mogul threw us out of work," one former employee recalls. "They knew their chances of finding other jobs were no good. Who wants to hire people in their fifties?"

By timing the plant closing as it did, Federal Mogul succeeded by five months in avoiding responsibilities it would have had when the 1974 pension reform act (ERISA) passed. Some workers did end up receiving pensions; most got termination payments amounting to $275 for each year of service, an average of about $5,800 per worker. That was the largest phase-out settlement the UAW had ever won, but the union had to take Federal Mogul to court to get it. Then too, prolonged unemployment for many of the company's employees quickly ate up the severance payments. Just about when the money ran out, the 1975 recession began putting thousands of other Detroit auto workers on the street.

Federal Mogul blamed the closing on many factors. Taxes were too high, it said; the markets for the bearings made in Detroit were changing, and it needed more "efficiency" to meet import challenges. At no time, however, did the company state publicly that it was losing money on its Detroit operations, nor did it claim during labor negotiations with the UAW that it needed relief on those grounds.

The year it shut down the Shoemaker Avenue plant, Federal Mogul reported record sales and more than $14 million in profit. The company's employees, however, didn't fare so well. In the aftermath of the closing, at least seven of Jim Farley's fellow workers took their lives.

Plant closings and relocations dominate the headlines throughout the industrial crescent of the North and Midwest. Since July 1977, for example, Ohio has seen the following:

- Youngstown Sheet and Tube's shutdown puts 5,000 employees out of work and Libby-Owens-Ford's Aeroquip closes out 390 workers.
- Goodyear Tire terminates 1,384 workers at its Plant 2 in Akron, while Firestone shuts down operations affecting 1,000 workers.
- Cleveland loses 300 jobs with 1,700 more to follow, as White Motor begins moving its truck production to Roanoke, Virginia; the city also loses 230 jobs in a Westinghouse shutdown.
- Dayton sees Sherwin-Williams close out 110 workers, while Canton loses 210 jobs in a Ferro-Alloys shutdown.

Exact numbers on plant closings and job loss are hard to come by: record keeping is inadequate, and methods of collecting data are suspect. Detroit, for example, used to determine the number of plant shutdowns by asking Detroit Edison how many factory electricity shutoffs had occurred in a given year. Today no one in the city planning department can provide figures on how many plants moved out of the city or how many jobs were lost as a result. A study by Wayne State University, however, reported that 278 plant shutdowns occurred in Detroit between 1970 and 1976.

One way Ohio's Bureau of Economic and Community Development determines plant closures is by counting the number of companies that stop filing franchise tax forms. The figures, which likely are understated, show that 271 plant closings displaced more than 50,000 workers between 1971 and 1976. An acceleration of shutdowns in the last two years may push official job loss figures close to 70,000.

These plant closures have a "ripple" effect on other employment. In Youngstown, for example, a recent study estimates the additional loss from the steel shutdown at 11,199 jobs, more than double the 5,000 jobs lost in steel itself. The study predicts employment losses in a variety of areas, such as 1,413 jobs in wholesaling and retailing, 372 in the office supply business, and even 35 in auto repair.

Overall, Bureau of Labor Statistics figures indicate that

the New England, Mid-Atlantic, and Great Lakes regions have lost 1.4 million manufacturing jobs since 1966. Major cutbacks—both plant closures and partial transfers of work to other areas without a total shutdown—have occurred in steel, clothing, textiles, rubber, auto parts, and electronics.

Where do these jobs go? Frequently, as in the case of Federal Mogul's relocation from Detroit to Alabama, they go to the South. In many other cases, they wind up in foreign countries. While states in the Northeast and industrial Midwest lost 14 percent of their manufacturing jobs, states in the Southwest gained a whopping 40 percent and those in the Southeast gained 18 percent. At the same time, American corporations overseas investment has gone from an estimated total of $11.8 billion in 1950 to $118.6 billion in 1974. A State Department study done by Cornell economists in 1976 reported that corporate movement overseas between 1966 and 1973 led to a net loss of 1.06 million jobs.

Some reasons for these shifts involve declining industries, outdated facilities, automation, access to new markets, energy cost and availiability, and transportation. No sound economy can be wholly static, and few would argue that the answer to economic dislocation lies in mechanisms that seek only to preserve the status quo. But the factors that precipitate a move frequently serve no one's interest but the corporate decision makers'.

Jobs go to some foreign countries, for example, because cheap labor is available. An unskilled laborer in South Korea earned an average of $1.90 a day in 1975. In the Philippines it was $1.74, Colombia $1.33, Taiwan $2.70. Arguments by "free market" economists that American consumers benefit from these low wages in the form of lower prices are not always true. Zenith may improve its profits by shifting production of television sets from Pennsylvania to Mexico, for example, but prices are unlikely to decline. Many shirts made in Taiwan at a low labor cost are sold in the United States at the same prices as comparable American-made shirts. In the auto industry, where imports account for 18 to 20 percent of the total U.S. market, there again is little evidence of "comparative advantage" benefits accruing to the American consumer these days, despite lower wage costs in most countries; in fact—partly because of changes in currency exchange rates—imports are generally leading on price increases now, and most comparable U.S. models are priced slightly lower than Rabbit, Honda, Datsun, et al.

In this country too, wage differentials are a prime cause of runaway plants. Wage rates in the South, for example, average close to $50 a week below the North in manufacturing operations. Federal Mogul, which paid an average of $6 an hour to UAW workers in Detroit, opened its Hamilton, Alabama, plant paying an average of $3.40 an hour. Fringe benefits there trailed far behind those required under the union contract up North, providing the company with an additional saving. Dennis Donovan, a vice-president of a consulting firm specializing in plant relocation, describes why corporations leave the North for the Sunbelt this way: "Labor costs are the big thing, far and away. Nine out of ten times, you can hang it on labor costs and unionization."

Plant closings in the North and relocations in the Sunbelt have ignited talk of another "war between the states." Because total manufacturing employment has stagnated since the early 1960s, job growth in one area often occurs at the expense of another. The opening of a new plant in one state may help lower its unemployment rate, increase its community payroll, and get the governor reelected. The community and state that lost these jobs, however, find themselves in a double bind of higher unemployment and decreased tax revenues.

Most states and localities fall all over each other seeing which can offer corporations the biggest package of tax breaks, low wages, and minimal regulation. Ohio, for example, has reduced taxes on corporations during the last five years, in part because of the campaign to attract new industry. First the state lowered tax rates on inventory and on machinery and equipment. Then, following a court decision in litigation brought by business, the legislature lowered corporate real property taxes. Additional reductions have made Ohio's taxes on corporations among the lowest of all the industrial states.

Rather than stem the plant closing tide, however, the tax breaks apparently have little impact. A study done in 1973, just as the reductions began to be enacted, reported that of 98 companies leaving Ohio, only 3 said Ohio's tax policies were a major factor. Today, even the Cleveland Growth Association, an industry group that has pushed tax abatement, admits that "tax abatement is not an incentive to prevent a relocation from Ohio to Alabama or Texas ... taxes probably would not play a major role."

Tax abatement does accomplish something: it makes it that much harder for states and localities to pay their bills. More than 70 Ohio school districts surveyed during the last school year reported severe financial difficulties. In large cities with thousands of students, such as Cleveland and Toledo, many closed for weeks. Police and fire protection, garbage collection, and other services have faced cutbacks. If states and localities didn't have to pay for so many services from their own limited tax revenues, they would be less vulnerable. Federalization of unemployment insurance, welfare programs, workers' compensation, and the health care system would limit the ability of corporations to play state against state and locality against locality in the search for the "better business climate" that always seems to exist elsewhere.

But it is the federal tax system itself that has the most deleterious effect on many communities, because it provides major incentives for plant relocations and closures. Under the current federal tax code, a company can write its old plant off against other profits in calculating taxes, and then deduct the cost of relocation as a business expense. Operating losses incurred as the plant is closed out can be used to offset profits elsewhere. New equipment at the new location normally is eligible for the federal investment tax credit, and both the plant and equipment are eligible for accelerated depreciation. Start-up costs at the new operation are deductible as well.

Even more significant in some cases are tax provisions that exempt foreign profits of American-based corporations from U.S. taxation until those profits are remitted to this country. And even when the profits are returned, foreign taxes already paid are treated as a credit (dollar-for-dollar) against U.S. taxes due. That enables a multinational to relocate a plant in a foreign country, deduct the expenses of the move, avoid paying U.S. taxes on the profits unless they are repatriated, and then take deductions under foreign tax credit provisions.

The taxes actually paid by corporations reflect plant movements of this sort. Thirty years ago, corporations contributed more than 25 percent of federal revenue; today the figure has dropped to about 15 percent. Congressman Charles Vanik (D-Ohio) recently released a study which found that the nation's 148 largest corporations paid about $20 billion in foreign taxes in 1975, while paying only $10 billion at home.

President Carter's tax reform proposals—which would remove the foreign profits deferral—fail to remedy other problems and, indeed, could further subsidize corporate runaways. He has proposed extending the investment tax credit (now providing write-offs for new equipment purchases) to plant structures as well. If this were enacted, the federal government would then be using taxpayers' money to help buy new plants for corporations.

Many years of corporate laissez faire relative to other countries have left the United States debating issues that were resolved elsewhere years ago. With the exception of South Africa, the United States remains the only industrialized nation without a national health insurance program. Similarly, while many countries enacted policies long ago requiring some public accountability for the economic dislocations caused by plant closures and relocations, the United States only recently has even begun serious discussion of the issue.

Workers in West Germany, for example, enjoy some protection from arbitrary plant closures or movements. Any relocation or transfer of work must be approved by the government, and must also be submitted to a works council elected by the employees. If they do not agree to the proposed shifts, binding mediation resolves the dispute. No plant may close without a permit from the state labor exchange, which can reject a proposed action when there is substantial unemployment in the affected area or when the corporation's reasons do not seem compelling.

France allows plant closings, if economically justified, but restricts them in a variety of ways. The French national labor code provides that no employee can be laid off or dismissed in a shut-down unless the corporation receives approval from the local government employment agency. That agency can refuse to approve shutdowns after considering the employment situation in the area and the economic rationale for the proposed closure. French law makes it illegal to close or relocate in order to avoid the terms of a collective bargaining agreement or to escape the consequences of government regulations. Companies there must provide notice to workers of proposed layoffs and shutdowns. They must also consult with factory committees representing workers. Failure to comply can result not only in reversal of the closure but also in cash damages for employees.

In England, a corporation that wants to relocate or build a new facility must first secure an industrial development certificate from the Department of Trade and Industry. The application is considered on the basis of whether or not the proposed action will be consistent with the proper distribution of job opportunities throughout the country. Not only have corporations been prevented from moving plants out of areas of high unemployment, they have also been *required* to locate new facilities in job-scarce areas. When shutdowns are permitted, workers must be offered suitable alternative employment by the company at another location. If such a transfer does not occur, the employee is entitled to a tax-free severance allowance, in addition to various other unemployment and supplemental benefits.

Belgium, the Netherlands, and other countries also have legislation that restricts corporate plant movement. In addition to notice and government approval, these countries' requirements include a variety of relocation, retraining, tax relief, and unemployment compensation payments to workers when closure or relocation is found to be necessary. In Sweden, a company gets no investment tax credits unless its outlays achieve social goals, such as generating jobs in high unemployment areas or among segments of the population traditionally underemployed (women, older workers, etc.) Notification and prior approval requirements in Sweden also make it possible for government to involve itself in specific problems that may have caused the shutdown or relocation proposal. That, in turn, makes it possible to develop alternatives—revised financing, government product orders, mergers, shifts in product—that may prevent the dislocation.

Regulation of plant movement does not automatically

strangle economic growth or result in massive stagnation of economic systems, as business interests charge. Indeed, many of the countries with the most stringent restrictions, such as West Germany, are also those with the highest growth rates and the lowest unemployment figures in the 1970s. The U.S. corporations that react angrily to proposals for limits on unfettered capital mobility often are the very same corporations that manage to live reasonably comfortably with those regulations in countries where they have foreign subsidiaries.

Dr. Sidney Cobb of Brown University and Dr. Stanislav Kasl of Yale have been jointly conducting longitudinal research on the health and behavioral effects of job loss from plant closures. Among the workers studied over a 13-year period, the two researchers found a suicide rate about 30 times the national average. Less drastic but far more pervasive were a variety of other health problems: higher incidence of heart disease, hypertension, diabetes, peptic ulcer, gout, joint swelling, dyspepsia, and alopecia in the displaced workers than among control groups of employed workers. Cobb and Kasl also found that the plant closings had serious psychological effects: extreme depression, anxiety, tension, insecurity, loss of self-esteem, and other mental strain.

Workers generally lose health benefits when they lose their jobs. Fewer than 30 percent of the unemployed have any health insurance at all. Those who do have to spend 20 to 35 percent of their unemployment benefits merely to continue their former coverage, in the infrequent cases where continuation is possible. Individual premiums average $169 a month—twice that of group plans—while non-group health insurance pays only an average of 31 percent of all medical costs. When the displaced worker has the greatest need for health insurance, coverage most often is out of reach.

The period of unemployment following a plant closure can be quite long. In a full employment economy this would not be the case, but with 6 to 9 percent official unemployment and real joblessness even higher, many of those displaced have great difficulty finding new jobs—particularly because many plant closings occurr in communities and states already hit by industrial exodus. Labor

Department studies of workers idled by plant closings indicate that about 40 percent remained unemployed two years after being laid off.

When workers displaced by plant closings do find new jobs, the jobs often do not provide wages and benefits equal to what they had. Pat DeFrank, for example, is a former Federal Mogul employee; after more than a year without a job, he now picks up and delivers dry cleaning. "I think I went to every shop in this city, but it was always the same story: 'We'll call you if we need you,'" he says. "They never call. I'm 59 now and make about half what I got paid at the plant before they moved out." A survey by the Ohio Public Interest Campaign of workers who lost jobs because of the Glidden Paint plant closing in Cleveland last year revealed that only 58 percent had found new jobs. Of those, 60 percent were receiving lower wages.

Plant closings and relocations are only a part of the overall economic dislocation problem. The threat of closure is important too: it is frequently a kind of Damoclean sword suspended over workers taking part in organizing drives or efforts to win first contracts. In other cases, the threat of shutdown inhibits workers from fighting for improved health and safety conditions.

The problem of dislocation also involves a variety of other private and governmental decisions that result in job loss. International trade policy, military conversion and shifts in defense expenditures, environmental regulation, energy policy, and similar factors often may displace small or large groups of workers.

As the number and rate of plant closings escalate, political support for actions aimed at preventing or mitigating the harm they cause will grow. The most visible force in favor of limiting plant closings is the labor movement. The UAW has been the most outspoken on the issue in recent years, but the Machinists, Rubber Workers, Steel-workers, and the various electrical workers unions have taken forceful stands as well. The labor movement has the necessary resources and political apparatus on a national level, and failing to use them against plant closures may seriously undermine its collective bargaining abiliy. Unions lose active members in a shutdown; they also lose bargaining strength when those jobs end up non-union.

At the community level—in the regions hardest hit by job loss from plant movements—local officials are beginning to indicate concern. In Ohio, support for state legislation advocated by the Ohio Public Interest Campaign and a number of trade unions has come from many such officials (who are conservatives on most issues). Taxpayers groups that have seen the tax burden shifted to individual citizens and homeowners because of the industrial exodus (and the push from the business community for further tax abatement) are showing interest in relocation restrictions. So, too, are some senior citizens groups, whose members normally depend more on governmental services than the population at large. Neighborhood associations and block clubs are another potential ally, because the devastation that follows a plant closing hurts neighborhoods in many ways. Merchants and owners of small businesses, traditionally conservative forces, also can be mobilized.

To have any serious hope of success, however, advocates of plant movement legislation must develop support in regions of the country other than those hardest hit by corporate flight. Business will work hard to exacerbate sectional rivalries—and to create the fear that any restrictions would mean an end to job growth in the South and West. Building support in areas that have experienced a net increase of jobs will not be easy, but already a number of southern communities have seen major plant closures (some because operations have been moved overseas, others because larger corporations purchased smaller firms and took write-offs after transferring operations, etc.). As these areas become more industrialized, plant movements that negatively affect individuals and communities can be expected to increase. Growth may also provoke a backlash—both from its psychological impact on traditional life styles and from the additional tax burdens that growth stimulates. The best legislation will be that which mobilizes support from diverse constituencies: those who might be affected by conversion, for example, and those who are simply affected by economic decline.

The rising number of plant shutdowns has sparked renewed interest in legislation that has been before Congress since 1970. Introduced by Representative William D. Ford (D-Mich.) and then-senator Walter Mondale, the proposal (and others like it) would establish a unit in the Department of Labor to deal with plant closings and relocations. Moves that idle more than 15 percent of a plant's workforce would require two years' written notice. If an investigation finds the move is justifiable, workers and the community would be eligible for federal compensation. If not, the labor secretary could deprive the company of various tax subsidies such as the investment tax credit, tax deferral on income earned outside the United States, tax deductions for moving expenses, and accelerated depreciation allowances.

The bill has the virtue of recognizing the need for public accountability. Its drawback is that it provides government tax money to subsidize the various social costs of plant movement instead of developing mechanisms that require corporations to bear their share of these costs. Nor does it provide specific criteria by which to determine what a "justifiable" plant closure would be—an oversight that leaves open the possibility of rubberstamp approval or, less likely, such stringent application that the economy would stagnate. The proposal includes provisions that could lead to subsidies for corporations to do what they would have done anyway. And if companies transfer work gradually rather than shut down an operation all at once, there is some question as to when and whether the 15 percent figure ever kicks in, causing the provisions to take effect.

No changes in legislation or public policy by themselves, of course, will be able to solve all the problems or reduce all the hardships that plant movements and other economic dislocations cause. But there are several avenues that should be seriously considered:

1. Limit existing subsidies. As noted above, present public policy actually encourages plant movements, regardless of their social impact. Ending current incentives to move would require subjecting all foreign profits of American-based corporations to U.S. federal income tax; treating taxes paid to foreign governments as an expense rather than as a tax credit; disallowing plant shutdown, moving, and relocation expenses as deductions unless stringent con-

ditions regarding workers and communities are met; refusing write-offs for abandoned plant and equipment and accelerated depreciation for runaway facilities; and ending the practice of using shutdown losses to offset profits. States and localities should develop "no raiding" pacts, and should end the spiral of additional tax incentives aimed at creating a "good business climate" to lure jobs from other states and localities. Federal "offset" taxes should be considered that would negate any tax benefits accruing specifically because of such incentives.

2. Enact relocation regulations. Few decisions have as much public effect as when private enterprises decide to shut down. The federal government should create mechanisms through which public bodies can exercise control over plant relocations. Specific criteria should be met before any plant is given approval to relocate or close. Is the plant profitable, for example—and moving only to increase profit rather than to avoid going out of business? To justify a move, gains from increased output and efficiency would have to outweigh not only private costs but certain social costs.

3. Provide worker rights. Workers who may be displaced by plant movement should have the right to notification in advance (as should unions, and all levels of government). Workers should be able to transfer to the new operations, and should get relocation allowances large enough to cover travel, maintaining two households for a period, and so on.

4. Strengthen contract protections. Current law requires companies whose workers are represented by unions to bargain over closure and relocation decisions, but the law's provisions need strengthening. Unions often negotiate wage and benefit increases in a three-year package, only to learn that the corporation intends to close the plant a year or less into the contract. If the union knew a shutdown was contemplated, its bargaining strategy normally would change dramatically to emphasize protections needed in case of closure.

Now, a union must honor a contract for its full duration, but a company can, at any time, close or relocate and sever the agreement (although it must bargain over terms of severance). Changes are needed that would require a corporation to honor all contract terms for the length of the agreement. In addition, further labor law revisions are necessary—along with renewed organizing efforts—to reduce the great wage-benefit disparity between unionized and nonunionized areas.

5. Adjustment benefits. Plant closings that are justified nevertheless displace workers. Corporations should pay for the human and social costs that their actions impose. Workers should get substantial lump-sum discharge payments and special adjustment assistance benefits (in addition to unemployment compensation) that raise transition income to that which would have prevailed had the dislocation not occurred. These benefits should be provided as necessary for periods of two, three, or four years based on seniority and age; so should continued health and medical insurance. When a worker must take a job at lower wages, a supplement should be paid to make up the difference, although that might phase down over a longer period. Expanded job search and retraining programs should be adopted as well. Unless the dislocation was caused by government action, these benefits should be financed directly and fully by the company at the time of closing.

6. Community assistance. Just as workers should be protected when plants shut down, so should their communities. Corporations that relocate should be required to pay a tax to a community-state readjustment fund equal to a percentage of the annual lost wages resulting from their action. These funds could be used to provide direct community aid in impacted areas as well as to leverage available federal funds.

7. Last resort panel. When plant closure is found to be justified, a "last resort" panel at the local or regional level should investigate the possibility of continuing operations under different auspices. The panel could assist in conversion to worker, community, or government ownership; in product shifts; or in other changes that might enable workers to continue their employment even if the corporation moves on.

8. Tougher takeover legislation. In recent years, larger corporations have taken over medium and small-size firms in ever-increasing numbers. Small, closely held firms tended to have stronger community roots than the larger, more mobile conglomerates and multinationals that have acquired them. Most existing takeover legislation is

designed to protect target companies and shareholder interests, but additional provisions are needed to protect workers and communities. Companies seeking to take over firms might be required to make broad disclosure of plans to transfer work, relocate, or shut down. Outright restriction of certain types of takeovers should also be considered.

9. Improved information flow. Sound public and private decisions in this whole area require far more detailed, accurate information on business closings, openings, and transfer of work, as well as data on workers displaced. Federal, state, and local governments should require the filing of such information regularly, and that information should be analyzed and made available to the public.

10. Public capital financing. As capital becomes increasingly mobile, banks and financial institutions contribute to economic dislocation. Corporate redlining has frequently resulted in plant closings that could have been prevented. Bank regulators should limit these practices, and should require banks to finance activities that have positive social impact. Also, new state or local public banks, state-run insurance companies, and state development corporations all could help channel capital to high unemployment or other depressed areas.

The men and women thrown out of work by Federal Mogul in Detroit might have been helped by measures like these. But they weren't. By now, some have found other jobs, others have retired, died, or, like Jim Farley, taken their own lives. Many are still unemployed. They sit in tiny, well-kept houses, mainly on Detroit's east side, and talk about what went wrong and what might have been. Sometimes the bitterness overflows, but most often now the tones are soft and questioning, like baseball fans replaying a promising season that went bad in the end.

To this day, some don't understand what happened, or why the American dream failed to work for them. They had played by all the rules. Many served in World War II fighting for that dream. They went to church, married, raised families, belonged to the VFW, put in a day's work for a day's pay, paid taxes and union dues, and sent their sons off to Vietnam.

The shutdown destroyed not only their security, but

their faith in the system as well. When Federal Mogul executives signed the shutdown directive, the workers were robbed of the future they had earned—not with a six-gun, but with a fountain pen.

For them, the victims of industrial exodus, it is too late.

From Brass Knuckles To Briefcases: The Modern Art Of Union-Busting

by Robert Georgine

There is a new form of terrorism stalking the factories, offices and job sites of America. It does not involve masked gunmen. There are no tales of bloody violence. It is not part of an extremist cause in a far away land. Today, working people are experiencing psychological terrorism in American industry. Drawn from the ranks of lawyers, labor relations specialists and psychologists, their weapons are emotional intimidation and subversion of the law, and their dress is not guerilla garb but three piece suits. Unlike the victims of company thugs during the first forty years of this century, today's workers have not been physically beaten or abused. Still, they have been the victims of violence—the psychological violence of a new breed of anti-union consultants.

Here is how consultants operate. First, they seek a psychological profile of the work force. Private files are opened. Supervisors are thoroughly interrogated on the union sympathies of each and every employee. Every worker is required to complete a so-called "attitude survey" to measure what some have termed "employee organizational loyalty."

Then, consultants work with supervisors to enlist them at foot soldiers in the anti-union campaign. Direct threats of dismissal are made to supervisors who lack the protection of the Taft-Hartley Act. After weeks of labor relations education, supervisors are given specific instructions for dealing with individual workers based on the psychological profiles. While the consultants stand behind the scenes, often without anyone knowing they exist, the supervisors carry out the anti-union game plan, by using such tactics as harrassment, interrogation, rumor mongering, discharge, selective promotions and special appeals to personal situations. Simultaneously, a series of legal maneuvers are begun. Unfair labor practices are often committed and dilatory motions are filed to delay the National Labor Relations Board.

In short, the consultants have no desire to pursue a rational dialogue. Their tactics are aimed at the worker's basic fears of isolation, powerlessness and insecurity. In the end, this "formula" has proven highly successful. One major consulting firm, Modern Management Hethods, has had a 98% victory percentage in NLRB elections.

The American trade-union movement is as old as this country and so is union-busting. Ever since a small group of colonial printers formed the first labor guild, there have been employers determined to prevent workers from organizing. The history books are filled with tales of Pinkertons, gun squads, blacklists and yellow dog contracts designed to frustrate the organizing efforts of workers. Illegal firings, spies, racism, sexism and company unions are part of an endless list of dirty tricks employed by anti-union employers. And while different tactics have been used through the years, the strategy of union-busting remains timeless: divide workers from one another to prevent them from organizing.

For more than 150 years after the first printing unions, American employers were free to pursue this strategy with *carte blanche*. The severity of company tactics was matched by stiff union resistance. Strikes often continued for months. Factories laid idle; workers went hungry, and violence became the rule of the day. In the end, everyone was a loser as the economy hobbled along well below capacity.

It took the Great Depression to raise our national aspirations above such narrow self-interests. With the passage of the Wagner Act in 1935, America began to recognize the wastefulness of sustained and continuing industrial conflict. The Act made every worker a full legal member of the American economy. Force and violence were removed from our working lives and union recognition was made available through the legal processes.

Since 1969, when the U.S. Congress last held hearings on union-busting, unfair labor practices of all kinds have sky-rocketed. Our records show that out of 6,000 organizing campaigns of 10 or more workers, two-thirds involve some form of outside anti-union expertise. By some estimates there are more than 1,000 firms directly and indirectly involved in union-busting activities with more than 1,500 individual practitioners engaged in full-time activity of preventing unionization efforts. Union-busting is now a major American industry with annual sales well over $1/2 billion.

We have identified five principal groups who teach or otherwise disseminate union-busting methods: (1) the seminar lecturer who gives companies a two or three day crash course in the art of anti-unionism; (2) the consulting firm composed of psychologists and industrial relations experts; (3) the anti-union law firm which handles the legal strategies of union-busting, including delays, discharges, bargaining to impasse and decertifications; (4) the industrial psychologist who develops and administers the surveys and psychological testing of anti-unionism and; (5) the trade association which combines all of these functions and specifically tailors them to the labor relations of an industry.

We have also indentified three basic techniques. First, there is what is politely called "preventive labor relations." Here an internal company program is established to extinguish union aspirations. Potential union sympathizers are denied jobs. Psychological profiles of employees are developed without the workers' knowledge. Consistent anti-union pressure is applied by the employer and an emergency legal strategy of delay and dismissal is developed just in case the situation gets out of hand.

The second category of union-busting techniques are those which occur during the ongoing organizing drive. Businesses have turned to consultants, lawyers, psychologists and trade associations for guidance in their day-to-day effort to defeat a union organizing campaign.

Finally, there are the de-unionizing efforts. While the employer's involvement is strictly regulated by law in these areas, consultants nevertheless coach firms in how to initiate such proceedings. Over the last ten years the number of decertification elections has increased threefold.

Seminars

Of all the union-busting delivery systems, none is more blatant than the anti-union seminar. Packaging their wares in slick glossy brochures, mailing them to hundreds of thousands of businesses each year, a handful of so-called "educational companies" are making big profits from employers who want to bust unions.

Whether these seminars are given by private companies or by trade associations, they follow a similar pattern. A group of 35-100 executives are invited to attend a one to three day seminar at a cost of roughly $400-500 each. This provides the seminar leaders with more than $20,000 for a few days work with some minimal overhead expenses. There is no way to determine the precise number of seminars given each year but a conservative estimate would place that number at well over two hundred. Thus, more than 10,000 business executives pay more than $450 each year to get a crash course on how to beat the union. That's a $4.5 million industry right there.

What are these seminars like? To answer that question, we have assembled a composite example from numerous reports. Much of the language is actual quotes from the seminar instructors or from the manuals which are distributed to seminar participants.

You are a businessman from Anywhere, USA, and receive a brochure in the mail entitled "Unions: How to Avoid Them. Beat Them and Decertify Them." It takes place over three days at a large hotel in a major American city. The first day is reserved for a psychologist who speaks on how to "Make Unions Unnecessary." He has practiced his art for more than two decades with major *Fortune* "500" companies, including IBM, Shell, du Pont, and Texas Instruments. He starts off the morning by stating:

> Gentlemen, we are here today because many of you already have a union problem. For some of you an organizing drive is now underway. For others, the union is already a reality and deunionization is desirable. And for a few, who believe that an ounce of prevention is worth a pound of cure, you are here to

insure that you never must face a union across a bargaining table.

There are really only two approaches to unions which I call the cactus and the plum. The plum is an easy target for a union since it is not even concerned with unionization. The cactus is tough and prickly—creating an environment clearly opposed to unions.

That first day you learn how to plant the cactus early. For starters the psychologist recommends screening workers in the interview process to weed out union sympathizers. Of course, since direct questions as to union sympathies are illegal, he recommends:

> Find out if they are involved in liberal causes; tenant organizations, consumer rights organizations or other activities which would reveal a pro-union tendency. Never hire workers with union backgrounds if you can help it.

The psychologist also urges you to pay particularly close attention to the sex and race of your workforce.

> Given a choice between a man and a woman for the same job, always choose a woman, because they are usually the secondary bread winner and because they are 'scared to death' of strikes and violence. Obviously it's absolutely legal to scare the beejesus out of your female employees with threats of strikes, violence and picket lines, and I suggest to you that this is a very good way to scare the hell out of them.

When you're dealing with minorities, look at it from the perspective of the average black. He sees that the only way that the blacks have gotten any place in this country in the last 20 years is collective action, getting together and raising hell. And there is a fair amount of evidence to support this. So, it is my very strong finding that blacks tend to be more prone to unionization than whites. Now you have EEOC these days and you have to follow the EEOC laws and have whatever the percentage of blacks you are supposed to have. There is no reason for you to be heroes about this and interested in abstract justice or upraising the downtrodden, so don't be heroes about the whole goddam thing and fill up the work force with blacks. If you can keep them at a minimum you're better off.

Screening, however, is just the first step to keeping a union out. You are given a checklist of cosmetic items which must be changed to foster a non-union environment.
- Don't call people workers or even employees and don't call bosses. Everyone should be considered part of the same firm. For instance, at IBM, everyone is an IBMer.
- Give people titles they respect like technician or engineer.
- Create numerous salary and job levels so that advancement comes early and often for everyone.
- Always stress their career at the firm. Emphasize that unions will hurt career advancement by emphasizing seniority.
- Always respond to employee inquiries from the highest possible level of the company.

Then perhaps you might receive a sample survey with multiple choice questions. The surveys are filled out at work and submitted anonymously. The psychologist explains:

> Anytime you get a bad score on anything having to do with supervisors or work pressure or competence of the management, you are going to have an organizing drive.

The psychologist stresses the recruitment of first-line supervisors who will do the bulk of the "dirty" anti-union work. He tells you how to motivate supervisors, stressing the danger unions would represent to their authority.

One such corporation's attempt to frighten its employees can be seen from reporter Beth Nissen's experience at Texas Instruments, chronicled by the *Wall Street Journal* in 1978. Nissen obtained a job at "TI" without revealing her identity as a reporter, conveying union sympathies to several people to see what would happen.

She describes a pervasive fear which overtook most

workers when the word "union" was mentioned. Said one employee, "It's like 1984. Big Brother is always watching for spies and for invaders from the union." The company's senior vice president told Nissen in a subsequent interview that this was false. He said "TI has no union policy with a capital 'P'. We just try to create a working environment which will make people not want a union."

But Nissen soon learned just how actively the company pursued the "non-union" environment. She reported:

> Be that as it may, the company made its feelings about unions clear to me and the other new "TI-ers'—as we're called—during our first hour of orientation. A TI-produced videotape told us that unions were detrimental and were unnecessary for progress. An orientation booklet warned us that we might be approached by union organizers and asked to sign a union card. We encourage you to do as a large majority of TIers all over the U.S. have done, the booklet ends, and reject the union attempts to organize.

Nissen soon discovered an intricate union reporting system in which all supervisors are required to report directly any union conduct to personnel executives. And there seemed to be plenty of places to go. Nissen estimates that out of every one hundred TI employees, there is one person whose main job is to thwart the union.

Finally, Nissen was fired less than three weeks after starting her job. Yet the grounds for her dismissal never mention union sympathies. As one worker put it:

> 'If TI finds out you're for the union, they won't fire you for union activity,' says Vicki Zuniga, my solder school teacher and a TI employee for six years. 'But they'll sure find something else they can fire you for.'

Indeed, Zuniga's predictions came true. Nissen concludes by reporting:

> Abruptly, right before Independence Day weekend, my supervisor pulled me from the assembly line and escorted me to the office of Herman King, chief of security at the Austin plant. Mr. King, a brusk, red-

faced man, charged me with a 'very serious, serious offense'—falsifying my application by omitting the fact that I am a college graduate.

The next morning, Gene Kise, the plant personnel director, told me the company won't tolerate falsification of an application unless there are extenuating circumstances—for example, if I hadn't understood the application. And he fired me. Mr. Kise denied that I was fired for pro-union activity.

In the second day of a typical anti-union seminar both the psychologist and a lawyer are present. You quickly realize that the lawyer's purpose is not so much to teach you the limits of the law as to teach you how to violate it strategically.

Many actions fall into the gray area of the law and some of them into the very darkest part of the fray.
Remember if you commit an unfair labor practice the union could have the election set aside. However, if an election is scheduled and it doesn't look good for the company, pull out all the stops, take the risk.

But of all the quasi-legal tactics the lawyer offers, delaying the election is singled out in importance.

Delay is crucial to your strategy. Delay in setting up in a first conference.
Dig up issues on appropriate units, supervisors, confidential employees, part-time workers. Don't consent to an election until all issues are resolved. Then delay hearings. Delay briefs with excuses.
Stall and delay wherever possible. When 30 percent of the employees have signed cards the union can file for an election. Can you stack the election? Yes—hire new people. Time is on the side of the employer.

With the legal ground rules of counter-organizing established, the seminar leaders move on to their next topic—how to plan and conduct the campaign. They give you a sample calendar which outlines steps to be taken against the union including delay tactics such as questioning the bargaining unit size and filing objections to the election if the union should win. Essentially, the campaign involves letters and speeches to workers pitched at certain sensitive issues. These include strikes, alleged union violence, the company's economic position, the viability of non-union firms in the same industry, the company's right to replace strikers, and the company's alleged right not to agree to union demands.

Yet the heart of the anti-union campaign like the non-union prevention program is the supervisor. Since there is little time once the campaign begins, you are advised to start early to slowly educate supervisors. The lawyer reminds you:

> The National Labor Relations Act has defined the term "employee" to *exclude* any individual employed as a supervisor. Therefore, it is clear that a supervisor does not enjoy the same legal protections as does a regular employee. Here are the rules:
>
> 1. A supervisor can be required AT THE PRICE OF HIS JOB not to engage in union activities.
>
> 2. He can be required, AT THE PRICE OF HIS JOB, not to become a union member.
>
> 3. A supervisor can be required, AT THE PRICE OF HIS JOB, to engage in lawful anti-union activity.

The supervisors, you learn, should be forced to follow the letters with conversations with their subordinates. The object: on a daily basis workers should hear new arguments against the union. The supervisor then should report back to the campaign coordinator on an almost daily basis. This permits an on-going refinement of strategy and allows management to repeat those themes which have the greatest effect.

The following is a previously unpublished interview with someone involved in a campaign where this supervisor strategy was used. I think you will see that it creates the most incredible disruption at a workplace. Long-standing rapport between people was destroyed in the effort to beat the union.

The pressure was intense. The pressure on supervisors was incredible. It was made clear in no uncertain terms that the victory of the university depended on the supervisors and if the university lost it would be the supervisors' fault and that it would be remembered. In each meeting they had to report back on how progress was going in their area.

The supervisor was a very gracious, very lovely kind of woman. Just one of those people that everyone likes. She's very even tempered, she's European and had that sort of elegance about her. They came down on her very hard. I was told that after one meeting with her superior, this woman was seen cussing at the top of her lungs, screaming and finally breaking down into tears. That's what it was like.

A lot of people associated that tenseness with the union. If the union had never come here, if people had never brought it up, all this wouldn't be happening.

On the third day of the seminar, the audience is much smaller in size. Many of the participants who face organizing drives have already left to begin their campaign. But those who remain want to learn about "deunionizing," a process which cannot legally be instigated by the employer.
Now, it is the psychologist who is absent. Only the lawyer remains. He begins.

During the last two days, we have given you an idea of how to keep the union out should they come knocking. Today we will be talking about what to do if your initial strategy fails and they should get in. This seminar is entitled "The Process of Decertification."

As he continues, he hands out a brochure on strike insurance which he suggests may come in handy if you plan to bargain to impasse. In addition, he urges:

Line up other employers who can handle your

work and take care of your customers during the strike. Train supervisors in advance to do the work of the bargaining unit. Find alternate means of transportation and extra security to ensure that everything goes smoothly.

Once the groundwork is laid, notify the union that you will put into effect your last offer. Don't give a better wage package, give the same. At that point the union will take their people out on strike. It puts the ball back in the union camp. It's put up or shut up for them at that point. The strike situation represents fertile grounds for decertification. If there are 75 people in and 75 people still out and you have hired 75 replacements . . . you can count on the scabs to vote with you. You will probably win the decertification effort.

Law Firms

Management law firms are nothing new. One such law firm is Jackson, Lewis, Schnitzler & Kruppman in New York City. Not only does this firm advise individual employers involved in union organizing drives, but an incorporated arm of the law firm also publishes a monthly report called "Preventive Labor Relations," which contains such articles as "Restrictions on Solicitation and Distribution," and "The Propriety of Discerning a Job Applicant's Union Sentiments." Subscribers to this report also receive a special offer for an anti-union campaign kit at bulk rates. The kit includes preprinted election material, anti-union posters, vote "No" buttons, and other anti-union campaign gimmicks, such as a sample collective bargaining agreements containing nothing but blank pages.

Another such firm is Seyfarth, Shaw, Fairweather and Geraldson, a traditional management law firm headquartered in Chicago. They have large offices in the District of Columbia, Florida and Texas. This law firm represented Tenneco at the Newport News Shipyards in Virginia where the United Steelworkers have only just won bargaining rights after years of delaying tactics; the *Washington Post* in their successful effort to bust one of its unions; and the lettuce growers in the strike by Cesar Chavez and the United Farmworkers. Seyfarth and Shaw have also just finished a 300-page looseleaf binder for the National Public Employee Labor Relations Association entitled "Maintaining Public Service: The NPELRA Strike Planning Manual."

On October 12, 1978, the Illinois State Chamber of Commerce held a decertification seminar. James Baird, a partner in Seyfarth and Shaw was a seminar leader. He told the audience which included a reporter from the Chicago Tribune:

> This is a forbidden subject, we're not supposed to care but obviously we do. So this is off-the-record. If you say we said it, we didn't say it . . . It's a delicate question—how does someone else make [deauthorization or decertification] happen . . . We'll talk about how to set it up so the employee comes in and asks the all important question on his own. . . .

Finally, Baird suggested that the Chamber of Commerce could act as a third party group to communicate with employees on their "rights to decertify the union." The Right-to-Work Committee was also recommended as a place to refer employees for advice.

There appears to be, at a minimum, widespread and substantial violations not just of legal ethics but of the laws of the land. The management labor bar is on the verge of abrogating its basic commitment to the law and legal process. I think it is necessary that responsible members of the legal profession speak out against these tactics, in all cases, which violate the spirit of the law.

Industrial Psychologists

Another vehicle through which anti-union expertise is traveling to employers is through industrial psychologists. The science of industrial psychology lies at the very heart of modern union-busting. Its basic objective is to understand the emotional undercurrent of the workplace and to harness that understanding in the interest of unfair profits. For the unscrupulous businessman it holds out the promise of a workforce silently manipulated into non-union status.

One recent study was performed by W. Clay Hammer

of Duke University and Frank J. Smith of the Sears Roebuck Company. They sampled 87,740 workers. Their test seeks to determine union voting patterns *strictly* on the basis of attitude survey questions which never refer to unions or labor organizations. These psychologists wrote:

> The present study takes advantage of a rare opportunity to examine the attitudes toward work of employees in 250 naturally occurring settings prior to any history of unionization activity. Subsequently, unionization attempts were made in 125 of these settings. A predictive model of unionization activity based on the attitudes of these employees toward work was derived and cross-validated to test our prediction.

An example of the use of these theories is Emery Air Freight which put its warehouse workers on a planned "reinforcement schedule." The following is a description of Emery's secret anti-union strategy:

> Each manager receives two elaborate, programmed instruction workbooks prepared in-house and geared to the specific work situation at Emery. One deals with recognition and rewards, the other with feedback. Under recognition and rewards, the workbook enumerates no less than 150 kinds, ranging from a smile and a nod of encouragement, to "Let me buy you a coffee," to detailed praise for a job well done.

> In bestowing praise and recognition, Emery follows Skinner pretty closely. There is the same emphasis on reinforcing specific behavior; the same insistence that the behavior be reinforced as soon as possible after it has taken place; the same assertion that you reinforce frequently in the beginning to shape the desired behavior, but that as time goes on, maintaining the desired behavior requires progressively less frequent and unpredictable reinforcement.

When questioned about the propriety of this system, an Emery official responded:

Actually, the charge that you're manipulating people when you use positive reinforcement—I prefer myself to say that you're shaping their behavior—is a hollow one to start with. People in business manipulate their employees all the time—otherwise they would go bankrupt. The only questions are, how effective are you as a manipulator and what ends do you further with your manipulation?

Clearly these tactics can be used to prejudice an election campaign without ever advancing good faith arguments. Moreover, these tactics pose a threat to our future as a society. Once we condone such conscious manipulation at the workplace, we are opening a deadly Pandora's box.

Consulting Firms

Today, the anti-union consultant remains the principal vehicle of union-busting in America. More than 1,000 of these so-called "labor management consultants" now make their presence felt in hundreds of NLRB elections every year. These are the individuals who do the employer's dirty work.

The consultant sets up shop in the company's personnel office or in a hotel near the workplace. Quietly, behind the scene, the consultant directs the daily action of front-line supervisors. He prepares campaign literature, writes captive audience speeches and in some cases directly seeks to persuade workers to vote against the union. In every case the consultant creates insecurities and confusion. Workers are frightened, supervisors pressured, and even the top management cannot escape the daily rigors of fighting the union tooth and nail. The only difference among consultants is one of sophistication and subtlety.

One example of such firms is Modern Management Methods (MMM). Located in Deerfield, Illinois but with branch offices across the country, it has been active in almost every state. Its clients are drawn from industries which employ high numbers of female employees, including hospitals, insurance companies, universities, banks and retail stores. The insurance client lists includes Equitable,

Aetna, Allstate, CNA, Prudential, Travelers and Massachusetts Mutual. Employing more than fifty full-time professionals, the firm is active in more than 100 representation elections a year. Raymond F. Mickus, Executive Vice President of MMM, claims to have been personally involved in more than 1,000 union elections in his career. Yet despite such impressive training and experience, the firm rarely leaves anything to chance, often assigning as many as seven full-time consultants to one organizing drive. According to the *Wall Street Journal*, such measures pay off, yielding the firm a 98% victory record. In fact, MMM reportedly offers prospective clients a fee reduction in the event their tactics are unsuccessful. They have been known to tell supervisors, "We never lose."

The stock in trade of MMM's work is the day-to-day practice of counter-organizing. For example, following an election at St. Elizabeth's Hospital in Massachusetts, the NLRB issued 38 unfair labor practice complaints against the hospital including charges of threats, intimidation, interrogation, surveillance, suspension and discharges for union activity. The organizer in this campaign reported that by the last week of the campaign "the tension was so thick you could cut it with a knife." Many supervisors stayed at home altogether while others found themselves suffering from chronic headaches or repeatedly breaking down in tears after being interrogated by MMM. Workers were in turn grilled by their terrified supervisors. In some cases three-hour long meetings took place betwen six supervisors and one worker after which the worker broke down in tears and left for the day. In other cases, dismissals or job changes severely disrupted people's lives. High pitched emotional appeals were made to worker loyalty. All the time, the day-to-day work of a hospital went by the wayside. Patient care became secondary in the effort to derail organizing efforts.

Trade Associations

In the construction industry, we have witnessed a conscious effort to build a major non-union trade association—the Associated Builders and Contractors. We have seen the major construction users work through the Business Roundtable to divert their jobs from union to non-union contractors. We have also watched them encourage union contractors to establish non-union subsidiaries, an operation known as double-breasting.

Another prominent example of the anti-union trade association is the National Association of Manufacturers Council on a Union-Free Environment. The Council was founded in December, 1977 and has grown to include 387 firms and trade associations. The co-chairmen are Edward J. Dowd, Jr., President of the Central Piedmont Employers' Association and Arthur C. Prine, Jr., Vice President of Personnel Service for R.R. Donnelly and Sons. Taken separately, these men have a formidable union-busting background.

Dowd's group, the Central Piedmont Employers' Association, coordinates anti-union activities for many employers in the Central Piedmont region of North Carolina. Their promotional brochure lists their members and services offered including attitude surveys, reports on local union activities, and professional assistance in dealing with "labor problems, psychological testing programs, E.E.O.C. and OSHA."

Arthus Prine has been a pioneer in union-free operations as Personnel Director for R.R. Donnelly, the world's largest non-union printer. He has lectured internationally on maintaining union-free operations and has been a leading advisor to the labor relations program of the Master Printers' Association.

All of these techniques are grave threats to the very heart of our labor law system. Now it is not just the consultants—the hired guns—who walk the tight rope of legality. It is corporations themselves acting in concert to bend and subvert the law.

Democratizing The Workplace: A Case Study

by Daniel Zwerdling

You'll find Harman International Industries on the edge of the sleepy town of Bolivar, Tennessee, population 7,000. Bolivar still has a monument to the Confederacy, only one movie theater, one radio station, two restaurants and no bars. Aside from the old-time southern courthouse, the biggest buildings in town are the agricultural supply stores where farmers pull up in their coveralls and pickups and chat about the crops and the weather.

Harman Industries, which makes most of the auto rearview mirrors in the U.S., is a crucial force in Bolivar and surrounding Hardeman County, for it is the second largest employer in the region next to the state mental hospital. But Harman has another distinction which gives it a more important niche in United States labor history: Harman is home for what was the first and perhaps most important management-union experiment in worker participation in the nation. The experiment—launched in 1972 by the United Auto Workers, the Harman management, and consultants form the Harvard Project on Technology, Work and Character—has involved virtually every worker in the factory.

The working core of the Work Improvement Program is a network of more than 30 shopfloor committees, in which employees initate changes from painting the walls to redesigning an assembly line. Some changes have been unusual: workers who achieve their production quota in less than the normal eight hours can leave their job and even go home if they like. But the most significant feature of the project isn't so much the specific changes that have taken place inside the factory—it's the fact that unlike other workplace participation projects, none of the changes have been imposed by top union officials or management.

The shopfloor employees have initiated virtually all of the changes on their own.

While most work participation projects stop at the factory gates, the Harman—UAW Work Improvement Program is reaching into the community. Workers have used their new influence to form a community child care center and a credit union, and even a school open to families and fellow residents in the community.

The organizers of the Work Improvement Program have deliberately attempted to make the Harman-UAW experiment a living model for corporations and unions across the nation. "The goal of the Bolivar project," writes former project director Michael Maccoby, "is to create an American model of industrial democracy: a model that is acceptable to unions and that might stimulate further union efforts. The project is based on the view that a national movement to improve the quality of work is unlikely to succeed without union support."

The Work Improvement Program did not come to Harman Industries in Bolivar because it was a comfortable, model plant. Far from it. The approximately 1,000 workers were housed in three huge Quonset huts left over from World War II. When the project was getting underway, one of the consultants, Robert Duckles, wrote this candid account:

"The production floor is dirty and disorderly, compared to many large factories belonging to richer companies. Like most engaged in this kind of work, it is noisy. A shortage of storage space and the pace of production which overworks the luggers and towmotor operators result in parts and materials being pushed into every available corner and sometimes strewing out into the aisles. No time is allowed for anyone to keep his work area clean and orderly. Many machines are kept in poor repair due to lack of replacement parts and a lot of ad hoc repairs with wire and roughly cut pieces of metal."

The Harman factory had been built in the Bolivar region because there were few unions and labor was cheap. The United Auto Workers didn't organize the plant until 1969. Historically, management and union officials agreed, labor relations had been strained.

"At the start of the project . . . the spirit was one of hostility, resistance and open conflict between management and workers." Maccoby writes. "The economics of the auto parts industry, fierce competition, price squeezing by the four customers, and fluctuating demand for cars, intensified insecurity and the dehumanizing conditions of work which fed this spirit." Workers, Maccoby says were treated as a "standardized replaceable part of the process," which bred "anger, hostility, depression and stifled creativity."

Some workers still talk about the notorious "buzzer incident" in 1972, as a symbol of management's once autocratic spirit: one day the factory's 10 a.m. buzzer, which signaled that workers could take their coffee break, failed. The management ordered workers to delay their cherished break half an hour, until the 10:30 buzzer, which still worked. Angry workers took their breaks at 10 a.m. anyway, timing themselves with watches and clocks. Top executives lashed back at this display of "autonomy" and independence by suspending some of the workers for three days without pay.

As Michael Maccoby remembers, the Work Improvement Project began when UAW vice president Irving Bluestone, a longtime advocate of industrial democracy, met then company president and owner Sidney Harman at a conference on workplace democracy. Like most union officials, Bluestone had strongly opposed workplace participation projects controlled unilaterally by management; unlike many union officials, he was eager to experiment with shopfloor democracy projects controlled jointly by management and the union. Harman had earned a reputation as a progressive businessman who insisted management "must have the courage to run risks." Before taking over Harman Industries, he had been president of the experimental Friends World College on Long Island. Harman had a "sense of mission." as Maccoby told the press. Harman and Bluestone agreed to launch the first management union workplace participation project in the nation.

The project began during the summer of 1973. The management, union and their consultants—a third party team led by Maccoby, who insisted the consultants would remain neutral—decided to take the experiment one step at a time, making sure they had a strong base before moving on to the next development. The first step was to gather accurate information about employee attitudes, so that researchers conducting future studies would have base data to which they could compare. The study, conducted with the help of the W.E. Upjohn Institute for Employment Research, was based on in-depth, four hour interviews with 60 workers, plus shorter interviews with about 300 more employees and 50 managers.

The results confirmed in detail what most people already knew: the employees were intensely dissatisfied with their work. As the researchers reported, "most workers don't trust the company": 55 percent disagreed that "when management says something, you can really believe it is true." Most workers felt management ignored them: 77 percent agreed, "It is hard to get people higher up in the organization to listen to people at my level." And the majority of the workers, 77 percent, asserted that, "This company cares more about money and machines than people."

Workers at Harman were so hostile toward management, in fact, that many went out of their way to be destructive: 57 percent said they or fellow workers had occasionally performed work "badly, slowly or incorrectly on purpose" to strike back at management. Employees seemed so turned off to the company, in fact, that when the consultants held some seminars to discuss the results of their study with any workers who wanted to attend, only three of four out of 1,000 workers showed up.

The next step in the experiment was to set up a management-union structure which would screen and approve all project developments. First, the project organizers created a top-level management-union "advisory" committee, including the corporation executives, members of the UAW International, and nationally known experts in the quality of work field. In the fall of 1973, the Working Committee was born, comprised of five representatives from the union and five from local management. One of the key strategies of the project structure, Maccoby stressed, was never to bypass the conventional management-union structures but to strengthen them, to "respect the existing authorities and try to improve them." If any part of the experiment, no matter how small, was initiated without the management and union playing an equal role,

Maccoby emphasized, it would be sure to generate "opposition"—and the project would collapse.

Next the management and union agreed to pursue a common set of principles. "The purpose of the joint management-labor Work Improvement Program is to make work better and more satisfying for all employees, salaried and hourly, while maintaining the necessary productivity for job security," the agreement began. But while many worker participation projects in the U.S. have aimed at boosting productivity, the Harman project declared pointedly, "The purpose is *not* to increase productivity." Project participants worried that if they increased plant production, especially given the stagnant economic climate, the management might lay off workers, ensuring the project's collapse.

The project's goals were "ambitious," as Maccoby has described them. While many previous worker participation programs have been motivated by management desires to reduce absenteeism, turnover, sabotage and other symptoms of worker malaise, the Harman-UAW Work Improvement Program set out "to reorganize the way the company itself operates." The union and management officials pledged to pursue four specific goals, described below.

(The Harvard Project on Technology, Work and Character insists that labor-management projects can flourish, and help workers to grow, only if they are committed to a set of "principles of human development." Labor-management projects which pursue only specific goals such as increased productivity, or nebulous goals such as "improved quality of work life"—tend to be gimmicks, project director Michael Maccoby says, with little impact and a brief lifespan.

Maccoby and Neal Herrick, formerly with the Department of Labor, conceived four principles which are considered sacred at the Harman plant. All workplace changes initiated by the Work Improvement Program, labor and management agree, must fulfill these principles:

- *security*—creating conditions which free workers from the fear of losing their jobs, and which maximize their financial income;
- *equity*—guaranteeing fairness in hiring, promotions and

pay; an end to discrimination against woman and minorities, and profit sharing if productivity increases;
- *individuation*—understanding that each worker is different. Individuation, as the participants define it, means that changes in the workplace should be structured to allow each worker to satisfy her or his individual development. The employee must not be forced to participate in a prescribed way that executives and social scientists have deemed is "satisfying" for them. Changes in the workplace should accomodate everyone as much as possible, and permit workers to get the job done at their own pace;
- *democracy*—making free speech, due process, and workers' participation in decisions which directly affect them a way of life in the corporation.)

Once the management and union participants had agreed on the four principles, they began to solve actual problems in the workplace. At first they concentrated on issues which the workers themselves had identified, in the survey interviews, as the most pressing-environmental problems, such as the temperature extremes in the plant, the irritating air pollution, and traffic jams in the parking lots. Workers had been infuriated by the company policy permitting bill collectors to track down debtors inside the factory; now, the Working Committee notified bill collectors, the factory was off-limits.

Early in 1974, the project organized a three-day seminar led by Einor Thorsrud, director of the Norwegian Industrial Democracy Project, to help spark some ideas for shopfloor experiments. By spring, the Working Committee had launched its first experimental groups, in three different departments.

The Working Committee decided to launch its first experiment in the assembly department, where the rearview mirrors are put together. The key to the experiment, as the principles of individuation and democracy implied, was that the workers themselves would analyze problems with their jobs and propose their own solutions; the work changes would not be imposed by either the consultants or the management. But the first day of the experiment, the project organizers discovered how much worker mistrust and apathy they would have to confront. The foreman asked for a few volunteers; none stepped forward. Then the foreman hand-picked some employees and assigned them to the experimental team, two insisted they did not want to participate, and backed out. Workers were suspicious, project consultants say, that management would use the experiment to boost their production—in spite of assurances from the union that production rates would not change. And furthermore, as project consultant Robert Duckles and manager John Lyle wrote, "Many people are not ready to plunge into something new, abandoning old customs..."

But enough volunteers finally stepped forward, and the experimental group finally got off the ground.

Despite the early tensions and anxieties, participants recall, the first meetings were productive. Workers soon began to propose, and then carry out, some small but effective changes. For instance, they decided to equip the production line with a backup screwdriver so the line wouldn't have to stop, as it normally did, every time the bit in the main screwdriver broke. They decided to teach the woman who operated the screwdriver to change bits herself so she wouldn't have to wait for another worker, who specialized in changing the bits, to be called from another part of the plant. And the employees decided they would install a special light which would signal the materials handler whenever extra parts were needed. Traditionally, workers would have to search for him all over the plant, wasting time.

After two months, the experimental group in the assembly department devised an even more ambitious plan: if the workers could achieve the production quota before quitting time on any given day, they would continue working anyway—and accumulate the extra hours as "bonus" hours, which they could take off some day in the future.

As the assembly department project was getting underway, other experimental groups were struggling to a start in other parts of the plant. A group of six workers in the polish and buff department collapsed when an employee grievance generated management-worker tensions— "worker members of the group informed us they did not have enough trust in management to continue with the experiment," Duckes and Lyle wrote. Undaunted, the Working Committee circulated a memo to workers describing the purpose of the experiment in detail, assuaging some of the employees' fears, and seven workers volunteered to join the experiment. After a few meetings, they decided to experiment with some workplace changes: the members of the group would decide work assignments as a team, rather than merely obey the directives of a foreman; workers who finished their jobs early would help out teammates who took more time; and the worker team would keep its own records of parts produced, efficiency, and the number of bonus hours the team members were accumulating.

A third experimental group was born spontaneously when women on the pre-assembly line, where the mirror shell is bracketed and screwed to its base, asked their foreman if they could join the project. The foreman passed their request to the Working Committee, which agreed, and the women began to organize their own meetings. They hammered out eight goals, including: helping each other achieve production quotas; gaining free time to learn new skills, and go home early; making their workplace more attractive; improving the quality of their work; reducing "downtime," and installing better tools and fixtures at their work stations.

Within a few months the women had increased their production speed so much that they began accumulating substantial chunks of bonus time. The workers began tagging their work so they could be held accountable, and recognized, for its quality. Within two weeks, Duckles and Lyle report, the value of wasted, carelessly stripped screws plunged from almost $40 a day to zero.

Morale in the experimental departments seemed high; "the work stations have been painted in colors chosen by the workers," Duckles and Lyle wrote. One of the Harman workers told the Third International Conference on Self-Management how her mood changed when employees became involved with the experiments. Before the project, she said, "it was just work, work, work, from 7 a.m. to 3:30 p.m. Sometimes we would finish earlier and we would be bored. Some of the ladies would bring cards, needlework. We would do anything so that we could go home earlier when our work was finished. We didn't know what we were volunteering for but we figured it couldn't be any worse. Now working there I feel just like it's a big family."

By late 1974 the experimental groups had become so successful that the factory was no longer plagued by worker resistance to the project. Instead, most workers in the plant, who were not participating in experimental groups, were becoming envious and hostile—hostile that they couldn't benefit too. Workers began to complain that their colleagues in the project groups enjoyed "more freedom, and they seemed to be elite or special," Duckles and Lyle said. Workers protested that they would have volunteered for the experimental groups long ago if only the company had explained more carefully what the groups would actually be doing; they charged that the company had failed to communicate carefully with the employees [today, both company officials and the consultants agree]. But more than anything else, the workers not participating in the experiment resented the "bonus" hours which project participants were enjoying. They saw fellow workers like Oscar Rivers, a polisher, leaving work after only five hours every day—yet getting paid for eight. And so in January 1975, one year after the Work Improvement Program had begun, the Working Committee voted to expand the project throughout the entire factory—that is, if the employees said they wanted it. In a special referendum, the workers voted that they did want to participate in the project, by a majority of 81 percent.

The guts of the factory-wide program is a network of more than 30 shopfloor committees, called core groups. Each department has at least one core group, some larger departments have several. Each core group operates like a grassroots-level, mini-working committee: a typical group includes at least one management representative (usually the foreman), one representative from the local union (the steward), and from one to four employee representatives elected by fellow employees in the department.

Most suggestions for work changes and new ideas in the factory are born in these core groups—all workers are free to attend the meetings, or to send their ideas through their representative. When a core group approves an idea, it sends it to the company Working Committee for final approval, or criticism. Sometimes the working committee and the core groups pass proposals back and forth several times, before everyone agrees on its final form.

The core groups have become the gears of the Work Improvement Program. Visit the Harman factory, and you'll probably be able to attend several different core group meetings in less than a day. The core group in polish and buff, for example, spent several months meeting once a week to discuss problems with the ventilation system, production methods in the department, quality control problems and departmental budget matters. The core group which represented workers producing the American Motors line of mirrors held numerous meetings to discuss the growing problem of work stoppages and "downtime," and, as one worker told the Third International Conference on Self-Management, the group decided to keep careful production records on the assembly line. Every time the line stopped, the employees would jot down the information in a log—why the line stopped, for how long—and then the workers on the line would analyze the information. When the workers took their report to their supervisor, "he just flipped over this information because he had never seen it all together before," the employee told participants at the conference. The data showed that one machine was causing most of the problems; the workers got a new machine, and the work stoppages were almost eliminated.

One important sign that the project is altering the way employees perceive their work, consultants say, is that the roles of the core groups and behaviors of the employees are continually changing. Early in the project, for instance, core group meetings "had to be initiated by the staff almost entirely," the Duckles report. "Now meetings are initiated by the core groups themselves" most often.

These changing roles and behaviors, consultants say, are the most important achievements of the experiment. Since the Work Improvement Program was first launched, the consultants and the Working Committee have agreed that the specific changes carried out in the factory are not as important as the way those changes were initiated and carried out. For the most part, the changes have been initiated and carried out by the workers.

"The *way* in which we do things is as important as what

we do," Duckles and Lyle wrote. "This program of work improvement is not one which is designed by concerned managers, with the help of social scientists, and imposed on the plant, but a program that is owned by everyone that it affects from the beginning ... This process is quite different from job enrichment, in which experts may enlarge a job for workers. The workers at Harman may decide to make changes similar to job enrichment ... but *they* have made the changes and reserve the right to modify them. The goal is to institute a *process* of democratic decision-making and evaluation rather than any specific changes in tasks."

So when some critics of the program have argued that it has not achieved many dramatic benefits for the workers—that many of the changes at Harman are little more than incentive plans such as bonus hours and the chance to go home early—Duckles and Lyle argue that "it is worth noting that these are the goals that the groups have chosen for themselves."

Most of the work participation projects in the United States have been limited to changes in the way work is performed on the factory floor. But the Bolivar Work Improvement Program has attempted to go beyond these projects by attempting to bridge the gap which separates most workers' lives inside the factory from their lives outside the gates. Perhaps the most unusual innovation is the in-plant school. Workers, their families, and even residents in the community can attend a rich variety of classes, which are held before the shift, after the shift, sometimes even during the shift, at lunch. "Improvement in the workplace and education go hand in hand," as one worker told the Third International Conference on Self-Management.

The school began early in 1975 when the experimental core groups began discussing different ways they could use earned idle time. Many employees said they would like to use their bonus hours not just for going home early—although that is an important benefit for workers with families and workers with part-time farms—and not just for socializing. Instead, many said they wanted the chance to learn new work skills or crafts which had always intrigued them. Others had never finished high school and wanted to get a degree. So a management-union committee was formed to draft an educational program for the working committee.

Today, more than 40 classes have been formed, with well over two hundred students. Teachers are paid by the union-management project fund, although some teachers are funded by the county under its vocational education budget. It's a little like the "free schools" which have sprouted in college towns across the country, except the Harman school is housed in a mirror factory.

Classes in the school are formed "when employees express an interest in them," according to the Duckles. "The first mention of a particular class or activity could come from anywhere. Some have arisen in core groups, others in the working committee, most are ideas that come up informally . . . Topically, an employee consults the program staff, and with our encouragement sets out to discover who else is interested in participating." A handful of employees in the paint department organized a course in paint technology, and tool room workers launched a class in die technology. Courses have included computer language, leadership skills, hydraulics, introduction to data processing, metric measurement, square dancing, theater group, ceramics, precision measurement instruments for quality control, typing, car care for women, and a class which earns its students a high school diploma.

Some workers study guitar during their lunch hour every Wednesday; others go to Bible class on Thursday afternoons, after their shift. One of the most popular courses has taught employees first aid, while another favorite has been art appreciation. This class, Robert Duckles writes, has "put pencils, pastels and brushes into the hands of people who 'came to watch' and 'can't even write good' and helped them come up with something they can feel some pride in."

The dingy Harman factory has been blooming with cultural renaissance of sorts: there have been free concerts in the cafeteria, with gospel singing and country music by workers and community musicians, and an arts and crafts fair. "We have . . . been struck by the fact that certain special interest classes, particularly those in art and Art Appreciation, have demonstrated an awakening of critical awareness and critical thinking," Duckles reports. "The fact that there are classes is a result of people expressing an interest and getting assistance in implementing them."

One expression of this critical "awakening" is the new factory newspaper, the Harman *Mirror*. Before WIP, there had long been a newsletter published by the personnel department, one of those typical corporate newssheets—a tepid collection of interviews with employees, items about a potluck supper and other innocuous information. As the Work Improvement Program got underway, employees began talking about the need for some real communication about issues. The result: the Harman *Mirror*, edited by employees. An editorial board composed of management, union and workers reviews the contents of each issue, not to censor any articles but to make sure that controversial views are paired with opposing arguments. The result, workers say, is a lively paper full of heated debates. Typical issues include articles proposing a four-day work week, a petition signed by about 60 employees asserting "We Want To Keep Second Shift ! ! ! !" and an attack on a recent U.S. presidential veto. One issue of the *Mirror* contained a heated letter from an employee, criticizing a quote by Harman president Sidney Harman in *Business Week*; the same issue carried a response by Harman. The paper also has a lighter side to it, such as poetry by employees, sports news, and even religious articles.

The paper has become so honest and often controversial, the Duckles report, that it has "been an irritant to a number of people."

"Some people say things used to be calmer and people got along better before the *Mirror* and this whole project started stirring things up," one Bolivar worker said. "That's what happens when you encourage people to bring their feelings to the surface, tensions burst out in the open. But I think it's a lot better for everyone in the long run."

The achievements of the Work Improvement Projects do not mean that the project is without its critics and faults. Some workers have charged that the changes in the "quality of work life" in the factory have actually been meager. "We cannot get a fan. We cannot get anything but a patchup job done on our dust system," a 12-year veteran of the plant told a local newspaper. "The program is in reality nothing but a scheme to get more work out of the employees, but it's done nothing to improve the quality of life for most of us in the plant." Some employees charge that they have little or no power, despite the core groups; "everything that works out seems to be the company's idea," one told the local press.

Part of the discontent seems to result from the gap between inflated worker expectations and the reality of what the project has delivered. Some workers expected the core groups and working committee to give the employees decision-making powers. But as project consultant Michael Maccoby has stressed, the project was nothing of the kind.

"The principle of democracy was interpreted as establishing the right of each individual to have a say in decisions directly affecting him. In fact, the factory was and is in many ways not democratic. Managerial authority is handed from the top down and workers have no say over who will be their supervisors, much less who runs the company. Decisions about investments and pricing are not usually discussed (although the company did consult with the union about pricing in order to save jobs). What the program has done is to create new areas of democracy and participation in analysis and decision-making which can grow as participants develop greater understanding about the business."

Other problems stem from the resistance among some managerial-level employees to the Work Improvement Program. When middle-line managers, such as foremen and supervisors, have endorsed the program, the core groups have often worked well. But when middle-level managers have resented the program, employees have confronted major obstacles to carrying out changes in their workplace. Some managers at Harman say the foremen are the most neglected employees in the plant.

"The foremen at our company don't know what the hell to do. They feel like no one's supporting them," a middle-level manager says. "We haven't had any training for them, and they don't really know what the program's supposed to be about or how far they can go with it. The workers want one thing from them but they aren't sure whether they have the authority to give it. And some of them are scared, they feel like they're being squeezed out of a job if the shopfloor employees and core groups get too much influence. How do we make the program a growth experience for them too?"

Still another problem which weakens the Work Improvement Program, according to some employees, is that many workers don't participate actively enough. "We sometimes get irritated and frustrated at griping without initiative," write the Duckles, who say that many employees complain about the way things are at Harman, without actively trying to create some alternatives. But they add, "When we get impatient in this way we are usually forgetting that the American industrial tradition is one in which energetic managers determine what needs to be done . . . The tradition is *not* to listen to employees and join with them in the search for alternatives . . . The Bolivar employee, like most others, is thoroughly socialized to expect this as 'the way things are done.' "

In late 1977, Sidney Harman sold the company to the Beatrice Corp., an international conglomerate. The Beatrice corporation has maintained that it supports the Work Improvement Program and will encourage the program to continue. Workers at Harman say the program is in a sort of limbo period: core groups are meeting, workers are initiating changes occasionally on the shop floor, courses in the school are beginning and ending. There have been no major new initiatives. Employees, the consultants say, have learned much about analyzing problems and proposing solutions on their own intiative, and making decisions in groups—and they have learned that changes are possible. These skills, more than any single change, are perhaps the main accomplishments of the Harman management-unit experiment.

THE CORPORATION AND HEALTH

The human body is the most intricate machine we know of. Exquisitely balanced and self-regulating, our bodies are sustained and powered by millions of simultaneous and dynamic processes.

Ironically, the twentieth century has proven to be not only the era in which we have perfected wondrous methods of medical care, but also an era in which we have created numerous new health hazards. Even as we conquer the infectious disease that wiped out whole populations, we must now contend with cancer in all of its more than one hundred varieties—a modern plague that is just as frightening and elusive as the earlier ones and that takes the lives of a thousand Americans a day.

Our food is sprayed with pesticides or soaked in additives. Our industries bring workers in contact with increasingly toxic substances such as vinyl chloride, benzene, kepone, and atomic waste. Our doctors, struggling to cope with this profusion of ailments, place fourteen million of us on medication *every week*.

The issue is straightforward: to what extent do corporations contribute to these problems by needlessly exposing us to toxic and carcinogenic substances that threaten our health?

In this section, Michael Jacobson describes the impact of business on our nutritional awareness and needs, and Amanda Spake explores the problem of drug advertising and overprescription. Harry Caudill and Samuel Epstein then address the health records of the mining and asbestos industries—where death can result from a blinding explosion or the slow agony of a cancerous tumor.

Nutrition and the Politics of Food

by Michael Jacobson

The foods we are eating are killing us. Shocking? Perhaps. But not as shocking as the fact that companies knowingly spend huge sums every year to encourage us to eat foods that promote some of the most common—and deadly—health problems.

The American food industry has changed dramatically in the past century. In the 1800s, farmers made up a majority of the population. Most people grew much of their own food. Diets were made up primarily of relatively unprocessed commodities. TV and radio commercials were undreamt of, and more mundane forms of promotion were rare.

Like an ancient piece of pottery that has been transformed by time from a useful implement into an investment, so food's role in society has shifted from being primarily a source of sustenance to a source of profits. Products like Bubble-Burger (a piece of bubble gum fabricated to look like a small Big Mac and packaged in a non-biodegradable plastic case), soda pop (a multi-billion dollar industry), breakfast cereals that contain more sugar than cereal, and Garbage Candy (small confections shaped like pieces of trash and marketed in miniature plastic garbage cans) illustrate how far the food industry has come from the early days of the eighteen-hundreds. In fact, in addition to the familiar "Basic Four" food groups, the food industry has coined the term "fun foods" for edible products that are not expected to provide significant sustenance to the eater. For the uninitiated, "fun foods" is industry's euphemism for what common folk call junk foods.

The modern food industry with giant farms, monopolistic food processors, slick food advertisers, and national food retailers—has had a major effect on the American diet:

- Sugar consumption has risen from 40 to 130 pounds per person in the past 100 years.
- Fat consumption has increased by one-third (as a percentage of total calories) since 1910
- Grain products were once made from whole unrefined grains; now virtually all grain foods are made from refined flour.
- Most processed foods are high in sodium coming from salt, monosodium glutamate, and other additives.
- Bread and potato consumption have declined by half since the early years of this century.
- The use of artificial colorings, flavorings, and other additives has soared in recent decades.

The changes in our diet would be of only academic interest to most people, if the changes were not accompanied by serious health problems. Unfortunately, they are. While we tend to think of Americans as a healthy people with a long life expectancy, our national diet has promoted a wide variety of diseases. Our increased life expectancy is due largely to improvements in infant mortality and control of infectious diseases. Consider some of the relationships between our diet and our health:

- Our high sugar intake (almost twenty percent of our diet) promotes tooth decay, which costs Americans several billion dollars a year; and obesity, which increases the risk of diabetes, stroke, and heart attack.
- Our high fat intake (about 40 percent of our diet) contributes to heart disease, the nation's number one cause of death; obesity; and probably bowel and breast cancer, two of the three leading causes of cancer deaths.
- The decrease in whole grains, potatoes, and beans has reduced our intake of dietary fiber. This reduction has been linked to various intestinal diseases, including constipation, diverticulosis, and bowel cancer.
- Diets high in sodium promote high blood pressure, which promotes stroke and heart disease.
- Some artificial colorings, other food additives, and contamination from pesticides and pollutants have been discovered to cause cancer; some of these chemicals are now banned, while several others are still being used (saccharin and sodium nitrite, especially). Some addi-

tives also appear to cause hyperactivity in children and allergic reaction for us all.

The American diet certainly provides energy and adequate amounts of protein, vitamins, and minerals that promote health in the short run. But that same diet contributes to our most widespread and deadly chronic diseases. All told, our diet contributes to about half of all deaths and costs us tens of billions of dollars a year in medical costs and time lost from work.

The United States is not the only nation that suffers from diet-related chronic diseases. Most other technologically advanced nations suffer from the same diseases at about the same rates. Japan, however, whose national diet has been quite different from our own, has much lower rates of heart disease and bowel and breast cancer, all these attributed to the traditional Japanese low-fat diets. On the other hand, certain regions of Japan have rates of high blood pressure which are linked to diets very high in sodium. As the Japanese begin eating more Big Macs and drinking more Coca-Cola, the Japanese medical community should expect to see increases in "Western" diseases.

Some so-called "backward" peoples, on the other hand, seem to be blessed with relative freedom from Western health problems. Dr. Denis Burkitt, a British physician and epidemiologist, spent many years in Africa and discovered to his surprise that rural Africans were relatively free of heart disease, tooth decay, bowel cancer, high blood pressure, and obesity. He correlated this health with diets high in fiber and low in fat. He demonstrated that once Africans migrate to the city they have higher rates of diseases, but still lower than those of black Americans. Similar studies have shown that Japanese people living in Japan have lower rates of several diseases than Japanese who migrated to Hawaii, who in turn have lower rates than Japanese-Americans in the continental United States.

The problem is not that food manufacturers are intentionally trying to shorten their customers' lives. Unfortunately their concern for the profit value of the food is so much greater than their concern for its nutritional value that they hardly think about their products' effects on the public's health.

To understand why companies market highly processed,

nutritionally worthless foods, it is helpful to understand the marketplace. In the "good old days" (and in certain cases now) a large number of producers marketed a relatively limited number of products. For instance, many farmers and distributors would be trying to market green beans. Potential customers could go from one vendor to another, comparing prices, and buying from the lowest-price vendor. This was possible, because one vendor's green beans were essentially identical to every other one's. It would be silly for one vendor to advertise his green beans, because since everyone knows that one green bean is the same as another, people persuaded by the advertising to buy green beans would be just as likely to buy another vendor's beans as the advertiser's beans. Actually, because of the cost of advertising, it would be possible that the vendor who advertised the beans would be forced to charge a higher price and lose customers.

The solution to the marketer's dilemma is called "product differentiation." If you can make your product distinguishable—by packaging, color, texture, taste, shelf life, or any other apparent improvement—from your competitor's, you can advertise it and be reasonably assured that customers will choose *yours* rather than any other brand because yours is unique. Thus, the first company to market a canned green bean, or a frozen green bean, or a green bean in New Orleans sauce, will reap the advantages of uniqueness. The real trick is that people who have been persuaded to search out a particular brand-name product will be willing to pay a little bit more for it and that can mean big profits.

Product differentiation has led to brand proliferation. Grocery stores several decades ago might have had hundreds of food items on their shelves. Supermarkets now have about ten thousand items. Brand proliferation is closely linked with declining nutritional value. Most old-time basic commodities—grains and grain products, vegetables, fruits, etc.—were nutritious. But as soon as the advertising department and food technologists get hold of a product and alter it for marketing purposes, they tend to impair its nutritional value. Once upon a time there was corn meal. Then millers refined the meal, eliminating the nutritious germ. Then processors learned how to bake degermed corn meal into corn flakes. Then thirty years ago

Tony the Tiger diluted out the corn by adding 30 percent sugar. And then in the early 1970s, General Foods' food technologists added the final insult to a once-good food by spraying sugar-coated corn flakes with a red dye. Presto! Pink Panther Flakes. (Not every modification of a product is nutritionally undesirable. For instance, removing some or all of the fat makes milk, cheeses, yogurt, and ice cream more healthful. But fortunately in the case of Pink Panther Flakes, American consumers had the good sense to let the product die on the shelves.)

While food manufacturers work feverishly to produce and market new products, good and bad, little is being done to arm consumers with the information they need to select a nutritious diet. The average person probably gets more information about food from packages and advertising than from all other sources combined. And even many of these other sources—such as newspapers, government leaflets, and textbooks—are heavily influenced by food industry pressure.

In public schools one of the biggest, if not the biggest, sources of nutrition information is the National Dairy Council. From offices in 129 cities, the Dairy Council dispenses filmstrips, pamphlets, and posters to tens of thousands of teachers and schools. Needless to say, not much is said about the relationship between saturated fat, which is abundant in most dairy products, and heart disease. The basic message is "all food is good food."

Americans have been called (and the same term could be applied to every other populace) "nutritional ignoramuses." However, since the early 1970s, hundreds of thousands, even millions, of people have educated themselves—with hardly any help from professional nutritionists—about nutrition and the politics of foods. This grassroots ferment blossomed into three National Food Day celebrations in 1975, 1976, and 1977. Gradually, this interest in nutrition percolated into the federal government, first in the Senate Select Committee on Nutrition and Human Needs, and in 1978-79 in the Departments of Agriculture and Health, Education and Welfare. The crowning stroke was the Surgeon General's July, 1979 report on disease prevention, *Healthy People*. This report recommended that people eat more whole grains, fish, poultry, beans, fruits, vegetables, and low-fat dairy products, and less fatty, sugary, salty, cholesterol-rich foods. This became the heart of America's national nutrition policy.

The activism in the federal government, not unexpectedly, spurred the food industry to new heights of its own activism. Consider:

- Representative Fred Richmond (D-N.Y.), who heads the House Subcommittee on Nutrition, sponsored a bill on nutrition education. Though "education" is usually considered a safe, harmless and ineffective activity, the meat and egg industries feared that an educational campaign might include information about fats, cholesterol, and heart disease. Quick, strong lobbying by the meat and egg industries killed the legislation in the House Agriculture Committee.
- Two citizens groups (Action for Children's Television, Center for Science in the Public Interest) petitioned the Federal Trade Commission to ban junk food ads on children's TV shows. The FTC responded by announcing a public hearing on the issues of advertising aimed at children. The FTC's staff proposed that all advertising directed to young children be banned. Industry, terrified that it might not be able to bombard tiny tots with thousands of slick advertisements a year, ran to its friends in Congress. In early 1980, the U.S. Congress was moving toward adoption of new legislation that would effectively prohibit the FTC from regulating ads on "kidvid." The kidvid market amounts to about $600 million a year in sales for the broadcasting industry.
- The Department of Agriculture has permitted vitamin-fortified cupcakes and doughnuts to be served in place of bread or cereal and fruit juice in the school breakfast program. In 1978, USDA proposed that the cupcakes no longer be allowed, because they constituted a poor nutrition education message. Though the proposal was generally applauded by parents and nutritionists, the baking industry got Congress to pass a law forbidding USDA from banning the cupcakes for at least a year.
- Junk foods have sprouted up everywhere, even in public school cafeterias, where they tempt kids to skip part or

all of their nutritious school lunch. The Department of Agriculture, which supervises the school lunch program, proposed that candy, gum, soda pop, and popsicles be prohibited in school, at least before the end of the last lunch period. The candy industry (represented by the former Chief Counsel of the Food and Drug Administration) threatened to sue USDA, if the rule was adopted as proposed, because it discriminated against candies, some of which contained measurable amounts of nutrients. USDA backed down and substituted a more limited proposal, which still drew industry opposition.

Whether or not industry gains its objective on each of these and other issues, it has certainly bought time and has forced government officials to advance new ideas and regulations very cautiously. In effect, government officials have been put on notice that every progressive proposal will be answered with lawsuits and massive lobbying on Capitol Hill. This phenomenon is not peculiar to nutrition issues, but to other areas where government regulations can promote the public's health and safety—at a cost to industry.

The lesson of the 1970s is that the problem of promoting health through better nutrition is not only a scientific one, but also a political one. The status quo has powerful advocates. Advocates for better nutrition and health will have to keep the lesson of the '70s in mind as they plan their activities for the '80s. Clearly, it will not be enough to publish pamphlets on nutrition, though that is a start. Achieving significant victories in the new decade will require action on at least three fronts:

1. Easiest is changing our own and our families' eating habits. This is a step everyone can take immediately. We should be eating more whole grains, fruits, starchy foods, vegetables, poultry, lean meat, and low-fat dairy foods, and less fatty, sugary, salty foods.
2. Local activism is vital and oftentimes less subject to corporate pressures. Start food coops and support existing ones. Encourage local schools, TV stations, and supermarkets to mount nutrition education campaigns; work with them. Grow your own food in

community-sponsored gardens. Help publicize school breakfast and lunch programs, and insure that the meals offered are nutritious and tasty. Good local programs serve as an inspiration for people in other communities and eventually have an impact on national policies.
3. Lobby your Senators and Representative on some of the more timely important issues being considered in Washington, such as advertising aimed at children; nutrition labeling and ingredient labeling on all processed foods; and maintaining the food stamp, school lunch, school breakfast, and other federally-subsidized food programs.

The Drugging Industry
by Amanda Spake

Langley High School in Northern Virginia, near Washington, D.C., looks like any other suburban, brown-brick set of classrooms. Langley has its prom queens, cheerleaders, and sock hops, its football games and jocks. It is not an unusual high school. But the birth and death of one of Langley's brightest students, Marilyn Malloy, had unique significance.

Marilyn's story could be played out in any high school in this country, and it undoubtedly will be in some. It is the story of America's pharmaceutical industry, too quick to sell doctors on prescribing drugs, and its physicians, too quick to believe in the drug houses. There is no way of knowing how many stories like Marilyn's are yet to be told.

Marilyn Malloy was an attractive seventeen-year-old with long, dark hair, wide eyes, and a desperate love for horseback riding. At Langley, Marilyn was an honors student, at the top of her senior class. She was serious about her studies; had she graduated, a wide range of colleges and career choices could have been hers. But Marilyn Malloy did not make it to her Langley graduation ceremonies. Early in the summer of 1974, while her friends celebrated their own commencement, she died.

Grace Malloy became pregnant with Marilyn in 1955. Early in the pregnancy, she noticed bloody spotting, a sign that she might be losing her baby. She telephoned her gynecologist to tell him she feared a miscarriage, and her doctor prescribed a drug to insure the pregnancy. "I had no reason to believe there might be anything wrong with it," Mrs. Malloy says. The miraculous pill was diethylstilbestrol or DES, and Mrs. Malloy took it throughout her pregnancy with Marilyn.

"I was reading the morning paper," Grace Malloy recalls, "and I saw this little article about DES and cancer." It was a cold, November day in 1971. Marilyn was fourteen years old. "I was worried. I took the drug with two of my girls." She hustled Marilyn and her sister Patti off to a gynecologist; her former doctor who had prescribed DES was now dead. Her physician said that Patti, then twenty, was in good shape, but the verdict was not so rosy for Marilyn. Barely a teen-ager, Marilyn Malloy had advanced cancer of the vagina.

"Then we went through the operations." Mrs. Malloy remembers. "You know they think they've 'got it all.' This is the tragic part. Marilyn was well after the first operation for a year and a half. We sat back relieved and thought it was over. The doctors told us that it was."

Grace Malloy's voice broke into a husky bitterness as she recalled the false hopes and bright promises of the doctors. "They were wrong. They were all wrong," she said. "It had already gone into her lung."

Adenocarcinoma of the vagina, Marilyn's disease and that most commonly found in affected DES daughters, spreads to the lungs in about 35 per cent of the cases discovered so far. The disease used to affect, primarily, women past the age of fifty. When an upsurge of cases was discovered in teen-agers in 1966, Dr. Arthur Herbst, a gynecologist at Massachusetts General Hospital, began to put the pieces of the DES puzzle together. By 1971, he was able to show a link in seven cases between DES taken during pregnancy and vaginal or cervical cancer in female offspring.

Since 1971, the number of DES-related cancers has escalated dramatically. Dr. Herbst reported in the *American Journal of Obstetrics and Gynecology* in 1974 that 138 DES-induced cancers had been recorded and that twenty-four of those young women, like Marilyn, were dead. Thirty-seven cases in the study experienced a cancer recurrence in less than two years. A spokesman for the National Cancer Institute said that by last year "at least 400" DES cancer cases had showed up in young women.

The drug was widely prescribed for threatened miscarriage between 1945 and 1965 and by some doctors until 1971. Only in the late 1960s did studies show DES was ineffective in preventing miscarriage. Dr. Herbst noted in his 1974 *Journal* article that "the peak incidence of these tumors may not have been reached." A study at the Mayo Clinic to determine DES-induced cancer rates shows that there may be four cancer cases for every 1,000 women who took the drug. All doctors who see women born between 1945 and 1965 should ask them if their mothers took DES, but they do not. DES daughters should be checked for the disease as soon as they reach puberty; millions of women took the drug during those years, and some half of them delivered girls. The scope of the DES tragedy is as yet undetermined.

"And it was all for nothing," Grace Malloy says. "DES doesn't even prevent miscarriage. I didn't want to say or do anything while my daughter was living, for fear it might embarrass her, but now that she's gone, I want people to know about Marilyn."

The nation's drug firms spend about $1 billion each year in prizes, trips, samples, and medical journal advertising to promote drug sales. In 1973, physicians received more than $14 million worth of gifts and reminder items from the pharmaceutical manufacturers. In addition, the companies gave doctors more than two billion free samples to encourage drug use; 18 million oral contraceptive packets were handed out by the twenty leading drug firms alone. The firms also control most of the drug information doctors receive, and physicians admit that drug salesmen are their first source on the uses of new drugs. As a result of this promotion, some pharmaceutical products become "best sellers"—like tranquilizers, oral contraceptives, and, in the past, DES. As one doctor put it, drugs are "merchandised like detergents or vacuum cleaners" and the patients pay at the pharmacy for the cost of marketing.

Each year, women visit physicians 25 percent more frequently than men. With the burden of contraception and pregnancy, women fill about 50 percent more of the prescriptions doctors write than do male health consumers. It is women, more often than men, who bear this advertising cost both in drug-induced illness and cold cash. What do they get for their money?

The Ortho Pharmaceutical firm, a division of Johnson and Johnson, is one of the largest pill pushers in the country. Ortho runs a "bonus point competition" for drug salesmen who successfully convince doctors to prescribe the company's oral contraceptives. In the competition, sales personnel selling the most contraceptives can participate in the "diamond aware program" and receive valuable art works and other prizes. Ortho also engages in "prescription surveys," in which the salesmen, called detailmen, are allowed to rifle through pharmacy files to see which doctors are prescribing contraceptives for their patients and what kinds. Ortho has said it may discontinue the practice but a detailman for Lederle (another producer of oral contraceptives) doubted the company would be able to enforce it. "Detailmen *have* to do 'script surveys' to sell drugs. I do them, everybody does them," he said.

Pfizer Pharmaceuticals relies in part on a "dinner program" for physicians, where doctors and spouses are treated to elaborate meals and an evening of drug promotion. When the company launched a campaign for one of its antibiotics the sales staff was told, "One of the most successful methods of quickly establishing Vibramycin intravenous has been the Vibramycin dinners. . . . Your district manager will be receiving fifty Vibramycin IV dinner kits. Each kit contains Vibramycin IV, reprints . . . and a small bottle of perfume." Presumably, the perfume was for the physician's spouse. Pfizer's president, Gerald G. Laubach, claims, "The dinner program is the heart of the informational and educational part of the thing." Yet a former Pfizer salesman told U.S. Senate investigators reviewing these promotional practices that the presentations were often unbalanced and reprints were seldom unfavorable to the product.

But the dinner programs are church socials compared to the almost 40,000 factory tours and seminar trips sponsored annually by drug firms. Food, entertainment, and transporation are often provided free to physicians and spouses and accommodations are never less than deluxe. On a plant tour of the Eli Lilly Company, one doctor commented, "We were afforded every luxury of bed and board," and on the Lederle tour, the doctors stay at the Waldorf Astoria in New York City.

One doctor, a dermatologist from Philadelphia, recounted his experiences at the generous hands of the drug companies: "I am chagrined to recall being a guest of a pharmaceutical house at the beautiful mountain retreat above New York City. Being wined and dined and then touring the plant. I also attended a symposium in a vacation spot, and I remember hearing at least five times that the meeting was a result of the Ciba-Geigy Pharmaceutical Company, as was our expensive roast beef dinner. I realized, on the way home, that it wasn't Geigy that was giving us all this, it was our patients."

The dermatologist also talked of gifts from the companies. "I remember accepting a tape recorder from a pharmaceutical company as well." Companies give tape recorders, books, or watches to doctors or pharmacists to convince them to prescribe or stock their brand of a drug that is similar to a competitor's, such as an antibiotic or oral contraceptive. The Lederle detailman added, "All drug companies have some incentive programs for physicians, pharmacists, and hospitals. If they say they don't, they're lying."

The G.D. Searle Company, makers of Ovulen, Demulen, and Enovid, decided one of its most effective sales tactics was to persuade nurses its oral contraceptives were superior. Realizing women often talk with gynecologists' nurses, the company directed its sales force to "Sell the nurse. Now talk to that gracious nurse, and tell the doctor she is well informed. She could better aid his patients. . . . She is as important in moving your product as gas is to moving a car. You cannot go far without either." Searle's training brochure next focuses attention on the physician: "He wants to be sold. He expects to be asked for the business. He is going to give it to the best sales person." Drawbacks of various oral contraceptives take a back seat to sales, when drug houses clearly feel the physicians' concern is "to be sold."

The pharmaceutical manufacturers may be right. One Maryland physician, commenting on this Madison Avenue operation, said, "It certainly influences prescribing practices and the patients might get the drugs prescribed to them which ordinarily would not have occurred had it not been for the impact of the detailmen."

Searle's promotional efforts have been extraordinarily successful in pushing a drug for the treatment of vaginal infections, Flagyl. Each year, 2.2 million prescriptions are written for Searle's Flagyl, the only drug used to treat trichomonas vaginitis, a minor disorder marked by itching, discharge, and sometimes burning during urination. Most women have had it at one time or another, and probably most have received Flagyl to correct it. Doctors often ask women if their husbands or lovers can take the pills as well, since some medical authorities believe males carry the tiny, one-celled organisms and women will be re-infected. Many women live with the protozoa all the time with no ill effects until there is an overgrowth and sometimes even the overgrowth symptoms disappear. Hot baths, loose clothing (air kills them), and relying on sanitary napkins instead of tampons can prevent overgrowth and eliminate the need for Flagyl.

Naturally, this old remedy is not promoted by Searle. Medical journal advertising proclaims Flagyl as "the only systemic Trichomonacide." But in the fine print, the company recommends white blood cell counts be taken before and after administration of Flagyl in both partners, and stresses that proof of the presence of trichomonas, verified by tests, should be present in both males and females before prescribing. Gynecologists rarely follow even these minor precautions, since the drug has been available for more than ten years and is considered safe. I have received the drug three times and never had a white cell count taken, nor have any women I have known, yet all but one have taken Flagyl. Only once did a gynecologist bother to take a smear to test if the organisms were actually there.

There is good reason for the blood counts, were doctors to read the warning. Flagyl reduces white cells, the body's main agents to fight all diseases. Furthermore, the drug causes tumors in rats and mice. When Searle submitted studies on the drug, about ten years ago, to the Food and Drug Administration for approval, the company apparently "misinterpreted" the results. The FDA overlooked the mistake. An article published in 1971 showed the drug caused lung and lymph tumors in mice. When the FDA pulled out the data submitted by Searle, the agency had one of its statisticians, Dr. M.A. Gross, look at the results. He concluded that Searle's findings, showing the drug was not cancer-inducing, were wrong. The drug caused twice as many breast tumors in rats when the animals were fed a dose comparable to that women receive, but over a longer period of time. "It is quite clear," Dr. Gross reported, "that the evidence of increased risk of development of mammary tumors as a result of treatment with this agent is overwhelming." The FDA is now considering criminal prosecution of Searle for "falsifying" its original animal tests.

Flagyl has not been used long enough to determine if the animal studies apply directly to humans as well, but most medical authorities agree that anything that causes cancer in animals could have the same effect on humans. Flagyl may turn out to be another DES in ten years, when the results of its massive administration are evident.

Anita Johnson, a lawyer with Ralph Nader's Health Research Group, is working to compel the Food and Drug Administration to pull Flagyl off the market. "With more than two million prescriptions each year, I think nearly every woman in the country has received Flagyl," she says. She points out that Ortho, eager to cash in on Searle's cornered vaginitis market, has started testing a related drug, Tinadazoil. Ortho animal tests showed that the drug, like Flagyl, caused cancer in mice. But under pressure from the company, the FDA is allowing Ortho to do tests on women.

"That is unprecedented," Johnson adds, "and very antifemale. They're saying it doesn't matter what the animal tests show, even if it's the worst. Now that they've gone this far, the FDA is going to be obliged to approve Tinadazoil." If Tinadazoil is approved, Ortho will undoubtedly move the drug into its promotional apparatus with full-page, glossy ads in the medical journals which now show only the glowing claims for Flagyl.

Medical journal advertising is an art in itself. Physicians' first information on new drugs may come through the companies' detailmen, but their second source, according to the FDA, is company ads in journals and by mail. Mailed ads are usually reprints of the journal ads. The drug houses invested $9 million in 1973 on advertising in the American Medical Association's journals alone.

The featured players in these medical advertising dramas are often women, and the most common disease in America today, one would guess from reading the ads, is female depression and anxiety. A wide range of drugs is promoted to physicians to "cure" depressions. Next to depression, the biggest "disease" in the journals is pregnancy, and it is in advertising contraceptives that the drug houses find their forte. Contraceptive ads usually appeal to a physician's paternalism, casting women as uninformed children. But the Lederle pharmaceutical company went one better in promoting its new, sequential oral contraceptive, Zorane. Here, women were chastised for trying to gain information about their bodies.

The ads featured two attractive young women, both with long, dark hair and dressed in slacks. They were pictured talking with one another in what was almost surely a food cooperative. One woman, gesturing and speaking, was obviously telling the other something that disturbed her greatly. The copy read: "Because her 'medical consultant' alarms her about 'the pill' . . . and because she runs to you for her answer—Lederle presents: Zorane. For her peace of mind . . . and yours."

This ad ran in medical journals for months before the FDA cracked down on it; it forced Lederle to change the copy and seized twenty-five million Zorane pills. The company's promotion, according to the FDA, was "not supported by substantial evidence" that these drugs are safer than any other birth control pill—a Madison Avenue style nuance that physicians who prescribed Zorane may have missed.

This promotional steamroller brings the drug houses more than $6 billion in prescription drug sales a year, about $30,000 per doctor. It also sends half a million people to the hospital with adverse drug ractions, and an estimated 30,000 to 160,000 unfortunate patients to the morgue. If the 160,000 figure is close, as indicated in studies from hospitals in Florida and Massachusetts, prescribed drugs could be the fourth largest killer in the nation. There are no exact figures on the numbers of Americans who die each year from over-prescribed or mis-prescribed drugs, and no figure could reflect the pain these drugs can cause. (Significantly, the FDA recently banned the production of three sequential oral contraceptives—Oracon, Ortho-Novum SQ, and Norquen—because of new evidence that they may be harmful.)

Legislation has been introduced by Senator Edward Kennedy, Massachusetts Democrat, to curb the pharmaceutical companies' voracious advertising appetite. His bill, S. 1282, would require licensing of detailmen, provide doctors with a drug compendium, and force sales personnel to present both the side effects and advantages of their products. The bill would also ban expensive gift-giving and limit trips and tours. If his legislation is supported by women (as it should be) and the bill passes, it is a start. But women will also have to inform themselves about the pharmaceutical products they take, realizing that the prescriptions may be the result of journal ads, gifts, dinners, free trips, or a detailman's efforts to earn a "diamond award."

It does not make much difference now to Grace Malloy's former gynecologist that he was undoubtedly receiving his share of gratuities from DES manufacturers. It does not make much difference to him now that he was merely following the prescribing practice of an era, a practice supported and promoted by the drug houses. It does not make much difference because he died a successful, old man. But it could have made a great deal of difference to Marilyn Malloy.

Unsafe in any Mine—
The Story of Big Black Mountain

by Harry M. Caudill

In March of 1976, a series of explosions in the mine operated by the Scotia Coal Company under Big Black Mountain in Letcher County, Kentucky, killed twenty-six men. The disaster was predictable, and when it was not predicted it became inevitable. Though by no means the worst tragedy in the history of coal mining in the United States, it was perhaps the most foolish.

Americans hug to themselves the comforting myth that their country leads the world in virtually all respects. Their cars are the roomiest and most gadget-laden, their homes the largest and most comfortable, their research programs the most productive and, until 1974, it was smugly assumed that their energy sources were amplest and least vulnerable. In a warm, expansive moment Lyndon Johnson once referred to America as "the richest and most powerful country in the history of the world." In reality such effusions of consoling rhetoric conceal the harsh fact that in some important respects the United States is a consistent laggard. In fact, when measured by well-established world standards, some aspects of our national life are shameful.

A shocking instance lies in the field of coal-mining safety. Under the best of circumstances digging coal is hard and ruinous work. Even strip mining, which now accounts for half the nation's output, takes its inexorable human toll. Bulldozers topple down the slopes of "spoil banks"; "highwall" rocks give way and fall onto benches; premature and delayed explosions hurl stones with cannonball force; loaded trucks lose their brake pressure on precipitous, winding roads. Such mishaps kill and maim workmen even in this segment of the industry, a segment that seeks to excuse its land-killing activities because it kills fewer men.

And in truth it is underground that coal mining reaches its deadly worst. In the long tunnels leading to the working areas, at the dust-choked "face" where machines rend the hard bituminous rock from the vein, and along the tracks and conveyor belts by which the fuel is carried to the outside, accidents occur with numbing frequency. The perils are legion. In the cramped confines of the mines the huge machines mangle bodies with the efficiency of sausage grinders. Roofs crash down despite wooden props and steel bolts. Poorly managed blasting snuffs out lives. Coal and rock dust suspended in the air that must be breathed cause slow strangulation from pneumoconiosis and silicosis. Most dramatic of all, methane gas can seep from the coal veins and blow up with a violence approaching that of gunpowder.

For most of the nation's history its coal mines operated in remote areas, received little attention from lawmakers and the public, and derived such safety standards as existed from feeble state mining bureaus and the well-sheltered consciences of mine owners. The former were always short of funds and routinely staffed by persons "friendly to the industry"; the latter could rarely abide safety procedures because they cost money and cut into profits. Consequently, miners died in small numbers, and large, crippled ex-miners limped along the streets of coal towns; by 1968 nearly 250,000 men were gasping, half-dead victims of pneumoconiosis, and half as many more had already been sent to inconspicuous graves by the same deadly ailment. A hundred thousand had died in mining accidents since the industry began.

Then on November 20, 1968 Consolidation Coal Company's mine at Fairmont, W. Va., blew up, killing seventy-eight men. There had been deadlier mine catastrophes in U.S. history—362 miners died at Monongah, W.Va., in 1907—but it was spectacular and television played it to the hilt, startling millions of viewers with the immense eruptions of black smoke that roared from the pit-head and drifted over the somber hills. The Governor rushed to the scene, to be photographed looking solemn and sympathetic, and used the opportunity to point out that mining is inherently dangerous, but that Consolidation had an unusually fine safety record. W. A. Boyle, then president of the

United Mine Workers, mouthed similar nonsense. "Consol" was part and parcel of the U.S. coal industry, its largest producer and general pace setter, and it shared fully in the industry's disgraceful casualty figures.

Sen. Harrison Williams of New Jersey took the lead in drafting and enacting legislation designed to prevent similar calamities. The Appalachian mining states were represented by influential legislators who might have been expected to initiate this legislation. But coal companies are so powerful in West Virginia, Kentucky, Virginia, Tennessee, Pennsylvania and Alabama, and coal miners and their families are so politically inert, that the elected Representatives from the region deemed it the better part of valor to leave the work to other hands. In any event, the time for a new law had come. The Federal Coal Mine Health and Safety Act of 1969 entered the U.S. Code, and two extremely reluctant Presidents—first Nixon, then Ford—took up the task of implementing it. The Mine Enforcement and Safety Administration (MESA) was created and charged to enforce the new safety code.

The voluminous and detailed safety requirements are laudably sound and reflect a desire on the part of Congress to introduce into U.S. coal operations essentially the same procedures, techniques and devices that have worked so well in Western Europe since 1950. The Act's principal weakness lies in the immense amounts of red tape that must precede the imposition of punishments for noncompliance, and the trifling extent of those punishments when actually levied.

Thus for the first time the federal government undertook to rein in and civilize the vast, fragmented, widely dispersed and still ideologically laissez-faire coal industry. Largely centered in Appalachia, were individualism and distrust of government are rampant, the industry's managers fully reflect these attitudes—and so do their employees. The chaotic conditions within coal can be measured by a comparison of fatality ratios per million manshifts worked underground in the ten years following World War II. Bear in mind that European mines were ravaged by that war, while U.S. mines were ravaged only by mismanagement and lack of foresight.

In Great Britain the death rate ranged from 0.44 in 1947 to 0.24 in 1954. In Belgium it declined from 0.66 in

1947 to 0.32 in 1955. In France the rate dropped from 0.48 in 1948 to 0.34 in 1955. In West Germany the figures went from a high of 0.77 in 1948 to 0.61 in 1955. In Holland, which almost certainly operates the world's safest pits, the fatality rate fell from a high of 0.53 to 0.15. In the United States during the same interval the high was 1.22 in 1947 and the low was 0.84 in 1952.

These data reflect a general unconcern with safety and lives that persisted with only minimal change through the Great Crusade, the New Frontier and the Great Society. That unconcern permitted the methane buildup along the miles of dusty, coal-black tunnels at Fairmont and culminated in the colossal explosion that roared with such deadly force under the West Virginia hills.

Gordon Bonnyman is 57, a slender man with restraint stamped in every line of his spare frame. He is one of the vanishing breed of American businessmen who have managed to hold onto inherited wealth and expand it for the next generation. The Bonnymans have left their everlasting mark on the torn and battered Appalachian landscape. The map reflects the names of their old operations at Bonnyman, Ky., and Bonny Blue, Va. Their new operations are conducted by Blue Diamond Coal Co. in the eastern Kentucky hills.

Blue Diamond is controlled and largely owned by Bonnyman and his family, and they do not give out information concerning stockholders and dividends. But in 1976 *Forbes* magazine reported that in 1975 Blue Diamond had increased its liquid assets by $55.4 million, that it had in fact, enriched its treasury by $150,000 per day throughout a year that most Americans recall as the most depressed in three decades. Nor is there any reason to suppose that the cornucopia ceased to flow as spring drew near in 1976.

Scotia Coal Co., a wholly owned subsidiary of Blue Diamond, generated more than a third of the profits *Forbes* had found so remarkable. Operating in thick, hard veins of heat-rich metallurgical coal in Letcher County, Kentucky, its strip mines and endless outpourings of wastes have done much to ruin a once beautiful tributary of the Cumberland River. But this immensely profitable mine was not without serious problems. The stripping operation attacked only the forest-heavy outcrops of the vein: tunnels followed the coal thousands of yards into the immense ridge.

The 4,200 foot Big Black Mountain has the appearance of absolute stability, but it has known eons of torment. A few miles to the north lies the long parallel Pine Mountain, a product of violent crustal upthrust. The pressures exerted by these processes reached far into the depths of the much older Black Mountain, twisting and folding its coal veins and the overlying layers of slate and stone. When the company began driving its tunnels at Scotia on the Poor Fork it encountered troublesome "top conditions," while the sinks created by the undulating coal deposits produced severe drainage problems.

But the principal difficulty was the bane of coal miners—methane. To most Americans this is highly beneficent "natural gas," the product delivered by public utilities to millions of homes, offices and plants. But when it is encountered 4,000 or 5,000 yards inside a mine, at the end of a long, dark, narrow tunnel, a methane "seep" is an entirely different matter. If the concentrations are high enough, breathing the stuff can be deadly. If a spark from machinery or an illegally smoked cigarette sets it off, the blast can ignite coal dust. The ensuing explosion converts the tunnels into gigantic gun barrels through which surge almost incalculable heat and power. In these circumstances, friendly natural gas becomes a demon.

In March 1976, Scotia's operations were about typical of at least half the nation's soft coal producers. No one connected in any way with the management of the company displayed any visible concern for land, air or water. They regarded environmentalists as nuts. To them the United Mine Workers of America with its royalty-supported Health and Welfare Fund was anathema, and the federal program to compensate disabled black-lung victims was a "give away." The poor people huddled in the hollows were disdained. Watching University of Kentucky basketball games on television was their most coveted form of entertainment, and the overriding goal of right thinking people was to dig coal and make money. The miners on their payrolls shared most of these views, seeing nothing wrong with the arrangements per se, but inclining to the notion that they should collect larger chunks of the profit pie.

Their share was already quite good. To keep them from being lured into the UMW, Scotia paid wages substantially higher than those received at unionized pits. Wages began at $52 per light-hour shift for the lowest categories and went to $64 for skilled machine operators. There was plenty of overtime, which drew 50 percent more. Generally the men worked six days a week, and sometimes on Sunday. There was a cash bonus of 10 percent for those who missed no workdays in a month. Thus wages ran from $12,000 to $16,000 and a few miners with a lust for work and no regard for Sundays or holidays boasted of $30,000 in 1975. Fringe benefits were meager, but they were of little interest to Scotia's 400 miners, most of whom were young and expected that pension funds—including Social Security—would "go broke" long before they reached retirement age.

For all this munificence Scotia demanded one thing: coal. It must clatter through the tipple and fill the railroad cars all day and all night, shift after shift, irrespective of injuries, pneumoconiosis, bad weather or state and federal safety laws.

On March 9, 1976, the third shift began as usual. The solemn enactments of Congress and the state legislature, and the regulations adopted pursuant thereto, provide the manner in which a new shift of workmen shall take place and the precautions that must be observed for their survival. Such laws and regulations are sound enough, but what actually happened on that ill-fated shift demonstrates the leaden inability of state and federal bureaucracies to carry public mandates into effect.

Charlie Fields is a short, plump, red-faced man whose physical appearance betrays many years in the air-short, dust-abundant mines. His breath comes in the labored gasps of incipient emphysema and black lung. Ambitious beyond most miners, he improved his lot by studying for the "mining papers" of a foreman. Because of a meager education this had come hard for him, especially the meaning of engineering terms used in the state's written examination. But his perseverance and ambition were rewarded and Charlie was eventually employed by Scotia to "fire-boss" the third shift. It is clear that he took his duties lightly, but there is scant reason to suppose he was appreciably less conscientious than most of his fellows similarly engaged in the industry. Perhaps he simply failed to appreciate the seriousness of the task with which he, as a licensed foreman, was charged by law.

It is the duty of a fire boss or "pre-shift safety examiner" to inspect all working places and all haulways leading into them within a three-hour span before a work shift begins. He must see that air circulation meets the required norms and that roof conditions are safe. He is expected to detect fire hazards, including such obvious risks as spark-emitting machinery, improperly stored combustibles of all kinds, accumulations of coal dust, and, most importantly and obviously, the presence of methane. The caged canary has long since disappeared and a methanometer now gives accurate readings of the percentage of the gas in the air. Methane becomes explosive at 5 percent and ceases to be explosive at 15 percent. Prudent supervisors are likely to empty a section when 0.75 percent methane is detected, the men being kept out until new airflows remove the gas.

At the official hearings held at the courthouse in the county seat two months later, it was made clear that Charlie Fields did not inspect that portion of the mine known as No. 2-Southeast Main, though he had entered in the log or journal that he had checked the area and that no gas was detected. When questioned by Robert Barrett, director of MESA on April 27, 1976, he admitted that the entry could have been erroneous. Someone had told him that the air was good and he had accepted that assurance as adequate and entered a notation that the ventilation was 14,-300 cubic feet per minute at the last "open cross-cut" in the "straight" of 2-Southeast Main. That is an immense volume of fresh air, surely enough to dilute to harmlessness any methane it encounters.

Fields conceded that he rarely made any inspections, relying instead on a subordinate, Arvil Cornett, to do so. On the basis of Cornett's reports to him he then made the log entries that constituted the mine's official record. He had been to the straight of 2-Southeast Main only twice in six weeks, though he knew of a "gas feeder" in that inactive dead-end tunnel that emitted such volumes that concentrations had risen to at least 5 percent at one time. He did not recall reporting that discovery. He had been instructed by higher level management to sign the log routinely on the basis of Cornett's reports.

As for Cornett, he told the hearing officers that he too had failed to inspect the long section at the end of the heading because he did not expect anyone to enter it. Weeks earlier a branch tunnel had been driven off at a right angle and "development work" was proceeding there. (This was done without advance notice to MESA, a serious violation of the safety code.) According to some miners who knew the area, brattices—barriers to shunt air from the fans to working places—had routed the oxygen to this new section, leaving 600 yards at the end of 2-Southeast Main temporarily abandoned and sealed off behind the brattice curtains. Even without these fixtures, air, following the line of least resistance, would enter the new section rather than push into the dead-end tunnel straight ahead. Thus the air in the idle length of tunnel was undisturbed as the days passed.

Then, on March 9, a crew from the third shift was directed to haul a load of track rails into the section, preparatory to bringing in a new "continuous miner." The inspection log showed the section to be free of gas and adequately ventilated, so two workmen blithely drove two electric locomotives, with their carloads of steel rails, into an area no methanometer had entered for at least a day and probably a month. Cornett noted that at the entry to the new branch tunnel he had found the air flow to be 10,120 cubic feet of air per minute, 30 percent less than was stated in the log. He had "heard rumors" of a methane feeder, but had not tried to track them down.

Just before the locomotive appeared in the area, problems had developed in the new working area, identified by the engineers on their maps as "2-left off 2-Southeast Main." The air was "bad" and there was "not enough" of it, according to miners, who said that Virgil Coots, the 23-year-old foreman, telephoned this information to James Bentley, ventilation foreman. Bentley, who had countersigned Charlie Field's log, denied that any such call was received, and testified that someone unknown to him and without authority to do so had opened an air regulator 4 feet. When this happened, Coots called to say "he had lost it [the air]."

Two minutes later fifteen men died as an immense,

booming ball of fire streaked out of the far limits of 2-Southeast Main, swept 1,800 feet to the entrance of 2-left off 2-Southeast Main, and flashed into it with a searing roar. The locomotives with the track layers had ventured into the long-deserted section and their arrival had set off gas accumulations that no one had bothered to suspect.

The Scotia mine had been inspected hundreds of times before March 9, 1976, and 652 violations of safety laws and regulations had been cited. Of these at least sixty infractions dealt with serious ventilation problems, including insufficient air circulating at the working face, line brattices out of position, inoperative methanometers, failure to follow the ventilation plan, and findings of imminent danger of explosions, due to methane concentrations of 1.2 percent. Penalties amounting to $164,352 had been imposed by assessment officers, but the company had actually paid only $78,877.

Neither the mine superintendent, the general foreman nor the vice president in immediate charge of the operation regularly checked on the work of the fire bosses or made routine inspections on their own initiative. As one of them put it, "Everybody knew what he was supposed to do and we just left it up to him to do it."

As for Gordon Bonnyman, who lives 150 miles away in Knoxville, he said that he knew nothing of any safety violations. At the courthouse hearings he described Blue Diamond as "a small, informally structured operation" that ran three coal mines in Kentucky and clay and mica mines in North Carolina. His time was spent at the Knoxville headquarters and from his demeanor and testimony one could surely conclude that the goings-on in the tunnels under Big Black Mountain were as remote to him as the harvesting procedures in Bulgaria.

The haphazard management practices at Scotia were matched by the equally haphazard and erratic conditions in the regional and Washington offices of MESA. As soon as he heard the news of the explosion, Herschel Potter, chief of the Division of Safety for MESA in the region, proclaimed that "Scotia stands tall in the industry" in matters of mine safety: he then rushed to the scene. There he met Robert Barrett, director of MESA, who had flown down from Washington with a covey of unimpressive looking "experts." After solemn conferences with company "management teams" and representatives of the anemic Scotia Employees' Association, a recovery team recruited from other mining companies brought out the dead bodies. It had not yet been discovered where the explosion originated or what had set it off, but coal production must go on "in these energy-short times" so, in the same shambling fashion, a crew was organized to go in and restore air circulation and rebolt the blast-weakened roof. This crew of men was accompanied by three MESA inspectors who were to see that the work was properly performed under the immediate supervision of foreman Don Polly. This time the "fire-bossing" was done by a MESA inspector and another company foreman. The former had no anamometer or carbon monoxide monitor. Incredibly, one of the workmen, P.D. Holbrook, was a machinist with absolutely no underground mining experience! The preposterous decision to include him in the crew was concurred in by MESA, the company, and the miners' "association." Toward the end of their shift a laconic notation was entered in MESA's log: "All O.K."

By then Barrett had flown back to Washington where, a few hours later, on March 11, he was confronted with the doleful news that another explosion had ripped out of that same deadly tunnel. This time eleven were killed, including all three of the MESA men.

Barrett and his experts reassembled at the gloom-and-doom shrouded mine where the lethargy at all levels had begun somewhat to dissolve.

A session of buck-passing and recriminations now ensued, as the company and the miners' association blamed MESA for the twin calamities, while the undaunted bureaucrats placed the entire responsibility squarely on the company.

At this point MESA began to formulate a theory to explain the blasts. It seems that one of the battery-powered locomotives, used to transport the steel rails into 2-Southeast Main, was equipped with pneumatic brakes instead of the usual manual type. A compressor automatically pumped up the pressure of these brakes at half-hour intervals, and each time this occurred it set off what was variously described as an electric "arc," "spark" or "flash." It was postulated that, when this machine was driven into the temporarily abandoned 2-Southeast Main section, the compressor ignited the accumulated methane. This kind of brake was a rarity necessitated by the uneven floor of the mine, so, quite naturally, MESA did not suspect its existence. The locomotive was still in the section, but the company did not inform MESA about the arc-producing mechanism, which would continue to function at half-hour intervals for weeks, until the battery was exhausted. Thus, the theory ran, MESA, misled by the company's silence, allowed the roof bolters and its own supervisors to enter a gassy pit in which a "possible ignition source" functioned every half hour. For a time this afforded MESA a tenuous escape hatch and it was clung to with the fervor of a drowning man holding to a life float.

Eventually the mine was sealed at all its openings to allow the air to "stabilize" and the battery to expire. It was reopened in July and miners working in oxygen respirators spent two months restoring brattices, pumping out immense pools of water, restoring electrical and telephone lines and shoring up the top. The bodies were reached and brought out in late November.

The Scotia explosions graphically illustrate all that is wrong with the nation's coal mines. Management is fascinated by the immense profits flowing from a bad and steadily worsening energy situation, and demands ever greater production. The gritty work of running the pits has been delegated to low-echelon foremen and superintendents of mediocre competence, and frequently, slight education. Top management avoids the tipples and tunnels and knows little about the guts of the operation. Management at the mine level delegates responsibility ever downward to foremen and sub-foremen, of whom there are seldom enough. For example, if Charlie Fields had lawfully "fire-bossed" the fatal third shift, he would have traveled more than 5 miles and stopped for inspections at dozens of working places, an obvious impossibility. The miners are hooked on high wages and resent any action that might cost them a shift. They are untrained for their dangerous work and few, even among the experienced, have any real understanding of the dangers they must encounter. In their ignorance on the one hand and greed on the other, they virtually court disaster. As for MESA, it is staffed with "experts" who know little more than the miners (from whose ranks they are recruited) and, like Herschel Potter, instinctively react in defense of the industry they theoretically police. And when a company increases its liquid assets by $55.4 million in a single year how can its anti-social propensities be checked by penalties totaling $78,877 or, for that matter, $164,352?

The corporation that drew such prompt encomiums from Potter had wholly omitted to educate its miners in safety procedures. Some of the men said they had never been shown how to put on a "self-rescue" respirator, designed to make survival possible in pits from which fire or explosion has removed the oxygen. They had been taught nothing about the geology of the mountain in which they worked and had no understanding of the nature of methane or the huge "kettle bottom" rocks that can drop with silent deadliness out of the roof. Methane escapes in increasing quantities as barometric pressures fall, but the mine did not even own a barometer. The mine had no rescue teams, trained to enter disaster areas and bring out survivors. It had never staged escape drills. The company did not keep an ambulance to carry injured miners to hospitals, the nearest of which was 15 miles away over a narrow and extremely winding road. When the men asked that one be bought, the company said it would put up half the cost, and the miners could pay the balance. Under these circumstances, hundreds of men were sent as far as 2.5 miles into a ridge that towered above their heads for thousands of feet, the twisted strata propped up on coal pillars and wooden beams, and strung together with tenuous steel bolts or pins. Such a ramshackle situation made catastrophe almost inevitable.

To a considerable extent the hearings into the March 1976, blasts were taken up with testimony of miners concerning the loose day-to-day operation of the mine. There were accounts of MESA-ordered ventilation curtains being routinely taken down during the working shift so as not to impede the passage of "shuttle cars," then rehung to impress inspectors expected with the fresh work crews. A continuous litany told of advance warning that MESA inspectors were on the way, whereupon all hands flew to making the mine passable. In such instances, it was reported, electrical facilities were quickly insulated, defective methane detectors were replaced, conveyor belts were cleaned up, and ventilation systems were put in order. Though company spokesmen denied it, some of the miners insisted that ventilation regulators were reset to keep bountiful air flowing in areas undergoing inspection, the excellent circulation accompanying inspectors as they moved from section to section. Meanwhile, stale air was the lot of the men whose areas had already met the eye of the "Secretary's representatives." This insidious and deadly game of cat and mouse continued, according to their accounts, right up to the fatal shift.

As it turned out MESA could not shelter for long behind a plea of ignorance concerning those arc-emitting brakes. At the agency's hearings Ben Taylor, chief of the Whitesburg district office, admitted that a foreman had told him about the brake compressor and that he knew it generated an electrical arc. He discussed this with William Clemons, his superior, but Clemons dismissed the idea as unimportant. Neither mentioned the information to Robert Barrett, a newcomer to the position and a conscientious man, who sadly noted that he would never have authorized the roof-bolting crew to enter the mine if he had known of the compressor.

The two miners who survived the second explosion testified that the "MESA men," the foreman and some of the miners discussed the compressor and its periodic electrical arcing as they went into the mine, agreed that it could ignite still another blast, and then with the innocence of children playing with a cocked and loaded .45, proceeded straight on to a fiery death a few hours later.

Neither Taylor nor Clemons had ever received any significant training in mine rescue work, and after the first explosion properly trained mine-rescue teams from nearby Bethlehem Steel and U.S. Steel operations had to be called in to bring out the fifteen bodies, this task being beyond the capacity of MESA and Kentucky's pitiable Department of Mines and Minerals.

This was too rich a field for Congressmen to avoid and in due time a hybrid group of Senators and Representatives came to Whitesburg for hearings. Chaired by Rep. Carl D. Perkins of the House Committee on Education and Labor, they spent six whole hours on a tragedy that had snuffed out twenty-six lives. They fulminated at the

MESA personnel, solemnly and respectfully slapped the wrists of company spokesmen, and poured out immense flows of sympathy on the widows, orphans and other relatives of the dead who filled the chamber. As the hearings adjourned one of the widows said with a disconsolate shrug, "You can see from what went on here why people ain't got no faith in Washington nowadays."

No foreman was indicted or punished for neglect of duty. Thirteen months later no charges had been brought against Blue Diamond Coal, Scotia, Gordon Bonnyman, the MESA bureaucrats or anyone else. Twenty-six men died under circumstances that reek of carelessness, lack of skill, illegality, incompetence and official neglect, but no noteworthy changes have been induced by the tragedy. The same stockholders own the mine, which is operated under the same management and supervisory personnel. The surviving miners, their ranks fleshed out with eager new recruits, go on as before. The MESA personnel still come round on inspection tours and have issued more than 500 new citations for safety violations since those fatal days in March 1976. If sleepless nights have been endured it was because of profits lost during the months when the coal vein was sealed, not because outraged justice demanded retribution.

A fantastic footnote must be added to this incredible story. After work resumed in the mine, the safety committee of the miners' association discovered some underground workmen smoking cigarettes, an act forbidden by both state and federal law. When the company fired them for thus endangering the lives of all and sundry, their fellow workmen struck to show their sympathy and support. Eventually the safety committee and mine management yielded and the smokers went back to work with the strong approbation of their "brother miners."

Because of the large-scale shift to Western strip mining, the mortality rate in U.S. mines was down in 1976 to 0.41 per million man-shifts, only about three times the casualty rate experienced in the mines of Holland twenty years ago. At this rate about 150 miners will die each year and another 11,000 will be injured.

The Asbestos "Pentagon Papers"

by Samuel S. Epstein

A new era in the history of asbestos has dawned with the discovery of a voluminous set of industry documents dating back from 1933 to 1945, dubbed the Asbestos Pentagon Papers. These were obtained during pre-trial discovery proceedings in recently-proliferating product liability suits against the asbestos industry. The documents (which were publicly released in San Francisco at the October, 1978, hearings of the Subcommittee on Compensation, Health and Safety of the House Committee on Education and Welfare) include correspondence among senior executives, lawyers, physicians, consultants, and insurance companies of Johns-Manville, Raybestos-Manhattan Inc., and other asbestos industries. According to South Carolina Circuit Court Judge James Price, the only judge to have reviewed the correspondence so far, "it shows a pattern of denial and disease and attempts at suppression of information" that is so persuasive that he ordered a new trial for the family of a dead insulation worker whose earlier claim had been dismissed. Judge Price noted that the correspondence "further reflects a conscious effort by the industry in the 1930s to downplay, or arguably suppress, the dissemination of information to employees and the public for fear of promotion of lawsuits."

The Asbestos Pentagon Papers afford unusual and detailed insight as to the mechanics of suppression and distortion by industry of information on the hazards of asbestos, as illustrated in the following series of incidents. By 1932, the British had fully documented the occupational hazard of asbestos dust inhalation. On September 25, 1935, the editor of the trade journal *Asbestos* wrote Sumner Simpson, President of Raybestos-Manhattan, requesting permission to publish an article on the hazards of asbestos, and referred to the magazine's past acquiescence to the American industry's desires that this dirty linen not be publicly aired.

> Always you have requested that for certain obvious reasons we publish nothing and naturally your wishes have been respected. . . . [However] discussion of it [the alleged asbestos hazard] in *Asbestos* along the right lines would serve to combat the rather undesirable publicity given to it in current newspapers.

While Simpson was unpersuaded, in a letter (October 1, 1935) to Vandivar Brown, Secretary of Johns-Manville, he praised the magazine for "not reprinting the English articles," and observed that "the less said about asbestos the better off we are . . ." Brown agreed and suggested that if an article on asbestosis had to be published, it should reflect "American data rather than English."

The American data referred to was a study by Anthony Lanza on behalf of Raybestos-Manhattan, Johns-Manville, and the Metropolitan Life Insurance Company, the insurance carrier for both manufacturers. The Lanza study, based on X-rays of 126 workers with three or more years asbestos exposure, was begun in 1929 and completed in late 1931, but the results remained unpublished until 1935.

Brown's confidence in the American (Lanza) data was well founded, as he and other industry officials and lawyers were to serve in an editorial capacity prior to its publication. Lanza submitted his galley proofs to Brown on December 7, 1934. Brown returned the galleys on December 10, 1934, commenting that Lanza had omitted from his final draft a sentence that had appeared in an earlier draft: "Clinically from this study, it [asbestosis] appeared to be of a type milder than silicosis." Hobart, Johns-Manville's New Jersey attorney, further explained in a letter to Brown (December 5, 1934) why Johns-Manville needed to portray asbestosis as a disease milder than silicosis. Referring to pending Workmen's Compensation legislation in New Jersey, Hobart stated that Johns-Manville opposed the inclusion of asbestosis as a compensible disease.

> It would be very helpful to have an official report to show that there is a substantial difference between asbestosis and silicosis: and by the same token, it would be troublesome if an official report should appear from which the conclusion might be drawn that

there is very little, if any difference, between the two diseases.

On December 21, 1934, Brown forwarded Hobart's suggestions to Lanza and asked that "all of the favorable aspects of the survey be included and that none of the unfavorable be unintentionally pictured in darker tones than the comments justify." Lanza agreed, and in his eventual publication concluded that asbestosis was milder than silicosis. Presumably in the further spirit of cooperation, Lanza omitted reference in his paper to the findings that 67 of the 126 workers (53 percent) he had examined were suffering from asbestosis.

Seeking ammunition for courtroom use "against ambulance chasing attorneys and unscrupulous doctors" (memorandum Brown, January, 1933), Simpson wrote F. H. Schulter, President of Thermoid Rubber Co., on November 10, 1936, suggesting that several manufacturers jointly fund asbestos experiments at Saranac Laboratories (Trudeau Institute). Simpson allowed that the benefactors "could determine from time to time after the findings are made whether we wish any publication or not." The decision to publish, of course, being a function of the nature of the results of the study. "It would be a good idea to distribute the information to the medical fraternity, providing it is of the right type and would not injure our companies."

Conferences between industry and Saranac representatives culminated in a deal being struck whereby certain experiments would be conducted, with the decision whether or not to publish the scientific results resting entirely with the sponsors. In a letter of November 20, 1936, Brown emphasized to Leroy Gardner of the Saranac Laboratories:

> It is our further understanding that the results obtained will be considered the property of those who are advancing the required funds, who will determine whether, to what extent and in what manner they shall be made public. In the event it is deemed desirable that the results be made public, the manuscript of your study will be submitted to us for approval prior to publication.

In a reply to Brown on November 23, 1936, Gardner agreed to accept the industry sponsors as the sole arbiters of publication of the results of the experiments. "The Saranac Laboratories agree that the results of these studies shall become the property of the contributors and that the manuscripts of any reports shall be submitted for approval of the contributors before publication." Even this arrangement was not watertight. On learning that Gardner was presenting papers which referred to his preliminary asbestos findings, Simpson complained to Brown (letter May 4, 1939): "The reports may be so favorable to us that they would cause us no trouble, but they might be just the opposite which could be very embarrassing."

In a survey of a Johns-Manville Canadian plant in which seven workers were found to have asbestosis, the medical director, Kenneth W. Smith, deemed it inadvisable that the workers should be warned of their peril.

It must be remembered that although these men have the X-ray evidence of asbestosis, they are working today and definitely are not disabled from asbestosis. They have not been told of this diagnosis, for it is felt that as long as the man feels well, is happy at home and at work, and his physical condition remains good, nothing should be said. When he becomes disabled and sick, then the diagnosis should be made and the claim submitted *by the Company*. The fibrosis of this disease is irreversible and permanent so that eventually compensation will be paid to each of these men. But as long as the man is not disabled, it is felt that he should not be told of his condition so that he can live and work in peace and the Company can benefit by his many years of experience. Should the man be told of his condition today there is a very definite possibility that he would become mentally and physically ill, simply through the knowledge that he has asbestosis.

The Johns-Manville policy of refusing to advise workers of early evidence of asbestosis was characterized in a sworn statement of January 11, 1978, by Wilbur Ruff, a former plant manager, as a "hush hush policy" and one that persisted until the late 1960s.

The mid-1950s found the asbestos industry embroiled in Workmen's Compensation litigation with asbestos workers who were lung cancer victims. The escalating cancer claims moved Smith in March, 1956, to request the Asbestos Textile Institute retain the Industrial Health Foundation to conduct a cancer study which would enable industry to "procure information which would combat current derogatory literature." Smith suggested an alliance with the Quebec Asbestos Mining Association (QAMA) which was conducting a similar study. After agonizing over this proposal for over four years, the Asbestos Textile Institute finally rejected it in March, 1957, for the following reasons:

(1) QAMA has a similar program.
(2) There is a feeling among certain members that such an investigation would stir up a hornets' nest and put the whole industry under suspicion.
(3) We do not believe there is enough evidence of cancer or asbestosis in this industry to warrant this survey.

Perhaps the most graphic illustration of the corporate mores of Johns-Manville comes from the testimony of Smith before he died in 1977. In response to whether he had ever advised Johns-Manville officials to place warning labels on asbestos containing insulation products, Smith replied:

> The reasons why the caution labels were not implemented immediately, it was a business decision as far as I could understand. Here was a recommendation, the corporation is in business to make, to provide jobs for people and make money for stockholders and they had to take into consideration the effects of everything they did, and if the application of a caution label identifying a product as hazardous would cut out sales, there would be serious financial implications. And the powers that be had to make some effort to judge the necessity of the label vs. the consequences of placing the label on the product.

In June, 1963, Institute members obtained copies of Irving Selikoff's cancer study of insulation workers, (as described in Institute minutes of June 6, 1963, and October 8, 1964) and braced itself for the 1964 New York Academy of Sciences Symposia on Asbestos by discussing the retention of a "public relations man to get accurate publicity to the public." In minutes of a February 4, 1971, General Meeting of the Institute, an industry medical consultant labelled Selikoff a "dangerous man." To the question as to whether the American Medical Association might be able to control him, the consultant replied that "pressure" on Selikoff's hospital, Mt. Sinai, might be "effective."

In a report of September 23, 1963, by Thomas Mancuso to Phillip Carey Manufacturing Co., he emphasized that the asbestos-cancer relationship was beyond dispute, and that the company should warn all concerned.

> Internally within the company the question has been raised as to why medical problems, particularly relating to cancer and asbestos were not recognized before. Actually, they were recognized, but the asbestos industry chose to ignore and deny their existence.

Phillip Carey responded by declining to renew Mancuso's contract, and failing to warn its workers and customers.

These documents are likely to affect more than 1,000 asbestos-related lawsuits, totalling more than $1 billion and involving more than one hundred different law firms all over the nation. Ronald Motley, a South Carolina attorney, who is informally directing these actions, has established an "Asbestos Litigation Group" for the purpose of disseminating information and coordinating this extensive litigation. While most plaintiffs have worked with asbestos for over thirty years, others include spouses who have contracted mesotheliomas from washing asbestos-laden clothes of workers, and a case involving Franklin Brooks, a former Georgia Tech All-American football player, who developed asbestosis although only exposed for three consecutive summers. The largest lawsuit to date was filed in Los Angeles in October, 1978, on behalf of five hundred present and former workers who contracted various asbestos-induced diseases at Todd Pacific Shipyards in San Pedro and the Long Beach Naval Shipyard. The suit asks for general and punitive damages, besides medical expenses and loss of earnings.

In the typical product liability or third-party insulator case (of which *Borel v. Fibreboard Paper Products Co.*, 493 F.2d 1076 [5th Circ. 1973] is precedential), there are often as many as ten defendants because the average worker has used products from that many different companies, such as Johns-Manville, Raybestos-Manhattan, Owens-Corning Fiberglas Co., Celotex, Pittsburgh-Corning Co., and Standard Asbestos Manufacturing and Insulating. Of pivotal importance is the question of whether the companies concerned knew about the hazards of asbestos products prior to the 1964 report by Selikoff, when they claimed they were first made aware of this, and what use if any they then made of this information. The primary defense in such cases is that there was no medical or scientific information on risks from asbestos-containing products prior to 1964. Additional lines of defense include statute of limitation exemptions, "contributory negligence" of workers, and their smoking. Johns-Manville's Kotin has been able to persuade the courts in four of five cases in which he has so far testified, that the pre-1964 studies were not definitive, thus absolving the industry from the need to have labelled their products and to have issued warnings. The asbestos "Pentagon Papers" are likely to diminish both the vigor of such arguments and the likelihood of their future success.

In September, 1978, at hearings before the Senate Human Resources subcommittee on labor on S.3060 (a bill designed to provide comprehensive reform of workers compensation programs including extended use of product liability suits to compensate workers or their heirs), Johns-Manville expressed the view that product liability suits were inadequate and inefficient methods of compensation. As an alternative, Johns-Manville proposed that government and labor join with industry to defray the costs of workers compensation through the creation at a state level of a "second injury fund," an alternative that industry, in general, is now vigorously supporting.

In 1960 an alarming report came from J. C. Wagner in South Africa of sixteen new cases of the rare mesothelioma. While six of these were in asbestos mine workers, none of the other ten had ever worked in the mines. All had lived in the vicinity of the mines, though, many as children. Public or non-occupational mesotheliomas have since been reported from nine other countries, including the United States. These cases are generally thought to be due to exposure of family members to asbestos brought home on the clothes of asbestos workers. Additional sources of exposure include contamination of the air with asbestos from nearby plants or factories. High concentrations of asbestos fibers have recently been demonstrated in communities adjacent to asbestos industries.

The indestructibility of asbestos, its indiscriminate use, and the careless disposal of its waste products make it difficult to predict the extent and level of exposure of the general public. For instance, Certain-Teed Products Corporation, an asbestos-cement pipe manufacturer, has in the past dumped about 2,700 tons each year of crushed asbestos pipe in an open-air landfill site in Ambler, Pennsylvania.

> The dump not only snakes diagonally through the very center of the town, which has a population of 8,000, but it is fifty feet high, anywhere from one to two city blocks wide, and about ten city blocks long. In fact, it is estimated to contain some million and a half cubic yards of waste material . . . Kids play on an asphalt basketball court that has been built smack on top of material from the dump, and is literally covered with loose asbestos fiber and wads of waste material containing (chrysotile) asbestos.

Drinking water is an additional possible source of non-occupational exposure to asbestos. Reserve Mining Company, a subsidiary of Armco and Republic Steel, for years has been dumping taconite mine wastes, rich in asbestos fibers, into Lake Superior at levels of about 67,000 tons a day. Not unreasonably, this gave rise to fears that polluting the drinking water of Great Lakes communities with asbestos would lead to excess cancer rates, especially of the stomach and colon.

In April 1974, Federal District Judge Miles Lord issued an injunction in Duluth, Minnesota, restraining the

Reserve Mining Company from further dumping its taconite mine wastes into Lake Superior. Reserve Mining witnesses attempted to prevent this ruling by testifying that there were no alternatives to this lake dumping, although it appears that the company had developed plans for land disposal sites as early as 1970.

It is not yet known whether the resulting asbestos contamination of drinking water of Lake Superior towns, including Duluth, will lead to cancer. Preliminary studies with laboratory animals have so far yielded ambiguous results. Certainly, it has been established that persons occupationally exposed to asbestos have an increased risk of alimentary tract cancer as well as lung cancer. Without waiting for answers to these questions, a Federal Appeals Court reversed Judge Lord's decision, on grounds that it was not based on adequate proof of risks to health, and permitted Reserve Mining to resume dumping its tailings into the lake, pending the development of alternate land disposal sites.

In May, 1975, Congress approved $4 million to build a water treatment plant in Duluth to filter out the asbestos fibers from drinking water. The State of Minnesota appropriated $2.5 million in local funds for the project, which became operative in November, 1976. Reserve Mining is now phasing out lake dumping, and is building a land disposal site, in accordance with a court order that dumping is to be terminated by 1980.

In addition to environmental exposure to asbestos in air and water, the general public receives a wide range of further exposures. Particularly important sources are construction operations involving the spraying of asbestos, the use of crushed stone containing unbound asbestos in roads and driveways, and demolition. Exposure to asbestos also results from its use in fireproofing and insulation, air ducts, automobile brake linings, cement water pipes, filter pads for beers, wine, and drugs, cosmetic talcs, and hand-held hair dryers.

In an ineffective attempt to protect the general public from asbestos air pollution, EPA developed an emission standard for asbestos as a hazardous air pollutant in April, 1973. The standard, however, is only based on visible emissions and on poorly enforced work practices, and not on asbestos fibril counts.

Acting on a petition from a public interest group, the Natural Resources Defense Council, the Consumer Product Safety Commission announced in December, 1977, that patching and spackling compounds containing asbestos would be banned from the $400 million market by June, 1978. Under the commission's order, fifty manufacturers ceased producing in January, 1978, leaving retailers the next six months to clear their shelves. While these patching compounds are used primarily by professional builders, about 10 percent of the market is for home hobbyists and craftsmen.

Realization is gradually dawning that, except under the most restrictive conditions, all forms of asbestos have become too expensive in terms of human disease for commercial use. Further illustration of this are the individual and class actions suits for asbestos cancer and disease, in the multimillion-dollar range now being filed by some of the four and one-half million workers employed in Naval shipbuilding yards during World War II.

The Navy has since abandoned the use of asbestos in shipbuilding in favor of alternative materials, including fiberglass. However, these are also reasons for concern on the use of fiberglass as an asbestos replacement. Experimental studies indicate that fiberglass, particularly the more modern short-fiber products which were introduced into large-scale use in the early 1960s, may produce a type of disease and cancer similar to that produced by asbestos. Epidemiological studies are now only suggestive of an increased cancer risk, probably because exposed workers have not been followed up for the three or so decades it generally takes for asbestos fibers to induce cancer. Industry is attempting to quiet these concerns in moves which reflect the growing shift from asbestos to fiberglass for insulation and a wide range of consumer products, including draperies. An interesting insight into such tactics was afforded by a recent letter to *New Times* by Johns-Manville's Kotin, bearing no reference at all to his industry employment, protesting that "epidemiological studies show that there is no chronic health effect in humans as a result of exposure to fibrous glass."

On April 26, 1978, HEW Secretary Joseph Califano issued the most explicit warning ever made by government on the dangers of asbestos. Califano estimated that as many as half of all workers exposed to asbestos could develop serious diseases such as cancer of the lung and gastrointestinal tract, mesotheliomas, and asbestosis. Califano also estimated that from 8 to 11 million workers may have been exposed to asbestos since the start of World War II. Besides urging exposed workers to have a chest X-ray, HEW has sent a "physician advisory" letter regarding the dangers of asbestos to the nation's 400,000 doctors. While Califano properly stressed the added danger of smoking to asbestos workers, an impression of "blaming the victim" appears to have been created by the absence of any balancing reference to the more urgent needs for control of exposures in the workplace.

Califano's statement appears to have been prompted by the growing number of lawsuits filed against federal agencies for having failed to notify workers in the past of the known hazards of asbestos exposure. As such, Califano's statement is also important for what it failed to say. Workers were not informed of their rights to sue the government. Nor were any plans announced for organization of a surveillance program, including contacting and examining former government workers. Nor was any mention made of the long overdue need to implement the recommendation of NIOSH for a 100,000 fiber standard as the only meaningful way to protect against asbestos-induced cancers and disease. Finally, no mention was made of the growing evidence of the hazards to the public-at-large, particularly those living in the vicinity of asbestos plants, quite apart from exposures due to asbestos-containing consumer products.

In spite of all the problems of omission and emphasis in the Califano statement, its significance is epochal and unique. It opens the door of national health care policies to preventive medicine. Specifically, the statement recognizes in principle that prospective surveillance is needed for groups at high risk of cancer, although how this will be achieved for asbestos workers is still unclear. It is likely that the high costs of surveillance may well act as future incentives to reduce risks of occupational exposure to carcinogenic and other highly toxic agents, forcing the ultimate realization that prevention is cheaper than "cure."

While the dangers of asbestos have been well recognized for over five decades, the industry was able to largely ig-

sent all U.S. Attorneys a set of enforcement guidelines for the 1899 Act. Essentially, these guidelines generalized the Gary precedent. Prosecutors were told not to inititate suits on their own, but to wait for referrals from the Environmental Protection Agency. Apparently there was substantial internal opposition by various U.S. Attorneys to this requirement, and on one occasion it was necessary to fire one who insisted on zealous enforcement.

In February 1971, the U.S. Attorney filed a civil suit against the Gary works under the Refuse Act, charging the corporation with a pattern of continuing discharges of iron, oil, ammonia, and suspended solids. The case was one of a group of thirty-eight intiated simultaneously by the Justice Department, most of which were settled out of court. The Gary works case has recently been dropped completely by the Justice Department on the grounds that the 1972 water pollution law amendments provide a better way to get results.

While this suit was pending, President Nixon reactivated the 1899 Refuse Act on December 23, 1970, by ordering the Army Corps of Engineers to begin implementing a section of the 1899 Act which required all industries discharging into the nation's waters to obtain a permit. Under the Corps regulations of July 1971, the application had to be approved by both the appropriate state pollution control agency and the EPA. If both bodies approved, the Corps would issue a five-year permit. But as it turned out, this set of procedures virtually made a dead letter of the 1899 Act. The basis for state approval of the permit application was to be the existing "water quality standards" under the Water Pollution Control Act. (Thus, for the Gary works, it was the inadequate standards of the Indiana Stream Pollution Control Board.) Then Director William Ruckelshaus indicated that EPA approval would be a formality; as a rule, his agency would simply follow the state guidelines. The effect was to increase the amount of paperwork and forms, while making actual change in the real world of sewer discharges less likely.

The permit program immediately began to collapse under its own weight as it proved impossible to provide adequate review for the 40,000 applications which had been filed. U.S. Steel's application for the Gary works alone ran to more than 500 pages. Few of the applications were

all effluent discharge patterns. The Federal Government then granted U.S. Steel a one-year extension. In January 1969, another conference was held to see how matters were proceeding. At this time, U.S. Steel obtained a second extension, until December 31, 1970. In December 1970 it demanded new extensions and made no pretense of intention to cooperate with the original requirements. No enforcement action has been taken by the Federal authorities under the Water Pollution Control Act.

The other main Federal anti-water pollution law is the 1899 Rivers and Harbors Act, more popularly known as the Refuse Act. In February 1970, responding to rising national concern about water pollution, the Justice Department filed a criminal suit under the Refuse Act against the Gary works. The Refuse Act has strong enforcement provisions, and in broad and sweeping terms—upheld by the Supreme Court—it forbids, in effect, any industrial water pollution. The only way one can legally pollute is to obtain a permit from the Army Corps of Engineers.

Initially, the Justice Department suit seemed to be a giant step forward. On June 8, 1972, U.S. Steel was found guilty and fined $5,000. But the amount of the fine was clearly far less than the cost of pollution control equipment to prevent the discharge, and more than four years had elapsed between the alleged offense and conviction. Even more significantly, the indictment was not based upon U.S. Steel's continual and massive water pollution; it simply alleged that on one specific day, October 11, 1967, discharges from two sewers opening into the Grand Calumet had occurred: one pipe discharging "a significant quantity of a red-brown substance," and the other "an oily substance."

This narrowly drawn indictment presaged a determined—and successful—effort by the Nixon Administration to prevent application of the Refuse Act to halt water pollution. The Nixon Administration clearly considered the law too powerful a weapon against big corporate polluters, and steps were rapidly taken to emasculate it. During the period when the Gary works case was intitiated, many U.S. Attorneys were instituting actions under the promising 1899 law, and it seemed likely to revolutionize water pollution enforcement.

On June 13, 1970, then Attorney General John Mitchell

There are two main Federal laws against water pollution. One is the Federal Water Pollution Control Act, originally passed in 1948 and amended to "strengthen" it by virtually every Congress thereafter. It is a textbook example of how complex standard-setting procedures and unwieldy enforcement can vitiate the noblest rhetoric.

As is the case with many progressive reform measures, insufficient funding makes it impossible to provide the staff necessary to implement the grand legislative design. With only enough resources to engage in spot enforcement, the agency must rely for its success on the voluntary collaboration of the regulated industry; if the industry actively resists, the agency is largely stymied. And since the statutes are never self-enforcing but require elaboration by the administrative agency, the framework is created for a hidden process of mutual accommodation with the regulated industry. Often the consequence is the virtual gutting of the legislative objectives.

Finally, when the agency does insist upon a standard the regulated group strongly opposes, the courts provide a method of delay. Powerful companies have both the resources and the incentives to spend millions of dollars on dilatory judicial tactics. For example, several pollution suits launched against U.S. Steel in the late 1960s are yet to reach final adjudication.

These enforcement problems can ultimately be traced to the immense economic and political power of American industry. Piecemeal attempts at reform legislation, such as the water pollution laws, do not attack the power; hence they often fail to achieve even their limited objectives.

Against this background, it is not surprising that the actions of the Federal Government to stop water pollution at the Gary works were quite limited. In March 1965, the Federal Government convened a conference on Lake Michigan pollution at which the Federal and state governments were to set "water quality standards" for the Calumet area and establish a timetable for compliance with these standards.

The standard adopted was the extremely lax set of regulations of the state of Indiana, and U.S. Steel was given three years—until December 31, 1968—to take some significant action regarding pollution. During this grace period, the Gary works did nothing to improve their over-to promulgate specific water quality criteria for the Grand Calumet, and these criteria were lax. Limits were placed on discharges of dissolved solids, ammonia-nitrate, and phenol, but no limits were placed on iron particles or cyanide, and the limits on suspended solids and oil were completely inadequate.

U.S. Steel was then, and still remains, in violation of these standards. After three years the Indiana Board decided to hold a hearing on the matter. On August 20, 1970, this procedure culminated in an order that U.S. Steel cease discharging "raw and inadequately treated waste water" into the Grand Calumet River and that it "institute at once the necessary procedures for the construction of additional waste treatment facilities needed to eliminate the pollution of waters." The corporation was to be given eighteen months to carry out construction work. U.S. Steel's response to this first legal demand that it stop polluting was to request a rehearing, at which time the Board reaffirmed its order. On appeal, U.S. Steel claimed that the Board had made numerous vital errors in its conduct—including failure to take a transcript at the initial hearing. The Indiana Superior Court reversed and remanded the case to the Board, which ordered a new hearing.

This court decision was attributable to the Board's inadequate case, not to pro-industry bias, for at virtually the same time, the same court upheld a far stronger order of the Gary Air Pollution Review Board with respect to the Gary works' air pollution.

Thus, in April 1971 the state of Indiana found itself beginning its laborious enforcement proceeding against U.S. Steel. The corporation's position was, "We all pollute." Since then, the state has taken no further actions leading to binding orders against U.S. Steel.

The public has come to expect failure from local and state government in solving pressing social problems. But despite the events of recent years, people still have faith in the power of the Federal authorites to regulate malefactors of great wealth. In the case of the Gary works' pollution, however, the Federal Government has been as ineffective as the city and the state. To understand this failure, it is necessary to disentangle a morass of laws, administrative regulations, and bureaucratic decisions.

1967 at the crest of the civil rights movement, local government had been notoriously corrupt—and particularly solicitous of U.S. Steel's preferences. Because of a variety of constraints, Hatcher himself did not press ahead on confronting U.S. Steel on this matter. But in 1971 he did appoint a new and activist health commissioner, Dr. Herschel Bornstein.

Bornstein's first effort to control U.S. Steel's water pollution involved a request to the Indiana Stream Pollution Control Board to perform laboratory tests on water samples from the Grand Calumet to determine whether there was a violation of state law. This request was refused on the grounds that this service was performed only for local health departments when drinking water samples were involved. (Soon thereafter, one of the key officials involved in this decision was appointed by a major steel company as its director of environmental control.)

Bornstein then attempted to proceed on his own; he obtained a search warrant from the Gary City Court on June 24, 1971—an action unprecedented in the city's entire history. Bornstein arrived at the Gary works with his warrant, took water samples from the Grand Calumet, and sent them off for analysis to a private laboratory. Gary works Superintendent J. David Carr angrily referred to the event as a "raid" and charged that it was a "carefully organized effort to create an incident." Bornstein found himself at an impasse, for neither state nor Federal authorities responded to his test results. Mayor Hatcher, too, did nothing to increase the health commissioner's legal powers so that he could effectively act on his own. The next year, Bornstein resigned, partly because he felt a lack of support for his initiatives from City Hall.

While the city has been moribund, the state of Indiana has been worse; it has, in effect, served as a legal shield for violations of the water pollution laws by U.S. Steel. The State Pollution Control Board has neither the funding nor the impetus to enforce water pollution regulations, and few violators have been prosecuted. Not until 1965 did the Indiana Stream Pollution Board even begin to go through the motions of industrial compliance with the Indiana law.

U.S. Steel officials have, understandably, expressed the highest regard for the Indiana Stream Pollution Control Board. It took the Board almost two years after 1965

tent that its entire bottom is composed of minute iron particles. The river is entirely unfit for any recreational activity. The ammonia-nitrogen discharged from the Gary works is a major contributor to the eutrophication of southern Lake Michigan. The cyanide level—due to a discharge of a ton a day from the steel mill—is perhaps sufficient to cause the death of anyone foolhardy enough to drink the reddish brown water covered with oil slicks. Not even sludge worms can live in the Grand Calumet, whose only life is blue-green algae.

The discharges from the Gary works do not exhaust the corporation's damage to Lake Michigan's ecosystem. The giant fleet of ore ships which the corporation maintains on Lake Michigan to transport iron ore to the Gary works periodically discharges oil into the lake. Three-fourths of the annual sixty million tons of cargo docked in the Calumet are materials for the steel industry. The result is visible to anyone's eye and, as the summer shipping season progresses, the Gary beaches are soiled by more and heavier oil slicks. In theory, the city of Gary, the state of Indiana, and the Federal Government can each require U.S. Steel to stop using the Grand Calumet River as an open sewer. None of them has done so.

When Gary's waterworks were constructed by U.S. Steel engineers between 1906 and 1908, they embodied the most advanced techniques and were constructed for an anticipated population of 200,000. (This plan was so farsighted that no further waterworks were needed until the mid-1960s.) The original waterworks have an intake tunnel which passes under the Gary plant and draws in water three miles from the lake's shoreline. The prevailing water flow in southwestern Lake Michigan is from south to north in a westerly direction, so the pollutants discharged from the Gary works (entering Lake Michigan west of the city at Indiana Harbor) do not pass into the city's own water system. Instead, some three to four days after discharge, they reach Chicago's water system. Consequently, although Gary's water has a high iron particle count which gives it an unpalatable taste, it is relatively safe for human consumption.

Within Gary itself, therefore, there has never been mass concern with the problem of water pollution. Until black reform mayor Richard Hatcher was elected to office in

Michigan, annihilating forever its natural state. Drastic changes were also wrought on the Grand Calumet River, which had meandered through Gary on what is now the demarcation between the Gary works and the city proper. The Grand Calumet River was first surveyed in the 1830s, and the original survey notes indicate that it was wide and, although shallow, navigable. Until early in the Twentieth Century, lumber and fruit boats traveled up the Grand Calumet from Lake Michigan and docked in Hammond, the city due west of Gary. There are pictures of three-masted schooners docked at Hammond in 1905, but by 1910, after the construction of the Gary works, regular commercial navigation had ceased.

From the outset of operations, the Gary works have used the Grand Calumet as a free disposal system for unwanted chemical effluents. Before the Gary works and the other large manufacturing plants were built in the Calumet region, the Gary beach was the center of a major fishing industry, with large commercial catches of whitefish and sturgeon. By the 1940s, however, the fishing industry had been destroyed. Algae growth in southern Lake Michigan (caused by industrial dumping of large amounts of ammonia-nitrogen and phosphates) had eliminated the environment necessary to support fish populations.

Industrial production is the main cause of American water pollution, and the steel industry alone is responsible for one-fifth of all the water used in manufacturing. The effluents of steel production are particularly harmful to the bodies of water into which they are dumped. It is not surprising, therefore, that those rivers which receive major steel plant discharges are among the most polluted in the country. And the newest steel industry technologies seem to be increasing the volume and toxicity of such pollution.

U.S. Steel's Gary works are a prime example. They currently employ 20,000 steelworkers and produce almost eight million tons of steel a year. This second-largest of all American steel plants (just barely behind Bethlehem's Sparrows Point Works outside Baltimore) occupies ten of the eleven miles of Gary's shoreline. Its dozens of sewers empty more than 600 million gallons of water into the Grand Calumet and Lake Michigan each day. The discharge of this water, after its use in steelmaking, has changed the Grand Calumet River downstream to the ex-

And Filthy Flows the Calumet

by Edward Greer

Judge Elbert Gary was a successful man. Because of his rectitude, J.P. Morgan chose him in 1901 to be chairman of the board of U.S. Steel. With his share of the profits, Gary turned to collecting works of art. After his death in 1928, his collection was sold for the highest price in an art auction up to that time. *The New York Times* of April, 28, 1928, described the invitation-only crowd as including "scores of persons prominent socially and financially." A two-volume illustrated and limited-edition catalog—itself now a collector's item—was printed for the occasion, and it contained this description of Jean Baptiste Corot's masterpiece, *Souvenir des Banque du Lac de Garde*, which had graced Gary's Fifth Avenue mansion: "The high bank in the left foreground is crowned with willows and saplings. . . . A traveler . . . stands under the trees looking out over the untroubled water."

Gary's ability to enjoy this idyllic scene had its costs to others—mainly to the immigrant steelworkers who reached "old age at forty" because of the rigors of U.S. Steel's labor policy, but also to the American landscape. Nowhere was—and is—this latter price more clearly signaled than in Gary, Indiana, originally built by U.S. Steel in 1906 as the first and most ambitious of all its works. All observers agreed at the time that the new steel city was one of mankind's most impressive engineering feats.

Today, however, Gary stands as a case study of industrial despoliation of the American environment. Its air pollution problem is evident to even the most casual traveler. Its water pollution problem is even more severe and intractable.

Among the factors which persuaded Gary to select the site for the steel works were its availability, price, access to transport and markets, and a favorable state legislature. Gaining the special acquiescence of the pliant Indiana legislature, U.S. Steel dumped massive landfill into Lake

cates how the cumulative effect of our industrial emissions has been to kill thousands of lakes and threaten international food supplies. And we witness, through the eyes of Michael Brown, the agony of the people of Love Canal, New York, when they discover that they had unwittingly built their homes above one of the most hazardous waste sites in America.

THE CORPORATION AND NATURAL RESOURCES

Our planet is a physical symphony, with oceans and mountains, animals and plants, earth and sky each playing a harmonious part in a majestic whole. How ironic then that the most recent addition to this global orchestra—the human being—should be the element to mar the environment's cadenced beauty.

For many years we have thought of the earth in two conflicting ways. We considered it to be our unlimited resource, from which we could take without fear of depletion. Yet we have also treated the earth as repository for our disposed garbage. Only now are we beginning to discover that what we wish to draw from the earth contains bits of what we thought we had thrown away.

The results of such an attitude are ominous. Lake Erie is dead. The Hudson river is contaminated by polychlorinated biphenyls (PCB's), largely the legacy of General Electric—chemicals which have so permeated the food chain that toxic levels have been found in some women's breast milk. Crops have been sprayed with 2,4,5,-T, a pesticide which contains dioxin, the deadly substance used in herbicides developed for the jungles of Vietnam. In Virginia, the James River has an estimated one hundred thousand pounds of kepone lying at the bottom, which would cost $8 *billion* to clean up. The riverbed of the Shenandoah is covered with more than two hundred and twenty thousand pounds of mercury, the legacy of twenty-seven years of dumping by the DuPont and Olin corporations.

In his article, Edward Greer recounts the struggle of the people of Gary, Indiana with the pollution of the Grand Calumet river by U.S. Steel. Then, an article from *Mosaic*, a publication of the National Science Foundation, indi-

nore or suppress these until studies in the 1950s by Doll in England and by Selikoff in the U.S. (sponsored by the asbestos insulators union) established the relationship between asbestos and asbestosis and cancers at various sites. Since then the industry has employed scientific expertise to advocate its position in professional journals and to successfully resist and prevent effective government regulations. With an estimated 8 to 11 million workers having been exposed since World War II, the toll of asbestos occupational disease and cancer is now reaching epidemic proportions. Workers have begun to exercise legal initiatives, including third-party and medical malpractice suits, resulting in multimillion dollar awards.

As the realization is dawning that asbestos is too expensive in terms of disease and death to continue using, the industry is beginning to develop the strategies of relocating in lesser developed countries and promoting the use of fiberglass as an asbestos substitute in the United States. There are serious unresolved questions as to the dangers of fiberglass and there are possibilities that it may be no less hazardous than asbestos.

The massive human toll taken by asbestos is probably the single most important incentive to the development of coherent national policies recognizing preventive medicine as a major future component in the delivery of health care.

granted, but while they were pending, legal action against industrial polluters was also held in abeyance.

As this nightmare unfolded, Congress again decided to amend the Federal Water Pollution Control Act. As the counsel to the relevant House committee put it in explaining why new legislation was appropriate, "Compliance with the existing laws in many cases was nonexistent. The superimposition of an 1899 law by EPA and the Corps of Engineers caused more problems than it solved, particularly when it broke down and collapsed of its own weight."

The new law has done nothing to solve the problem. Under the 1972 amendments—hailed by the politicians responsible for them as providing unprecedented power to curb polluters—all the permit applications filed under the Refuse Act were automatically transformed into applications under the new law. All of the practical problems of processing the permit applications (which have now grown to 57,000) remain. But everyone who has applied for a permit is immunized from prosecution for polluting under the 1972 amendments until the permit has actually been processed; thus, as late as mid-1975, about 600 of the 4,600 major industrial polluters were still awaiting initial decisions on their applications.

As to the general thoroughness of review where permits have been issued, one need only compare the handful of agency personnel available to review them with Ruckelshaus's estimate that the applicants spent "in excess of $100 million" in their preparation. Among environmentalist partisans the consensus is that the new law has resulted in the widespread issuance of "permits to pollute."

In support of this conclusion an examination of the handful of cases chosen by the EPA for intensive attention—such as the Gary works—is most instructive. For several years the EPA unsuccessfully attempted to reach a negotiated agreement with U.S. Steel over the terms of the Gary works permit. These negotiations ultimately broke down, and on October 31, 1974, EPA unilaterally issued a permit. The corporation appealed under the administrative review process provided for under the new law. An adjudicative hearing was held in August 1975, and no decision has yet been reached. But it is virtually certain that if the decision is adverse to the corporation's preferences, it will pursue its legal options in the courts—a process which will certainly result in several years of additional delay.

In the meantime, U.S. Steel continues to defer expensive capital investments for water pollution control equipment. The monitoring group set up under the 1972 amendments to report on the progress of enforcement recently indicated that industry has been spending at less than half the rate needed to meet the 1977 interim water clean-up goal. EPA data on the Gary works reveal that in 1975 the mill was still discharging suspended solids at the same rate as in the late 1960s—forty-five tons per day.

Recently, the continuing intransigence of U.S. Steel has provoked EPA to attempt to subject the corporation to public pressure by identifying it as a flagrant environmental scofflaw. In a widely reported speech before a group of leading industrialists on February 5, deputy administrator John Quarles singled out U.S. Steel and charged that it "has compiled a record of environmental recalcitrance which is second to none." Summarizing the national situation, Quarles indicated that seventeen of U.S. Steel's twenty major facilities had substantial compliance problems. The corporation immediately retorted that its violations were only marginal and that its pollution record was typical of other manufacturers.

But regardless of the long line of enforcement failures by the Federal and Indiana regulatory authorities, U.S. Steel may finally be brought into line by a combination of an activist Illinois state's attorney, a responsive court, and the old common law of nuisance. If so, it will be a true irony of history. Judge Gary made the decision to locate his new mill in Indiana—rather than expand the existing South Works in Chicago—largely because reformist Illinois Governor John Altgeld had blocked the use of landfill in Lake Michigan. Gary decided that the Indiana legislature would be more pliable, and it was; it passes special legislation to permit such landfill. So if the state of Illinois brings U.S. Steel to heel, it will be a belated vindication of Altgeld's concern to protect the Lake Michigan environment.

What has happened in the Illinois courts in this: In 1967, the state of Illinois and the Chicago Sanitary District brought suits against both the Gary works and the neighboring Inland Steel plant in East Chicago, Indiana.

After many years of delaying tactics, the Illinois courts have ruled that it is appropriate, under the old common law of nuisance, for Illinois to bring suit against water pollution which affects Chicago's water supply—even though the origin of that pollution is in another state.

Moreover, in the U.S. Steel case, the Illinois court has specifically rejected the defense that the Federal EPA permit is paramount and excludes state remedies. Instead, the court ruled that in nuisance cases both the Federal and state authorities have concurrent jurisdiction. And not only can the state of Illinois bring the steel companies into court, but it can also hold them to more stringent standards than those embodied in the EPA permit system. Traditional common law remedies and our old-fashioned Federal system have combined to produce results after all the modern regulatory processes failed.

In the Inland Steel case, the company capitulated and filed a consent decree before the Circuit Judge Nathan Cohen in which it agreed to install an advanced waste recovery system to be operative by 1983 and even to pay Illinois $400,000 in court costs. The U.S. Steel case has not yet reached final adjudication, but there is good reason to believe that the ultimate judgment will be similar. That U.S. Steel is worried about the outcome is revealed by its action a few days before the Inland Steel consent decree was made public: It announced a new $30 million pollution control system would be installed in its Chicago South Works.

It would be premature to decide that U.S. Steel has finally met its match. The corporation's delaying tactics may well continue for a long time, as it takes full advantage of the opportunities presented by our complex administrative and judicial systems. The stockholders can continue to clip their coupons while corporate lobbyists try to extract additional tax benefits from Congress to reduce the cost of capital expenditures when or if they become unavoidable. Meanwhile, Lake Michigan continues its ominous ecological decline.

The legacy of Judge Elbert Gary is not just a ghost over the peaceful and polluted Calumet waters. It is a palpable injury, each day renewed and intensified by his corporate heirs.

Acid From The Sky

from *Mosaic*

"The water was so clear it looked transparent. Nothing broke the surface. No frogs croaked. Nothing moved on the shore."

This is what ecologist Anne LaBastille saw not long ago when she hiked into Brooktrout Lake in a wilderness area of New York's Adirondack Park. Brooktrout Lake had been a prime fishing spot for anglers who didn't mind the 15-kilometer roundtrip hike from the end of the nearest road. But now, LaBastille, a commissioner of the Adirondack Park Agency, wrote in *Outdoor Life*, the trout are gone from Brooktrout Lake. So are other life forms that were linked to the trout and to each other in a complex aquatic ecosystem. The water in the lake, crystal clear with a faint tinge of blue, is so acidic that fish cannot reproduce and survive in it.

Brooktrout is one of the more than 2,000 lakes and ponds in Adirondack Park, 2.4 million hectares of mountains and forests set aside as parkland more than 80 years ago. Then Carl Schofield, a Cornell University biologist, sampled more than 200 Adirondack lakes in the mid-nineteen-seventies, he found that about half of them were so acidic that fish could no longer live in them.

Schofield and other scientists see convincing evidence that much of the excess-acid in the high mountain lakes of the Adirondacks falls from the sky—from rain and snow made acidic by sulfur and nitrogen compounds from power plant and factory smokestacks as far away as Ohio and Indiana. As they travel through the atmosphere and react chemically with water droplets and other airborne substances, these compounds form sulfuric and nitric acid which is then incorporated into raindrops and snowflakes.

Trout fishermen and ecologists are not the only ones who are concerned about acids that fall from the sky. Although the evidence is not conclusive, there are indications that acid precipitation may stunt the growth of forests and reduce agricultural productivity. It certainly is contributing to the deterioration of ancient stone structures like the Parthenon and the Colosseum, as well as other concrete and metal structures all over the industrial world.

Further, the impacts of acid rain have national and international implications. The affected areas may be hundreds or even thousands of kilometers from the sources of the pollutants that form the acids. The United States "exports" ingredients of acid precipitation to Canada; England sends them across the North Sea to Scandinavia; acid haze over Alaska may come from as far away as Japan.

Because emissions from electric power plants appear to be the likeliest major source of acid precipitation, the problem has become a component of energy policy deliberations. "In terms of our domestic energy policy, the acid precipitation problem is pivotal," says Kay Jones, senior adviser for air pollution to the President's Council on Environmental Quality in Washington, D.C.

Although a number of universities and research centers in the United States are studying acid precipitation, Jones says, a carefully planned and closely coodinated national program is badly needed. He has been working with scientists and administrators from other Federal agencies to develop such a program. "I believe we will have a cohesive plan for a national research program on acid rain before the end of 1979," Jones declares.

The focus will be an array of unknowns, including the relationships and interactions among fossil-fuel combustion products, the chemistry of the atmosphere and the acidity of the precipitation that falls from it. The evidence for links between specific pollution sources and particular acid precipitation episodes is mainly circumstantial. The chemistry is still little understood. As ecologist Gene Likens of Cornell University puts it, "The correlations are convincing, like those between cigarette smoking and lung cancer. But I can't prove conclusively that the sulfur in my rain collector in New Hampshire came from a power plant in Ohio."

As an example of the lack of knowledge of the mechanisms of acid precipitation, notes Allan Lazrus, a chemist with the National Center for Atmospheric Research and principal investigator for its Acid Precipitation Experiment, more and more nitric acid has been turning up in precipitation samples in the northeastern United States, although sulfuric acid has been predominant in the past. It seems probable, says Lazrus, that the reduction in sulfates reflects the trend in fossil-fuel use from high-sulfur to low-sulfur coal and natural gas. Automobile emissions would account for the higher nitrogen-compound levels, he says. But this, he concedes, is an informed guess. It can be neither rigorously supported nor successfully refuted on the basis of present knowledge.

Whatever the precise sources of acid precipitation, it is an increasingly pressing environmental threat. Almost anyplace investigators seek it, it is being found. Recent examinations in the Front Range of the Rocky Mountains by William Lewis of the University of Colorado have uncovered elevated acidity there. And in the Venezuelan tropics acidity levels are being reported "unbelievably" high.

Although long-term data on trends in acid precipitation over large areas are scarce, it appears that the acidity of rain and snow has probably increased slightly since around 1930. And, according to Cornell's Likens, a pioneer in acid precipitation research, in the last two or three decades "the areas affected by acid precipitation in both Europe and North America have increased rather dramatically." (Chemists rate acidity in terms of hydrogen ion concentration, expressed as a factor known as pH, which ranges in value from 0 to 14. A pH of 7 is neutral; values less than 7 indicate increasing acidity, and values higher than 7 indicate increasing alkalinity. The pH scale is logarithmic—a solution with a pH of 5 is ten times as acidic as one with a pH of 6, and a drop of pH from 6 to 4 indicates a hundredfold increase in acidity.

Rain with a pH of 4 may fall on plant foliage from a sudden summer thunderstorm. When the storm passes and the sun comes out, drops of water standing on leaf surfaces can evaporate rapidly. As the drop grows smaller, the acid becomes more concentrated, possibly to the point that it can physically damage the protective surface structure of the leaf.

Samples of "fossil precipitation" taken from glaciers that formed centuries ago usually have pH values greater than 5. The lower limit of a natural acidity from rain or snow is a pH of around 5.6, caused by dissolved atmospheric carbon dioxide that produces a weak solution of carbonic acid. Thus acid precipitation is often defined as rain or snow with a pH of less than 5.6.)

The first comprehensive precipitation pH data for the United States were collected from a 33-station network by the National Center for Atmospheric Research between 1960 and 1966. Those data showed pH levels ranging from less than 4 in New England to more than 7 in the Western United States.

The seriousness of acid precipitation as a regional problem in the United States was recognized largely as a result of field research done by Likens, Herbert Borman of Yale University and their colleagues at Hubbard Brook Experimental Forest in New Hampshire. Precipitation sampling and biogeochemical cycling studies that started at Hubbard Brook in the early nineteen-sixties revealed that rainfall with a pH of less than 4 was a common occurrence there. Other measurements in New England and the Adirondacks, at sites remote from local pollution sources, also showed precipitation pH values around 4. The lowest precipitation pH ever recorded at Hubbard Brook was 2.85, which Likens describes as acidic enough to do serious direct damage to vegetation.

Although there are still contentions that cause-effect relationships have not been demonstrated. "It's generally accepted," says the University of Virginia's James Galloway, "that precipitation in the Eastern United States has become acidified by fossil-fuel combustion and that this has acidified many lakes in the northeastern United States.

"A few people," he notes, "attribute this to natural mechanisms rather than fossil fuels; the areas of dispute have to do with the amount and quality of the monitoring that's been done."

Not all lakes that receive acid precipitation become highly acidic. If a lake has a bed of rock and soil that contains alkaline substances, such as the calcium carbonate of limestone, acids may be neutralized as they mingle with lake water.

But in areas where the underlying rock is granite or lava, there is a shortage of such buffering chemicals. Lakes there are acid-vulnerable.

The Canadian Shield, for instance, is a huge formation of granitic rock that extends down across the eastern half of Canada into the Eastern United States. Lakes in this vast, hard-rock region, such as those in the Adirondacks, face a double threat: They are in the path of acid precipitation, and they lack the capacity to neutralize the acid that falls into them.

More than 2.5 million square kilometers of North American land surface overlie such acid-sensitive hard-rock formations. So does most of Scandinavia. Even if a lake has a modest buffering capacity, it can be overridden by large and continuing inputs of acid precipitation.

Likens sees solid evidence that fish cannot reproduce in lakes in which acidity has risen above a certain level. Lakes like those of the Adirondacks seldom grow acid enough to kill mature fish directly, but the acidity can interfere with the more delicate and acid-sensitive reproduction stages of fish.

Some indirect effects of acid rain can also have serious impacts on fish. Investigating a drop in the trout population of lakes in which acidity did not seem to be strong enough to account for high fish mortality, Cornell's Carl Schofield discovered a lethal side effect. Strong acid in the rain was releasing aluminum from the soil and carrying it into the lakes.

"We found that the aluminum in this situation is very toxic to fish." Schofield says. The acid runoff with aluminum added was more poisonous to the trout than the acid precipitation alone would have been.

Swedish and Canadian scientists have identified another serious side effect of acid precipitation: elevated levels of mercury in fish that live in lakes and rivers that are consistently acidic. A Canadian researcher, G.H. Tomlinson, presented a report on this subject to the Panel on Mercury of the U.S. National Research Council in 1977. Tomlinson and his colleagues found that fish in lakes and rivers draining into James and Hudson Bays in northwestern Quebec contained mercury concentrations well above the 0.5 part per million prescribed as the standard for safe human consumption in the United States and Canada.

The mercury apparently reaches the rivers and lakes in very low concentrations in rain and snow and, possibly, by leaching from soil. When the mercury enters well-buffered water having a pH higher than 8, however, it forms dimethyl mercury, a volatile compound that tends to evaporate promptly back into the atmosphere.

But if the pH is 6 or less, highly toxic monomethyl mercury is formed and accumulates in the tissues of fish. Pike in the isolated Broadback River system, for example, often contain more than 2.5 parts per million of mercury, more than five times the level considered safe for human consumption.

Sport fishermen who eat their catch from occasional fishing trips are not endangered by these mercury-contaminated fish. But Indians who eat fish almost every day can absorb dangerous amounts of mercury. In a Canadian Government survey, almost half of more than 700 Indians tested in Quebec, Ontario and the Northwest Territories showed abnormally high levels of mercury in hair and blood samples.

Likens says the question of the effects of acidity on aquatic biological populations other than fish is less certain. But he sees evidence that a variety of other aquatic organisms in the food web may be adversely altered by acid precipitation. In general, fewer or different species of algae and invertebrates are found in acidic lakes and streams. And the rate of organic decomposition is slower. Swedish researchers believe that decreased decomposition of organic matter on lake bottoms, along with increased growth of mosses and fungi, leads to a depletion of nutrients and reduced biological productivity in acidic lakes. In short, acidity appears to reduce the ecological diversity and vigor of lakes and streams.

The effects of acid precipitation on soils and terrestrial vegetation are more difficult to document. "Acid rain is a popular name for something that sounds—or that is—very threatening," says Ellis Cowling of the School of Forest Resources at North Carolina State University, "but it's only one part of a phenomenon that is usually called atmospheric deposition." Cowling points out that many kinds of airborne substances are deposited on vegetation and soils and in surface waters as dry particulate matter, aerosols (tiny liquid particles suspended in air) and gases, as well as in precipitation.

Some of the substances deposited by the atmosphere are injurious, but others, including airborne matter from natural sources, are beneficial. These include spores and pollen from plants, sea spray from oceans, soil particles picked up and transported by the wind, dust from volcanic eruptions and cosmic sources and gaseous compounds of sulfur and nitrogen released by decomposing organic matter.

Cowling maintains that it is important to understand the whole process of atmospheric deposition before attempting to alter any part of it. Atmospheric deposition is a source of plant nutrients as well as damaging substances, he emphasizes, and most plants are nourished through the atmosphere as well as through the soil. "It takes 15 elements to make a plant grow," Cowling says, "and all of them are available in the air. Man is augmenting the supply of both good and bad things in the atmosphere and is changing their rates of flux, but the net effect may not be bad in every situation."

When moderately acid rain falls on a forest, for example, the net effect could be positive because of additional nutrients deposited along with the acid or released more rapidly from the forest-floor humus by the action of the acid. Cowling feels that we need much more detailed and comprehensive knowledge of atmospheric deposition and its effects on forests, grasslands and agricultural systems before we can prescribe effective remedies for the adverse effects of acid precipitation.

Having delivered this *caveat*, Cowling is quite ready to point out that acid precipitation can have many direct and indirect adverse effects on plants. Some potential direct effects are:

- Damage to protective surface structures of foliage.
- Poisoning of plant cells by diffusion of acidic substances into leaves, flowers, twigs and branches.
- Disturbances of normal metabolic or growth processes such as photosynthesis.
- Interference with reproductive processes.

Potential indirect effects may include:

- Leaching of mineral elements and organic substances from foliage.
- Increased susceptibility to drought and other environmental stresses.
- Alteration of host-parasite interactions.

Cowling feels that a simplistic view of the acid precipitation problem may lead to some dangerously oversimplified attempts to deal with it. "One solution that has been suggested," he says, "is to inject ammonium into stack gases to produce ammonium sulfate instead of sulfuric acid. But when plants take up ammonium sulfate, they produce still more acid, which is more harmful than the acid precipitation alone would have been. Instead of solving the acid precipitation problem, you have replaced it with an acidifying precipitation problem."

Cowling was one of four scientists who recently produced a national plan for research on atmospheric deposition for the President's Council on Environmental Quality. They noted that "reliable research will give no 'quick-and-easy' solutions to the problems of atmospheric deposition, because lakes, forests and agricultural and range ecosystems are complicated communities of organisms. The amount of time required to answer the key questions will vary from months to years. Key questions on the sensitivity of species, lakes and soils to acidification can be answered relatively easily compared to the long-term questions of ecosystem stress and alteration."

If such research efforts, and others that are in progress or being planned, are fruitful, will it be possible to translate their results into effective action to deal with the acid precipitation problem? Or is the whole tangled web of ecology, politics, energy, chemistry, agriculture and other factors too intertwined and sticky to be unraveled? One example of an effort to deal with the problem can be found in the Netherlands, a nation that is much smaller than the United States and much less diverse geographically, politically and economically.

In 1966, the highest acid precipitation measurements in the world were made in the Netherlands. But from 1967 on, the acidity of the precipitation decreased, simultaneously with a general reduction in sulfur dioxide emissions from manufacturing and power plants.

One element in the reversal in the Netherlands was effective action by the Government. In 1967, according to Arend Vermeulen of the Netherlands Department of Environmental Control, it was easy to see that a constant increase in energy production, with oil continuing to be the main energy source, would double the emission of sulfur dioxide in five years. "In order to keep the Netherlands habitable," Vermeulen says, "drastic measures were required immediately."

The Dutch Clean Air Act was enacted in 1968 and, in response to its requirements, facilities were built to remove sulfur from industrial emissions, the use of high-sulfur oil was prohibited, and imports of low-sulfur oil were increased.

Total sulfur dioxide emissions dropped dramatically in the Netherlands after 1968, and the acidity of precipitation went down, along with air pollution. But these benefits resulted from luck as well as design and deliberate action. About the time that the clean air act became law, the Dutch discovered the largest coherent natural gas field in the world, and they promptly began to substitute gas for oil. Between 1967 and 1975, the fraction of Dutch energy needs supplied by natural gas rose from 18 to 85 percent, dramatically reducing the emission of sulfur into the atmosphere.

The point of the Dutch experience is not that the United States should hope and pray for natural gas discoveries, but rather that acidity in precipitation seems to be tied closely to patterns of energy production.

As James Galloway puts it, "If scientific research provides good evidence that the ecological impacts of acid precipitation are unacceptable, or that its economic or social costs are excessive, it should be possible for the policy-makers to use that knowledge as a basis for intelligent and effective action."

Love Canal And
The Poisoning of America

by Michael H. Brown

Niagara Falls is a city of unmatched natural beauty; it is also a tired industrial workhorse, beaten often and with a hard hand. A magnificent river—a strait, really—connecting Lake Erie to Lake Ontario flows hurriedly north, at a pace of a half-million tons a minute, widening into a smooth expanse near the city before breaking into whitecaps and taking its famous 186-foot plunge. Then it cascades through a gorge of overhung shale and limestone to rapids higher and swifter than anywhere else on the continent.

The falls attract long lines of newlyweds and other tourists. At the same time, the river provides cheap electricity for industry; a good stretch of its shore is now filled with the spiraled pipes of distilleries, and the odors of chlorine and sulfides hang in the air.

Many who live in the city of Niagara Falls work in chemical plants, the largest of which is owned by the Hooker Chemical Company, a subsidiary of Occidental Petroleum since the 1960s. Timothy Schroeder did not. He was a cement technician by trade, dealing with the factories only if they needed a pathway poured, or a small foundation set. Tim and his wife, Karen, lived in a ranch-style home with a brick and wood exterior at 460 99th Street. One of the Schroeders' most cherished purchases was a Fiberglas pool, built into the ground and enclosed by a red-wood fence.

Karen looked from a back window one morning in October 1974, noting with distress that the pool had suddenly risen two feet above the ground. She called Tim to tell him about it. Karen then had no way of knowing that this was the first sign of what would prove to be a punishing family and economic tragedy.

Mrs. Schroeder believed that the cause of the uplift was

the unusual groundwater flow of the area. Twenty-one years before, an abandoned hydroelectric canal directly behind their house had been backfilled with industrial rubble. The underground breaches created by this disturbance, aided by the marshland nature of the region's surficial layer, collected large volumes of rainfall and undermined the back yard. The Schroeders allowed the pool to remain in its precarious position until the following summer and then pulled it from the ground, intending to pour a new pool, cast in cement. This they were unable to do, for the gaping excavation immediately filled with what Karen called "chemical water," rancid liquids of yellow and orchid and blue. These same chemicals had mixed with the groundwater and flooded the entire yard, attacking the redwood posts with such a caustic bite that one day the fence simply collapsed. When the chemicals receded in the dry weather, they left the gardens and shrubs withered and scorched, as if by a brush fire.

How the chemicals got there was no mystery. In the late 1930s, or perhaps early 1940s, the Hooker Company, whose many processes included the manufacture of pesticides, plasticizers, and caustic soda, began using the abandoned canal as a dump for at least 20,000 tons of waste residues—"still-bottoms," in the language of the trade.

Karen Schroeder's parents had been the first to experience problems with the canal's seepage. In 1959, her mother, Aileen Voorhees, encountered a strange black sludge bleeding through the basement walls. For the next twenty years, she and her husband, Edwin, tried various methods of halting the irritating intruson, pasting the cinder-block wall with sealants and even constructing a gutter along the walls to intercept the inflow. Nothing could stop the chemical smell from permeating the entire household, and neighborhood calls to the city for help were fruitless. One day, when Edwin punched a hole in the wall to see what was happening, quantities of black liquid poured from the block. The cinder blocks were full of the stuff.

More ominous than the Voorhees basement was an event that occurred at 11:12 P.M. on November 21, 1968, when Karen Schroeder gave birth to her third child, a seven-pound girl named Sheri. No sense of elation filled the delivery room. The child was born with a heart that beat irregularly and had a hole in it, bone blockages of the nose, partial deafness, deformed ear exteriors, and a cleft palate. Within two years, the Schroeders realized Sheri was also mentally retarded. When her teeth came in, a double row of them appeared on her lower jaw. And she developed an enlarged liver.

The Schroeders considered these health problems, as well as illnesses among their other children, as acts of capricious genes—a vicious quirk of nature. Like Mrs. Schroeder's parents, they were concerned that the chemicals were devaluing their property. The crab apple tree and evergreens in the back were dead, and even the oak in front of the home was sick; one year, the leaves had fallen off on Father's Day.

The canal had been dug with much fanfare in the late nineteenth century by a flamboyant entrepreneur named William T. Love, who wanted to construct an industrial city with ready access to water power and major markets. The setting for Love's dream was to be a navigable power channel that would extend seven miles from the Upper Niagara before falling two hundred feet, circumventing the treacherous falls and at the same time providing cheap power. A city would be constructed near the point where the canal fed back into the river, and he promised it would accommodate half a million people.

So taken with his imagination were the state's leaders that they gave Love a free hand to condemn as much property as he liked, and to divert whatever amounts of water. Love's dream, however, proved grander than his resources, and he was eventually forced to abandon the project after a mile-long trench, ten to forty feet deep and generally twenty yards wide, had been scoured perpendicular to the Niagara River. Eventually, the trench was purchased by Hooker.

Few of those who, in 1977, lived in the numerous houses that had sprung up by the site were aware that the large and barren field behind them was a burial ground for toxic waste. Both the Niagara County Health Department and the city said it was a nuisance condition, but no serious danger to the people. Officials of the Hooker Company refused comment, claiming only that they had no records of the chemical burials and that the problem was not their responsibility. Indeed, Hooker had deeded the land to the Niagara Falls Board of Education in 1953, for a token $1. With it the company issued no detailed warnings of the chemicals, only a brief paragraph in the quitclaim document that disclaimed company liability for any injuries or deaths which might occur at the site.

Though Hooker was undoubtedly relieved to rid itself of the contaminated land, the company was so vague about the hazards involved that one might have thought the wastes would cause harm only if touched, because they irritated the skin; otherwise, they were not of great concern. In reality, as the company must have known, the dangers of these wastes far exceeded those of acids or alkalines or inert salts. We now know that the drums Hooker had dumped in the canal contained a veritable witch's brew—compounds of truly remarkable toxicity. There were solvents that attacked the heart and liver, and residues from pesticides so dangerous that their commercial sale was shortly thereafter restricted outright by the government; some of them were already suspected of causing cancer.

Yet Hooker gave no hint of that. When the board of education, which wanted the parcel for a new school, approached Hooker, B. Klaussen, at the time Hooker's executive vice president, said in a letter to the board. "Our officers have carefully considered your request. We are very conscious of the need for new elementary schools and realize that the sites must be carefully selected. We will be willing to donate the entire strip of property which we own between Colvin Boulevard and Frontier Avenue to be used for the erection of a school at a location to be determined. . . ."

The board built the school and playground at the canal's midsection. Construction progressed despite the contractor's hitting a drainage trench that gave off a strong chemical odor and the discovery of a waste pit nearby. Instead of halting the work, the authorities simply moved the school eighty feet away. Young families began to settle in increasing numbers alongside the dump, many of them having been told that the field was to be a park and recreation area for their children.

Children found the "playground" interesting, but at times painful. They sneezed, and their eyes teared. In the days when the dumping was still in progress, they swam at the opposite end of the canal, occasionally arriving home with hard pimples all over their bodies. Hooker knew children were playing on its spoils. In 1958, three children were burned by exposed residues on the canal's surface, much of which, according to residents, had been covered with nothing more than fly ash and loose dirt. Because it wished to avoid legal repercussions, the company chose not to issue a public warning of the dangers it knew were there, nor to have its chemists explain to the people that their homes would have been better placed elsewhere.

The Love Canal was simply unfit as a container for hazardous substances, poor even by the standards of the day, and now, in 1977, local authorites were belatedly finding that out. Several years of heavy snowfall and rain had filled the sparingly covered channel like a bathtub. The contents were overflowing at a frightening rate.

The city of Niagara Falls, I was assured, was planning a remedial drainage program to halt in some measure the chemical migration off the site. But no sense of urgency had been attached to the plan, and it was stalled in red tape. No one could agree on who should pay the bill—the city, Hooker, or the board of education—and engineers seemed confused over what exactly needed to be done.

Niagara Falls City Manager Donald O'Hara persisted in his view that, however displeasing to the eyes and nose, the Love Canal was not a crisis matter, mainly a question of aesthetics. O'Hara reminded me that Dr. Francis Clifford, county health commissioner, supported that opinion.

With the city, the board, and Hooker unwilling to commit themselves to a remedy, conditions degenerated in the area between 97th and 99th streets, until, by early 1978, the land was a quagmire of sludge that oozed from the canal's every pore. Melting snow drained the surface soot onto the private yards, while on the dump itself the ground had softened to the point of collapse, exposing the crushed tops of barrels. Beneath the surface, masses of sludge were finding their way out a quickening rate, constantly forming springs of contaminated liquid. The Schroeder back yard, once featured in a local newspaper for its beauty, had reached the point where it was unfit even to walk upon. Of course, the Schroeders could not leave. No one would think of buying the property. They still owed on their mortgage and, with Tim's salary, could not afford to maintain the house while they moved into a safer setting. They and their four children were stuck.

Apprehension about large costs was not the only reason the city was reluctant to help the Schroeders and the one hundred or so other families whose properties abutted the covered trench. The city may also have feared distressing Hooker. To an economically depressed area, the company provided desperately needed employment—as many as 3000 blue-collar jobs and a substantial number of tax dollars. Hooker was speaking of building a $17 million headquarters in downtown Niagara Falls. So anxious were city officials to receive the new building that they and the state granted the company highly lucrative tax and loan incentives, and made available to the firm a prime parcel of property near the most popular tourist park on the American side.

City Manager O'Hara and other authorities were aware of the nature of Hooker's chemicals. In fact, in the privacy of his office, O'Hara, after receiving a report on the chemical tests at the canal, had informed the people at Hooker that it was an extremely serious problem. Even earlier, in 1976, the New York State Department of Environmental Conservation had been made aware that dangerous compounds were present in the basement sump pump of at least one 97th Street home, and soon after, its own testing had revealed that highly injurious halogenated hydrocarbons were flowing from the canal into adjoining sewers. Among them were the notorious PCBs; quantities as low as one part PCBs to a million parts normal water were enough to create serious environmental concerns; in the sewers of Niagara Falls, the quantities of halogenated compounds were thousands of times higher. The other materials tracked, in sump pumps or sewers, were just as toxic as PCBs, or more so. Prime among the more hazardous ones was residue from hexachlorocyclopentadiene, or C-56, which was deployed as an intermediate in the manufacture of several pesticides. In certain dosages, the chemical could damage every organ in the body.

While the mere presence of C-56 should have been cause for alarm, government remained inactive. Not until early 1978—a full eighteen months after C-56 was first detected—was testing conducted in basements along 97th and 99th streets to see if the chemicals had vaporized off the sump pumps and walls and were present in the household air.

While the basement tests were in progress, the rains of spring arrived at the canal, further worsening the situation. Heavier fumes rose above the barrels. More than before, the residents were suffering from headaches, respiratory discomforts, and skin ailments. Many of them felt constantly fatigued and irritable, and the children had reddened eyes. In the Schroeder home, Tim developed a rash along the backs of his legs. Karen could not rid herself of throbbing pains in her head. Their daughter, Laurie, seemed to be losing some of her hair.

The EPA test revealed that benzene, a known cause of cancer in humans, had been readily detected in the household air up and down the streets. A widely used solvent, benzene was known in chronic-exposure cases to cause headaches, fatigue, loss of weight, and dizziness followed by pallor, nose-bleeds, and damage to the bone marrow.

No public announcement was made of the benzene hazard. Instead, officials appeared to shield the finding until they could agree among themselves on how to present it.

Dr. Clifford, the county health commissioner, seemed unconcerned by the detection of benzene in the air. His health department refused to conduct a formal study of the people's health, despite the air-monitoring results. For this reason, and because of the resistance growing among the local authorities, I went to the southern end of 99th Street to take an informal health survey of my own. I arranged a meeting with six neighbors, all of them instructed beforehand to list the illnesses they were aware of on their block, with names and ages specified for presentation at the session.

The residents' list was startling. Though unafflicted before they moved there, many people were now plagued with ear infections, nervous disorders, rashes, and headaches. One young man, James Gizzarelli, said he had missed four months of work owing to breathing troubles. His wife was suffering epileptic-like seizures which her doctor was unable to explain. Meanwhile, freshly applied paint was inexplicably peeling from the exterior of their house. Pets too were suffering, most seriously if they had been penned in the back yards nearest to the canal, constantly breathing air that smelled like mothballs and weedkiller. They lost their fur, exhibited skin lesions, and, while still quite young, developed internal tumors. A great many cases of cancer were reported among the women, along with much deafness. On both 97th and 99th streets, traffic signs warned passing motorists to watch for deaf children playing near the road.

Evidence continued to mount that a large group of people, perhaps all of the one hundred families immediately by the canal, perhaps many more, were in imminent danger. While watching television, while gardening or doing a wash, in their sleeping hours, they were inhaling a mixture of damaging chemicals. Their hours of exposure were far longer than those of a chemical factory worker, and they wore no respirators or goggles. Nor could they simply open a door and escape. Helplessness and despair were the main responses to the blackened craters and scattered cinders behind their back yards.

But public officials often characterized the residents as hypochondriacs. Every agent of government had been called on the phone or sent pleas for help, but none offered aid.

Commissioner Clifford expressed irritation at my printed reports of illness, and disagreement began to surface in the newsroom on how the stories should be printed. "There's a high rate of cancer among my friends," Dr. Clifford argued. "It doesn't mean anything."

Yet as interest in the small community increased, further revelations shook the neighborhood. In addition to the benzene, eighty or more other compounds were found in the makeshift dump, ten of them potential carcinogens. The physiological effects they could cause were profound and diverse. At least fourteen of them could impact on the brain and central nervous system. Two of them, carbon tetrachloride and chlorobenzene, could readily cause narcotic or anesthetic consequences. Many others were known to cause headaches, seizures, loss of hair, anemia, or skin rashes. Together, the compounds were capable of inflicting innumerable illnesses, and no one knew what new concoctions were being formulated by their mixture underground.

Edwin and Aileen Voorhees had the most to be concerned about. When a state biophysicist analyzed the air content of their basement, he determined that the safe exposure time there was less than 2.4 minutes—the toxicity in the basement was thousands of times the acceptable limit for twenty-four-hour breathing. This did not mean they would necessarily become permanently ill, but their chances of contracting cancer, for example, had been measurably increased. In July, I visited Mrs. Voorhees for further discussion of her problems, and as we sat in the kitchen, drinking coffee, the industrial odors were apparent. Aileen, usually chipper and feisty, was visibly anxious. She stared down at the table, talking only in a lowered voice. Everything now looked different to her. The home she and Edwin had built had become their jail cell. Their yard was but a pathway through which toxicants entered the cellar walls. The field out back, that proposed "park," seemed destined to be the ruin of their lives.

On July 14 I received a call from the state health department with some shocking news. A preliminary review showed that women living at the southern end had suffered a high rate of miscarriages and had given birth to an abnormally high number of children with birth defects. In one age group, 35.3 percent had records of spontaneous abortions. That was far in excess of the norm. The odds against it happening by chance were 250 to one. These tallies, it was stressed, were "conservative" figures. Four children in one small section of the neighborhood had documentable birth defects, club feet, retardation, and deafness. Those who lived there the longest suffered the highest rates.

The data on miscarriages and birth defects, coupled with the other accounts of illness, finally pushed the state's bureaucracy into motion. A meeting was scheduled for August 2, at which time the state health commissioner, Dr. Robert Whalen, would formally address the issue. The day before the meeting, Dr. Nicholas Vianna, a state epidemiologist, told me that residents were also incurring some degree of liver damage. Blood analyses had shown hepatitis-like symptoms in enzyme levels. Dozens if not hundreds of people, apparently, had been adversely affected.

In Albany, on August 2, Dr. Whalen read a lengthy statement in which he urged that pregnant women and children under two years of age leave the southern end of the dump site immediately. He declared the Love Canal an official emergency, citing it as a "great and imminent peril to the health of the general public."

When Commissioner Whalen's words hit 97th and 99th streets, by way of one of the largest banner headlines in the Niagara *Gazette*'s 125-year history, dozens of people massed on the streets, shouting into bullhorns and microphones to voice frustrations that had been accumulating for months. Many of them vowed a tax strike because their homes were rendered unmarketable and unsafe. They attacked their government for ignoring their welfare. A man of high authority, a physician with a title, had confirmed that their lives were in danger. Most wanted to leave the neighborhood immediately.

Terror and anger roiled together, exacerbated by Dr. Whalen's failure to provide a government-funded evacuation plan. His words were only a recommendation: individual families had to choose whether to risk their health and remain, or abandon their houses and, in so doing, write off a lifetime of work and savings.

On August 3, Dr. Whalen decided he should speak to the people. He arrived with Dr. David Axelrod, a deputy who had directed the state's investigation, and Thomas Frey, a key aide to Governor Hugh Carey.

At a public meeting, held in the 99th Street School auditorium, Frey was given the grueling task of controlling the crowd of 500 angry and frightened people. In an attempt to calm them, he announced that a meeting between the state and the White House had been scheduled for the following week. The state would propose that the Love Canal be classified a national disaster, thereby freeing federal funds. For now, however, he could promise no more. Neither could Dr. Whalen and his staff of experts. All they could say was what was already known: twenty-five organic compounds, some of them capable of causing cancer, were in their homes, and because young children were especially prone to toxic effects, they should be moved to another area.

Dr. Whalen's order had applied only to those living at the canal's southern end, on its immediate periphery. But families living across the street from the dump site, or at the northern portion, where the chemicals were not so visible at the surface, reported afflictions remarkably similar to those suffered by families whose yards abutted the southern end. Serious respiratory problems, nervous disorders, and rectal bleeding were reported by many who were not covered by the order.

Throughout the following day, residents posted signs of protest on their front fences or porch posts. "Love Canal Kills," they said, or "Give Me Liberty, I've Got Death." Emotionally exhausted and uncertain about their future, men stayed home from work, congregating on the streets or comforting their wives. By this time the board of education had announced it was closing the 99th Street School for the following year, because of its proximity to the exposed toxicants. Still, no public relief was provided for the residents.

Another meeting was held that evening, at a firehall on 102nd Street. It was unruly, but the people, who had called the session in an effort to organize themselves, managed to form an alliance, the Love Canal Homeowners Association, and to elect as president Lois Gibbs, a pretty, twenty-seven-year-old woman with jet-black hair who proved remarkably adept at dealing with experienced politicians and at keeping the matter in the news. After Mrs. Gibbs' election, Congressman John LaFalce entered the hall and announced, to wild applause, that the Federal Disaster Assistance Administration would be represented the next morning, and that the state's two senators, Daniel Patrick Moynihan and Jacob Javits, were working with him in an attempt to get funds from Congress.

With the Love Canal story now attracting attention from the national media, the Governor's office announced that Hugh Carey would be at the 99th Street School on August 7 to address the people. Decisions were being made in Albany and Washington. Hours before the Governor's arrival, a sudden burst of "urgent" reports from Washington came across the newswires. President Jimmy Carter had officially declared the Hooker dump site a national emergency.

Hugh Carey was applauded on his arrival. The Governor announced that the state, through its Urban Development Corporation, planned to purchase, at fair market value, those homes rendered uninhabitable by the marauding chemicals. He spared no promises. "You will not have to make mortgage payments on homes you don't want or cannot occupy. Don't worry about the banks. The state will take care of them." By the standards of Niagara Falls, where the real estate market was depressed, the houses were in the middle-class range, worth from $20,000 to $40,000 apiece. The state would assess each house and purchase it, and also pay the costs of moving, temporary housing during the transition period, and special items not covered by the usual real estate assessment, such as installation of telephones.

First in a trickle and then, by September, in droves, the families gathered their belongings and carted them away. Moving vans crowded 97th and 99th streets. Linesmen went from house to house disconnecting the telephones and electrical wires, while carpenters pounded plywood over the windows to keep vandals away. By the following spring, 237 families were gone; 170 of them had moved into new houses. In time the state erected around a six-block residential area a green chain-link fence, eight feet in height, clearly demarcating the contamination zone.

In October 1978, the long-awaited remedial drainage program began at the south end. Trees were uprooted, fences and garages torn down, and swimming pools removed from the area. So great were residents' apprehensions that dangerous fumes would be released over the surrounding area that the state, at a cost of $500,000, placed seventy-five buses at emergency evacuation pickup spots during the months of work, in the event that outlying homes had to be vacated quickly because of an explosion. The plan was to construct drain tiles around the channel's periphery, where the back yards had been located, in order to divert leakage to seventeen-foot-deep wet wells from which contaminated groundwater could be drawn and treated by filtration through activated carbon. (Removing the chemicals themselves would have been financially prohibitive, perhaps costing as much as $100 million—and even then the materials would have to be buried elsewhere.) After the trenching was complete, and the sewers installed, the canal was to be covered by a sloping mound of clay and planted with grass. One day, city officials hoped, the wasteland would become a park.

In spite of the corrective measures and the enormous effort by the state health department, which took thousands of blood samples from past and current residents and made uncounted analyses of soil, water, and air, the full range of the effects remained unknown. In neighborhoods immediately outside the official "zone of contamination," more than 500 families were left near the desolate setting, their health still in jeopardy. The state announced it would buy no more homes.

The first public indication that chemical contamination had probably reached streets to the east and west of 97th and 99th streets, and to the north and south as well, came on August 11, 1978, when sump-pump samples I had taken from 100th and 101st streets, analyzed in a laboratory, showed the trace presence of a number of chemicals found in the canal itself, including lindane, a restricted pesticide that had been suspected of causing cancer in laboratory animals. While probing 100th Street, I had knocked on the door of Patricia Pino, thirty-four, a blond divorcee with a young son and daughter. I had noticed that some of the leaves on a large tree in front of her house exhibited a black oiliness much like that on the trees and shrubs of 99th Street; she was located near what had been a drainage swale.

After I had extracted a jar of sediment from her sump pump for the analyais, we conversed about her family situation and what the trauma now unfolding meant to them. Ms. Pino was extremely depressed and embittered. Both of her children had what appeared to be slight liver abnormalities, and her son had been plagued with "non-specific" allergies, teary eyes, sinus trouble, which improved markedly when he was sent away from home. Patricia told of times, during the heat of summer, when fumes were readily noticeable in her basement and sometimes even upstairs. She herself had been treated for a possibly cancerous condition on her cervix. But, like others, her family was now trapped.

On September 24, 1978, I obtained a state memorandum that said chemical infiltration of the outer regions was significant indeed. The letter, sent from the state laboratories to the U.S. Environmental Protection Agency, said, "Preliminary analysis of soil samples demonstrates extensive migration of potentially toxic materials outside the immediate canal area." There it was, in the state's own words. Not long afterward, the state medical investigator,

Dr. Nicholas Vianna, reported indications that residents from 93rd to 103rd streets might also have incurred liver damage.

On October 4, a young boy, John Allen Kenny, who lived quite a distance north of the evacuation zone, died. The fatality was due to the failure of another organ that can be readily affected by toxicants, the kidney. Naturally, suspicions were raised that his death was in some way related to a creek that still flowed behind his house and carried, near an outfall, the odor of chlorinated compounds. Because the creek served as a catch basin for a portion of the Love Canal, the state studied an autopsy of the boy. No conclusions were reached. John Allen's parents, Norman, a chemist, and Luella, a medical research assistant, were unsatisfied with the state's investigation, which they felt was "superficial." Luella said, "He played in the creek all the time. There had been restrictions on the older boys, but he was the youngest and played with them when they were old enough to go to the creek. We let him do what the other boys did. He died of nephrosis. Proteins were passing through his urine. Well, in reading the literature, we discovered that chemicals can trigger this. There was no evidence of infection, which there should have been, and there was damage to his thymus and brain. He also had nosebleeds and headaches, and dry heaves. So our feeling is that chemicals probably triggered it."

The likelihood that water-carried chemicals had escaped from the canal's deteriorating bounds and were causing problems quite a distance from the site was not lost upon the Love Canal Homeowners Association and its president, Lois Gibbs, who was attempting to have additional families relocated. Because she lived on 101st Street, she was one of those left behind, with no means of moving despite persistent medical difficulties in her six-year-old son, Michael, who had been operated on twice for urethral strictures. [Mrs. Gibbs' husband, a worker at a chemical plant, brought home only $150 a week, she told me, and when they subtracted from that the $90 a week for food and other necessities, clothing costs for their two children, $125 a month for mortgage payments and taxes, utility and phone expenses, and medical bills, they had hardly enough cash to buy gas and cigarettes, let alone vacate their house.]

Assisted by two other stranded residents, Marie Pozniak and Grace McCoulf, and with the professional analysis of a Buffalo scientist named Beverly Paigen, Lois Gibbs mapped out the swale and creekbed areas, many of them long ago filled, and set about interviewing the numerous people who lived on or near formerly wet ground. The survey indicated that these people were suffering from an abnormal number of kidney and bladder aggravations and problems of the reproductive system. In a report to the state, Dr. Paigen claimed to have found, in 245 homes outside the evacuation zone, thirty-four miscarriages, eighteen birth defects, nineteen nervous breakdowns, ten cases of epilepsy, and high rates of hyperactivity and suicide.

In their roundabout way, the state health experts, after an elaborate investigation, confirmed some of the homeowners' worst fears. On February 8, 1979, Dr. David Axelrod, who by then had been appointed health commissioner, and whose excellence as a scientist was widely acknowledged, issued a new order that officially extended the health emergency of the previous August, citing high incidences of birth deformities and miscarriages in the areas where creeks and swales had once flowed, or where swamps had been. With that, the state offered to evacuate temporarily those families with pregnant women or children under the age of two from the outer areas of contamination, up to 103rd Street. But no additional homes would be purchased; nor was another large-scale evacuation, temporary or otherwise, under consideration. Those who left under the new plan would have to return when their children passed the age limit.

Twenty-three families accepted the state's offer. Another seven families, ineligible under the plan but of adequate financial means to do so, simply left their homes and took the huge loss of investment. Soon boarded windows speckled the outlying neighborhoods.

The previous November and December, not long after the evacuation of 97th and 99th streets, I became interested in the possibility that Hooker might have buried in the Love Canal waste residues from the manufacture of what is known as 2,4,5-trichlorophenol. My curiosity was keen because I knew that this substance, which Hooker produced for the manufacture of the antibacterial agent hexachlorophene, and which was also used to make defoliants such as Agent Orange, the herbicide employed in Vietnam, carries with it an unwanted by-product technically called 2,3,7,8-tetrachlorodibenzo-para-dioxin, or tetra dioxin. The potency of dioxin of this isomer is nearly beyond imagination. Although its toxicological effects are not fully known, the few experts on the subject estimate that if three ounces were evenly distributed and subsequently ingested among a million people, or perhaps more than that, all of them would die. It compares in toxicity to the botulinum toxin. On skin contact, dioxin causes a disfiguration called "chloracne," which begins as pimples, lesions, and cysts, but can lead to calamitous internal damage. Some scientists suspect that dioxin causes cancer, perhaps even malignancies that occur, in galloping fashion, within a short time of contact. At least two (some estimates went as high as eleven) pounds of dioxin were dispersed over Seveso, Italy, in 1976, after an explosion at a trichlorophenol plant: dead animals littered the streets, and more than 300 acres of land were immediately evacuated. In Vietnam, the spraying of Agent Orange, because of the dioxin contaminant, was banned in 1970, when the first effects on human beings began to surface, including dioxin's powerful teratogenic, or fetus-deforming, effects.

I posed two questions concerning trichlorophenol: Were wastes from the process buried in the canal? If so, what were the quantities?

On November 8, before Hooker answered my queries, I learned that, indeed, trichlorophenol had been found in liquids pumped from the remedial drain ditches. No dioxin had been found yet, and some officials, ever wary of more emotionalism among the people, argued that, because the compound was not soluable in water, there was little chance it had migrated off-site. Officials at Newco Chemical Waste Systems, a local waste disposal firm, at the same time claimed that if dioxin had been there, it had probably been photolytically destroyed. Its half-life, they contended, was just a few short years.

I knew from Whiteside, however, that in every known case, waste from 2.4,5-trichlorophenol carried dioxin with it. I also knew that dioxin *could* become soluble in groundwater and migrate into the neighborhood upon mixing with solvents such as benzene. Moreover, because it had been buried, sunlight would not break it down.

On Friday, November 10, I called Hooker again to urge that they answer my questions. Their spokesman, Bruce Davis, came to the phone and, in a controlled tone, gave me the answer: His firm had indeed buried trichlorophenol in the canal—200 tons of it.

Immediately I called Whiteside. His voice took on an urgent tone. According to his calculations, if 200 tons of trichlorophenol were there, in all likelihood they were accompanied by 130 pounds of tetra dioxin, an amount equaling the estimated total content of dioxin in the thousands of tons of Agent Orange rained upon Vietnamese jungles. The seriousness of the crisis had deepened, for now the Love Canal was not only a dump for highly dangerous solvents and pesticides; it was also the broken container for one of the most toxic substances ever synthesized by man.

I reckoned that the main danger was to those working on the remedial project, digging in the trenches. The literature on dioxin indicated that, even in quantities at times too small to detect, the substance possessed vicious characteristics. In one case, workers in a trichlorophenol plant had developed chloracne, although the substance could not be traced on the equipment with which they worked. The mere tracking of minuscule amounts of dioxin on a pedestrian's shoes in Seveso led to major concerns, and, according to Whiteside, a plant in Amsterdam, upon being found contaminated with dioxin, had been "dismantled, brick by brick, and the material embedded in concrete, loaded at a specially constructed dock, on ships, and dumped at sea, in deep water near the Azores." Workers in trichlorophenol plants had died of cancer or severe liver damage, or had suffered emotional and sexual disturbances.

Less than a month after the first suspicions arose, on the evening of December 9, I received a call from Dr. Axelrod. "We found it. The dioxin. In a drainage trench behind 97th Street. It was in the part-per-trillion range."

The state remained firm in its plans to continue the construction, and, despite the ominous new findings, no further evacuations were announced. During the next several weeks, small incidents of vandalism occurred along 97th and 99th streets. Tacks were spread on the road, causing numerous flat tires on the trucks. Signs of protest were hung in the school. Meetings of the Love Canal Homeowners Association became more vociferous. Christmas was near, and in the association's office at the 99th Street School, a holiday tree was decorated with bulbs arranged to spell "DIOXIN."

The Love Canal people chanted and cursed at meetings with the state officials, cried on the telephone, burned an effigy of the health commissioner, traveled to Albany with a makeshift child's coffin, threatened to hold officials hostage, sent letters and telegrams to the White House, held days of mourning and nights of prayer. On Mother's Day this year, they marched down the industrial corridor and waved signs denouncing Hooker, which had issued not so much as a statement of remorse. But no happy ending was in store for them. The federal government was clearly not planning to come to their rescue, and the state felt it had already done more than its share. City Hall was silent and remains silent today. Some residents still hoped that, miraculously, an agency of government would move them. All of them watched with anxiety as each newborn came to the neighborhood, and they looked at their bodies for signs of cancer.

One hundred and thirty families from the Love Canal area began leaving their homes last August and September, seeking temporary refuge in local hotel rooms under a relocation plan funded by the state which had been implemented after fumes became so strong, during remedial trenching operations, that the United Way abandoned a care center it had opened in the neighborhood.

As soon as remedial construction is complete, the people will probably be forced to return home, as the state will no longer pay for their lodging. Some have threatened to barricade themselves in the hotels. Some have mentioned violence. Anne Hillis of 102nd Street, who told reporters her first child had been born so badly decomposed that doctors could not determine its sex, was so bitter that she threw table knives and a soda can at the state's on-site coordinator.

In October, Governor Carey announced that the state probably would buy an additional 200 to 240 homes, at an expense of some $5 million. In the meantime, lawyers have prepared lawsuits totaling about $2.65 billion and have sought court action for permanent relocation. Even if the latter action is successful, and they are allowed to move, the residents' plight will not necessarily have ended. The psychological scars are bound to remain among them and their children, along with the knowledge that, because they have already been exposed, they may never fully escape the Love Canal's insidious grasp.

THE CORPORATION AND COMMUNITY

Some people shy away from the problems of corporate power and accountability because they seem so abstract, so distant from our experiences as we go on about our lives. But the presence and the attitudes of big corporations in an area often has the most decisive effect on the quality and direction of the community's life.

In this chapter, we examine some of the innumerable ways in which corporation have an effect on us at the most local levels—on jobs, on education, on politics, on development, on the environment, on health. After a broad overview of the spheres of corporate influence by Mark Green, we move, with Sheila Harty, to explore an often over-looked corporate presence: in the classrooms of our secondary schools.

Then, two articles describe the manner in which corporations control the financial health of our states and municipalities. James Rosapepe analyzes the alarming extent to which corporations avoid paying state taxes, and Jack Newfield recounts the successful campaign by a group of angered New Yorkers to force local banks to stop the destructive practice of "redlining."

Big Business as Neighbor

by Mark Green

The average American often has great difficulty comprehending the economics of his immediate environment. He knows the air is foul, his job and pension insecure, his taxes up, his political influence marginal. But those who could explain the paradox of a malfunctioning economy with a two trillion dollar-plus GNP have been busy elsewhere. Economists pay passionate attention to impersonal economics (monetary and fiscal policy); at the same time, they traditionally ignore the multiple and very personal interreactions between the corporation and the community. There is a dearth of economic data and studies on the local effects of corporate enterprise. It has consequently devolved to occasional newspaper stories to describe the blemished reality: what happens when a corporation monopolizes not a product but the work force? What is the effect on a community when it is obliged to "consume" a company's pollution? What recourse does a citizen have when political intimidation and racial discrimination are inspired and promoted by a dominant corporation?

These are telling questions to which the decade of the eighties must respond. For the concentration of corporate activity—accelerated by the merger waves of the late 1960s and late 1970s—intimately affects in two ways communities supporting such economic enterprises. First, local families and owners can become appendages of national and multinational conglomerates. A system of financial, economic, and political cues by absentee owners replaces community self-rule. Justice William Douglas described the pattern:

> [T]here is the effect on the community when independents are swallowed up by the trusts and [when] entrepreneurs become employees of absentee owners.

Then there is a serious loss of citizenship. Local leadership is diluted. He who was a leader in the village becomes dependent on outsiders for his action and policy. Clerks responsible to a superior in a distant place take the place of resident proprietors beholden to no one. These are the prices which the nation pays for the almost ceaseless growth in bigness on the part of industry.

Second, rather than absentee-owned firms disregarding a community's welfare, a large local corporation may utterly dominate the town simply by flexing its economic and political muscles. As with absentee ownership, democratic self-determination then becomes more homily than reality. Examples range from state domination, like Anaconda and Montana Power in Montana and DuPont in Delaware, to the company towns which erupted with the sudden expansion of infant industries at the turn of the century. Often in mining, lumber, and textile regions—usually unhealthy, hazardous, grim, and grimy—company towns made their citizens dependent on the company for their work, their homes, and their daily purchases. Employers both underpaid their laborers, and then exploited them as consumers. It was a closed circle which inspired the popular lament, "St. Peter don't you call me 'cause I can't go, I owe my soul to the company store."

The impact of a corporation on a community can be reflected by such factors as *civic welfare, political sway, industrial pollution, corporate philanthropy, local investment* and *racial discrimination*. And whether the source of the impact stems from absentee-run corporations or local dominants, the community damage is often quite similar.

As conglomerates have burgeoned in the past few years, many local enterprises became branch offices of financial centers in New York City and Chicago. The acquiring corporation has a national if not an international market and perspective. Birmingham, Alabama, or Providence, Rhode Island, is where it manufactures the goods, not where it sells them; hence, the economic committment extends well beyond the community. The branch managers who run the plants understand this point well. "The man who years ago might have been a 'big man in the community' because he headed a large local company," Senator Philip Hart observed, "now finds himself No. 1 in Company Z, which is a subsidiary of Company Y, which is in turn a subsidiary of Company X." For them the town in which they reside may be only a rung on a corporate success ladder. Such managers are transients, staying a few years before being shifted to another corner of the conglomerate's jigsaw puzzle. "[T]heir community roots were the most shallow," said sociologist Robert Schulze, "—if indeed it could be said that they had any community roots at all. The data led us to suspect that perhaps Cibola (Cibola, the town's name is this study, as well as those names in the studies which follow, are fictious.) . . . was of no great importance to their lives." They are *in* the community, not *of* the community. In fact, the branch manager often views local affairs as something of a risk, more likely to mire his firm in controversial issues than to further his corporate career. One study asked community leaders in three cities whether they thought branch managers were more or less interested in the community than were local businesses; 95 percent, 79 percent, and 57 percent respectively, said "less." One branch manager noted:

> I would try to get into things more if I honestly felt it would help the company, but I honestly don't see how it would. . . . Nobody [here] decides whether or not to use our product. . . . So I've never really tried to get into things here. What we need most—any company does—is business, and this town can't do anything about that,

A manager who *was* interested in some local activities in Worcester, Massachusetts, called his home office to get further cooperation—only to be told by a high-ranking executive, "We couldn't care less what happens in Worcester." Thus, although they occupy positions usually associated with community leadership, these citizens tend to abstain from local activities. This indifference can leave a corrosive effect on a community's civic welfare. For power unused is not an open road but an obstacle to citizen action. One empirical study observed that "in the relative power vacuum which exists in Bigtown, community projects are usually doomed if they lack the approval of the industrial, absentee-owned corporations."

Yet even when absentee-run firms *do* become involved in civic affairs, it is often in rearguard actions to protect their own economic interests. They may threaten to leave the town or city, exercising an effective veto over proposals they dislike. Or they support local puppets who utilize power in their behalf—a kind of local imperialism which both paralyzes the civic will and engenders a hostility not unlike that which Chile must feel toward ITT.

As a result of corporate withdrawal or surreptitious control, the independent political infrastructure of a community can collapse and with it the community's well-being. The seminal study documenting this pattern was conducted for a Congressional committee in 1946 by Professor C. Wright Mills. Noting that by 1944 2 percent of all manufacturing concerns had employed 60 percent of our industrial workers, Mills asked, "How does this concentration of economic power affect the general welfare of our cities and their inhabitants?" To find the answer he studied three pairs of cities. In each pair was a "big-business city," where a few big absentee-owned firms provided most of the industrial employment, and a "small-business city," where many smaller, locally owned firms comprised the community's economic life. His specific conclusions:

- Big-business cities witnessed sudden and explosive jumps in population, leading to real estate booms, speculation, and unplanned suburban sprawl radiating around center city slums; homes were built quickly and poorly. As a result, the operating cost of municipal services was quite high. Growth in the small-business cities was more evolutionary and planned. Homes were better built, the city was better laid out, and municipal costs were lower.
- A quarter of those employed in the small-business city were proprietors or officials of corporations; only 3 percent were self-employed in the big-business city. Plant shutdowns in bad times were obviously more catastrophic in a big-business city, since the local economy was so much more dependent on a few major firms.
- Income was more equitably distributed in small-business cities, as an average of more than twice as many people earned over ten thousand dollars. Thus, while the "independent middle class thrives" in the small-business cities, it does not in the big. There "the independent

middle class is . . . being displaced by a middle class consisting largely of the salaried employees of the giant corporations."

Mills attempted to gauge the relative overall welfare in each pair of cities, employing a number of indicators developed by sociologist E.L. Thorndike. They included, among others, measures of general death rates, infant mortality, the number of libraries, museums, recreational facilities, and parks, per capita expenditure for schools and teachers, extent of gas, electrical, and telephone installations, and frequency of home ownership. Of the three pairs of cities, the civic welfare of small-business city substantially exceeded that of the big-business city. Mills concluded that "big business tends to depress while small business tends to raise the level of civic welfare."

These findings were reinforced by another special Congressional study that same year. A group of sociologists compared two California communities which differed in that Arvin was surrounded by large-scale corporate farming, Dinuba by small-scale independent farming. While Dinuba was incorporated in 1906, Arvin had not been by the time of the study. Interviews revealed that the large farmers were satisfied and uninterested in incorporation; one minister said that in fact the large landowners were afraid the laborers "would run the town." Also, the large corporations and absentee landowners could see no benefit to themselves in higher taxes for civic improvements. Arvin residents, therefore, had to approach county officials for any local request, while Dinuba exercised self-rule. By many local standards—high schools, garbage disposal, retail sales, wages and the distribution of income, local clubs, municipal services, and the standard of living—Dinuba was clearly superior. For example, Arvin lacked a high school, its only playground was on loan from a corporation, and it had a teacher turnover rate five times that of Dinuba. The report stated that "Large-scale farming does, in fact, bear the major responsibility for the social differences." This differential, in turn, can be traced to the lack of self-rule in Arvin, as distant entrepreneurs and county officials made the decisions which affected local citizens. The community lacked both the means and the resolve to redeem the situation, and the large corporations who *could* have done something simply didn't care.

In the twenty-five years since these studies were conducted, aggregate economic concentration has significantly increased. Mergers often aggravate the community cankers discussed previously—which should hardly be surprising given the buccaneering attitude of merger managers. While synergistic payoffs are forever cited to justify conglomerate takeovers, often the motive is pure empire-building. Edward Krock, the financial wizard of two holding companies (controlling fifteen firms) listed on the American Stock Exchange, can pick up his telephone, as he reports with some pride, and order a company president fired in Illinois or a factory closed down in Ohio. Why do big companies buy small ones, he was asked. "Because of men's ambitions. They are hungry for money and influence." While such a consuming drive may get the conglomerateur listed in *Who's Who*, it is unlikely to be good news for the community.

Acquisitions by absentee owners can also reduce the use of local professional services. It has been found that most of the acquired firms shifted away from local accountants and lawyers and toward the accounting and legal services of the parent firm. These findings discredit the argument that such mergers contribute to the growth of local firms and communities due to the financial resources, management skills, and research and development programs of the acquiring corporations.

At times company towns have had surface glitter. Pullman, Illinois, created by George M. Pullman of the Pullman Palace Car Company, was built in the 1880s as a model town. Mr. Pullman alone invested eight million dollars in apartment buildings, parks, playgrounds, churches, theaters, arcades, casinos, and more. The town won awards at international expositions for its layout and maintenance. But beneath this classy exterior, there was something politically rotten in the town of Pullman. It was rife with fear and suspicion, as company spies probed for tips on "union infiltration" or "dangerous" and "disloyal" employees. This company town showed its true constitution during the crunch of the 1893 depression, when it laid off workers, cut wages 25 percent, but did not reduce rents. After investigating Pullman, economist Richard T. Ely concluded that "the idea of Pullman is un-American. It is a benevolent, well-wishing feudalism, which desires the happiness of the people but in such a way as shall please the authorities."

Pullman has its modern parallels, as some five million Americans live in company towns. While *Time* magazine was lauding Kannapolis, North Carolina, because its dominant company, Cannon Mills, "has given money and land for a number of the town's eighty-four churches, built a golf club for its fourteen thousand employees, and contributed most of the cash for a civic auditorium," local citizens reeled under a barony out of the Middle Ages. Philanthropy here was a small contribution indeed in lieu of greater tax payments. The town of thirty-nine thousand is unincorporated and was subject for decades to the whim of "Mister Cannon," chairman of the board of Cannon Mills, who died in 1971. Until then, he selected and paid the town's twenty-two policemen, he owned the central business district, he controlled the town's only newspaper, his firm dumped four million gallons of industrial waste into the Irish-Buffalo Creek every day, and he opposed incorporation because of the taxes he would have to pay. Did the townspeople want incorporation? Said one, "nobody with mouths to feed is eager to tangle with the guy who owns the grocery store."

Centralia, Missouri, is an extension of the Chance Electric Company and its former chairman, F. Gano Chance (he retired in 1972), whose authoritarian rule insured that dissidents did not flourish there. One unidentified citizen of Centralia, Missouri, his back to the camera, recently described the political tyranny of his company town to an educational television network:

> Mr. X: I realize that any time you have a large factory in a town that the owner of such factory or the one who controls the largest interest in the factory will have great influence, but I am firmly convinced that this is a conspiracy to rule. They control jobs. They control credit. And if they don't control you directly they control your relatives, your son, your daughter. If you're a trustee in a church or have a position of other honor or duty, they will see that

you're relieved of it, if you dare to oppose them. You'll also be attacked in such ways as harrassment by phone calls. These calls usually come in the night. When you answer the phone, no one is there. That is the standard form. Although occasionally the caller will abuse you with vicious and vile and profane language. I know of no one employed by the Company who has ever tried to run for public office against one of the Company-sponsored candidates. All of those who have ... no longer live in Centralia.

The type of dominance and intimidation represented by a town like Pullman still thrives in company towns throughout America—from paper-pulp towns in Maine, to mining towns in the West, and to textile and paper-mill towns in the South. We realize how one-crop economics in underdeveloped countries can lead to political authoritarianism and economic instability; American analysts often lack the same perception of communities in their own country.

Corporate dominance, however, can occur at the state as well as the local level. DuPont in Delaware is the best (but not the only) example of a "company state." The firm employs 11 percent of the state work force and generates 21 percent of the state's gross product. The DuPont family controls the DuPont company through board membership and the Christiana Securities, the family's holding company, which owns the company that publishes the state's two biggest newspapers, the *Morning News* and the *Evening Journal*. The presence of the family and firm in Wilmington is everywhere—from the DuPont Building, housing the company's huge office complex, to the Playhouse, Wilmington's only legitimate theater and owned by DuPont, to the Wilmington Trust Company, Delaware's largest bank and controlled by the DuPonts. In the city-county complex in Wilmington works the county executive, a former DuPont lawyer, and Wilmington's mayor, whose father was a prominent DuPont executive. The state's governor is Pierre S. DuPont IV; another family member is attorney general; DuPont firm or family-connected members comprise a fourth of the state legislature, a third of its committee heads, the president pro tempore of the Senate, and the majority leader of the Delaware

House. Twenty-two of the twenty-six Delaware campaign donations of five hundred dollars or more in 1969 were given by DuPont family members or employees, and all the contributions went to Republicans. Finally, DuPont's twelve-million-dollar annual donation to groups around the state gives the family and firm (called "Uncle Dupie" by Delawarians) added political leverage.

The result of this lockhold? The state legislature has failed to reform the tax system, which favors both the DuPont firm and family due to its extremely low property tax assessments and the lack of any tax on either individually owned or business personal property; in fact, a 1970 state law abolished one of the most progressive aspects left in the Delaware tax system—the treatment of capital gains as ordinary taxable income. When the DuPont-connected Wilmington Medical Center wanted to rezone a few hundred acres of county land from industrial to institutional usage in order to move its facilities, it had little trouble convincing the New Castle County Council—although the rezoning, according to professional planners queried, destroyed the land use balance in the county. Five of the seven members of the Council, including the president, were elder DuPont employees or family. When the county had to choose between general aviation (business and pleasure flying) or commercial aircraft for the expanded Greater Wilmington Airport, it favored wealthy users by increasing general aviation; no public hearings on the issue were ever held.

Dominant local corporations often deploy their political power to pollute without challenge. There is little encouragement to stop polluting when a dominant corporation controls the local authorities who supposedly monitor it. Take, for example, Savannah, Georgia, and its mighty Savannah River. They have become garbage dumps for local industry. American Cyanamid, producing, among other materials, the pigment with which to write the m's on M & M's, pours six million gallons of waste water, including over six hundred thousand pounds of sulphuric acid, into the Savannah every day. The Union Camp Corporation, producing paper bags, dumps *thirty-seven million* gallons of waste water daily. According to two scientists at a local pollution conference, Union Camp has so fouled the air with its kraft pulp emissions that the long-range community effects include:

1. reduced desirability of the community as a place in which to live;
2. reduced attraction to the community for other new industries and commercial enterprises;
3. reduced attraction to hotels, motels, and resorts for the traveling business and touring public;
4. depreciation in property values and rentals in summertime areas;
5. hazard or inconvenience to travelers because of reduced visability . . .

In addition, of course, there is the damage to the health of local residents, an unquantifiable but palpable penalty for local "progress."

Union Camp's response to such criticism is arrogance, the arrogance of power high in the political saddle. The firm refuses to divulge the extent of air pollution particulates it emits per day. The state's Air Quality Control Branch, whose responsibility includes obtaining just this type of information, is discouraged from doing so due to Union Camp's power. But then Georgia's air pollution law itself was drafted by Glen Kimble, the firm's Director of Air and Water Pollution, who proposed it on "behalf of all Georgia industry." It was Kimble who said of the ecological crisis ". . . it probably won't hurt mankind a whole hell of a lot in the long run if the whooping crane doesn't quite make it." When John Lientz, Union Camp manager, was asked about the likelihood that heavy industrial pumping might dry up the Savannah area's underground water supplies, he answered, "I don't know. I won't be here." A study of Savannah, sponsored by the Center for Study of Responsive Law, asked a Union Camp executive vice president whether there were *any* limitations on their depletion of ground water. "I had my lawyers in Virginia research that," he said, "and they told us that we could suck the state of Virginia out through a hole in the ground, and there was nothing anyone could do about it."

Although Union Camp perpetrates an invisible violence on the city of Savannah daily, it remains largely immune to effective local control. Essentially, the city is hostage to the corporation. Union Camp entered Savannah in 1935 during the Depression, for which the firm has exacted *quid pro quos* ever since. Among other concessions, the following were contained in a 1935 contract between the two sovereigns:

> The parties hereto agree to use their best efforts to secure the necessary action and if possible legislation on the part of the governmental bodies concerned, to protect and save you [Union Camp] harm from any claims, demands, or suits for the pollution of air or water caused by the operation of the plant.
> It is agreed in case litigation arises or suits are brought against you on account of odors and/or flowage from the proposed plant that the Industrial Committee of Savannah will pay all expenses of defending such suits up to a total of $5,000....

In return for these concessions, the city is being slowly poisoned by its corporate benefactor. And the city's economy is stagnant since new industry hesitates to enter Union Camp's satrapy due to the already polluted environment, the dwindling water supply, and the dominance of the local labor market. Yet Savannah remains in bondage, intimidated by threats that Union Camp will run away to another city if local restrictions become too severe. But it is an unequal contest, for Savannah cannot run away from Union Camp.

Another example of the corporate "donor" poisoning its municipal donee is the Johns-Manville plant in Manville, New Jersey. The plant employs 40 percent of Manville's employees; its payroll accounts for 60 percent of the town's total income. It pays more than half the taxes and has made gifts to hospitals, schools, and recreational facilities. But all is not well in this small industrial town. "People are dying in Manville "of diseases virtually unknown elsewhere" wrote Philip Greer in the *Washington Post*, "and at rates several times the national norms. They are dying, medical experts agree, because they work in the biggest asbestos processing plant in the world." Johns-Manville claims it is doing all it can to reduce the dust levels which lead to disease. Any more costly improvements, the firm warns critics, could lead to plant shutdowns instead.

There are other examples of such Faustian relationships, where a locale looks to a firm or investment to resuscitate its economy—only to find unintended side effects. Union Carbide in Anmoore, West Virginia, U.S. Steel in Gary, Indiana, Anaconda in Butte, Montana—in each place, the town tolerates its own poisoning since it perceives itself to be in hock to the dominant corporation. But such self-destructing obedience is not inevitable. Between 1968 and 1971, the American Smelting and Refining Company dumped eleven hundred tons of lead from its towering 828-foot-high smokestack onto neighboring El Paso, Texas. Of 416 children tested by town and firm doctors, 102 had dangerously high lead levels and 25 of the children spent a week or more in hospitals for treatment or observation. El Paso and the Texas Air Quality Board filed suit against ASARCO in early 1972 for its failure to meet air quality standards and its consequent damage to El Paso residents. As a result of a May 1972 judgment, ASARCO agreed to pay fines of $80,500 for eighty-eight specific pollution violations, post $30,000 with the court for any future violations, install $750,000 of additional emission control equipment, and, in a remedy tailored to fit the offense, agreed to pay all the medical expenses for at least thirty months of the 134 children being treated.

In terms of corporate giving to local causes, corporate gifts in 1968 totaled 912 million dollars or some 6 percent of all philanthropy in the country. Yet even these gifts amount to only about 1 percent of pretax profits, well below both the Internal Revenue Code's permissible charitable deduction of 5 percent and the average individual taxpayer's contribution of 2.5 percent of adjusted income. But however one views the current level of corporate giving, "the concentration of a large proportion of the wealth of [the] community in the hands of business corporations has made corporate gifts essential if charities are to be privately financed," according to the basic law text on corporations. For example, DuPont firm and family gifts in Delaware have become "essential" there. As already mentioned in passing, the family's thirty-six foundations in the state, with assets of more than four hundred million dollars, give away over twelve million dollars a year in Delaware; this is almost as much as the city of Wilmington and the county of New Castle each spend for local government functions.

Clearly this infusion of private funds leads to some community benefits. And equally clearly, there are benefits to the donors: gifts can reduce federal, state, and local estate taxes, thereby limiting public revenue; the donor may retain control over the disbursement of funds; the firm reaps invaluable publicity over its community concern; corporate policies can be indirectly promoted.

But there are costs of dependency, and the more dominant the firm, the more dependent the community. "Dependency on DuPont foundations take two major forms," assert James Phelan and Robert Pozen, authors of *The Company State*; "some private groups change their programs to suit the needs of a DuPont family member and some governmental bodies come to rely on foundations to perform public functions." Private groups can become supplicants to corporate largesse, trying to get a DuPont family member on their boards of Directors, currying favor with foundation decision-makers, fearing the effects of corporate retaliation on controversial programs. Donations are made by a corporate elite without standards of checks or community involvement. With one funding source dominating private donations, citizen initiative is discouraged and the diversity of possible citizen projects limited.

DuPont, therefore, represents the problem of the dominant local firm contributor. Its philanthropic monopoly encourages civic dependence and its donations can be an unspoken *quid pro quo* for property tax and other regulatory leniency. Thus, a firm can take more out of a community through tax underpayment than it returns, although publicity over its generosity convinces communities they are net beneficiaries.

But what about the reverse problem, the paucity of business giving? Communities can also suffer if the corporate donations they have come to expect suddenly decline. And corporate giving can in fact decline when a local operation is acquired by an outsider. "Every time a company changes hands, we worry," says Robert F. Cahill, campaign director of the Golden Rule Fund of Worcester, Massachusetts. "Experience has taught us that it wouldn't be surprising if we were to suffer a sharp cut in the company's corporate gift, even if employee giving is not affected." A study of the effect of mergers on Rochester, New York, showed a drop in postmerger corporate contributions; "it was clear that these absentee-owned firms lagged behind the locally owned firms in response to rising community needs."

Professor William Shepherd has shown, contrary to conventional assumptions, that competitive industries are less racially discriminatory than non-competitive ones. When a few large firms have the power to discriminate, they do so; competitive firms, compelled to hire the best employees, are more colorblind. (For example, until recently prodded into more affirmative action, General Motors had a dismal record on black dealerships, managers, or directors.) So too in local communities. If dominant corporations are indifferent to minorities, the ethos of the community will reflect this attitude.

—Dearborn, Michigan, is essentially a fiefdom of the Ford Motor Company. Ford is the city's major employer and pays one-half of its taxes. Ford's River Rouge plant, the largest factory in the world, is there; so are the company's headquarters. But while Ford identifies itself with neighboring Detroit—getting favorable publicity as a leader of Detroit's renaissance and redevelopment movement—it underplays its role in Dearborn. There, Mayor Orville Hubbard has ruled for thirty years as an avowed racist; there are thirteen blacks, mostly domestics, out of a population of over one hundred thousand. ("Lincoln was ready to ship them back to where they came from. Now Mrs. Nixon is in Ghana courting them," he complained in 1971.) Recently, Ford built its Fairlane Project in Central Dearborn, where houses sell for between twenty-eight thousand dollars and forty thousand dollars. Michigan groups trying to persuade Ford to include low-income housing in the development were told by a Ford official of an exchange of letters between Mayor Hubbard and Ford officials agreeing to keep the price tag high in order to keep out "undesirables."

—Big local banks can often set a racial investment pattern. When they show reluctance to advance mortgage money to black areas of a community, they can initiate that section's physical decline. The same syndrome occurs when insurance companies "redline" a geographic area—often black—and then refuse to extend insurance there. In both cases white citizens then realize that the influx of blacks into their neighborhoods would depreciate the value of their homes and property. They behave accordingly.

Control of local banks by corporate cliques has repercussions beyond the racial. The small inventor, the maverick entrepreneur, the politically unpopular enterpriser all would benefit from a diversity of funding sources since it increases the likelihood that someone would risk advancing them money. And the community benefits in turn from the funding of innovative and diverse initiatives. But with centralization comes conservatism, as dominant banks shun risky ventures in favor of servicing their corporate clientele. Wilmington Trust, a DuPont-dominated bank, invests heavily in corporate and government bonds rather than local loans. While the value of these securities was a staggering 60 percent of the loans outstanding for Wilmington Trust in 1969, it was 42 percent for the U.S. Trust Company of New York, 23 percent for the Philadelphia National Bank, and 26 percent at the Girard Trust Company of Philadelphia.

Large corporate interests can tie up local funds in other ways. They often keep large amounts in demand deposits for their special needs; thus, Lammot duPont, Jr. had 2.5 million dollars in his Wilmington Trust checking account and Irence DuPont, Sr. had up to eight million dollars deposited in four cash accounts at Wilmington Trust in 1964. Banks must keep much cash on hand to meet big depositor demands for ready access. Wilmington Trust, therefore, retains from 10-15 percent more of its assets in cash and its equivalents than do other Delaware banks. This amounts to some 66.8 million dollars, a huge loss of potential investment for the local economy. Inherited wealth passed on for generations can also freeze large amounts of capital. Frequent turnover and reinvestment of funds, on the other hand, is necessary for a vigorous local economy.

Again, the problems of absentee-controlled firms differ in form, but not effect, from situations of local corporate dominance. The Rochester study previously mentioned concluded that merged companies no longer banked as much locally; big city banks prospered at their expense.

The Wisconsin study of outsider acquisitions estimated that 70 percent of the acquired firms shifted to the financial institutions of the parent corporation. The Gulf & Western conglomerate has a specific policy of insisting that local firms it acquires transfer their banking business from local banks to the Chase Manhatten Bank in New York City. Or take Teledyne's acquisition of the Monarch Rubber Company of Hartville, Ohio. An official of the First National City Bank of New York City went to Hartville to make an appeal for the company's deposits. When he later called New York he was told, "Forget it. Teledyne just picked them up and we'll get the deposits." They did—and the First National Bank of Canton lost most of Monarch's deposits, and the Harder Bank and Trust Company lost Monarch's two-and-a-half-million-dollar pension fund. As a top official of one Connecticut bank said, "As soon as a national company picks up some local outfit, the money just shoots down to New York."

But it is cities just like Canton, Ohio (1970 population 108–872, down from 113,631 in 1960) which need local investment from local banks. From community capital investment to the residential home mortgage market, available loan money is like a blood bank to a patient. Without infusions when necessary, it can die. Thus can "banking practices operate like a regressive tax, funneling the money of communities with declining economics to those with brighter economic prospects."

That communities can be harmed *either* when absentee-owned corporations ignore community interests *or* when local corporations dominate community affairs is not a contradiction. Each damages the polity in its way, albeit in different ways. Common to both, however, is an underlying causation: corporate sway over a community is bad whether exercised or not. Like sleeping with an elephant, every thrashing, grunt, or inaction cannot but have major consequence on its bedmate.

Still, problems of local corporate dominance seem like benefits to many communities: a local hospital is built (which corporate employees use); government contracts for housing or job training are negotiated (permitting diversification and ample profits); a cultural center is constructed (attracting top executives and unbuyable publicity); corporations give money away to local groups and foundations (controlling public policy along the way, and tax deductible as well); research and development centers are promoted (attracting students and contracts). Should corporations police the streets, educate the young, rebuild the slums? Some think that if corporations perform such functions, it is free. But there is no such thing as free corporate benevolence. We gave away the airwaves to corporations expecting free television but paid for it via higher priced advertised products and other costs; towns invite corporations in to enhance their tax base and economy, only to find themselves being taxed by corporate pollution and added service burdens. Our largest cities are collapsing right alongside prosperous corporations, whose officials thrive from the city but live in the suburbs. Ultimately, then, the company's contributions accrue to the company's benefit, often in conflict with community benefit; and ultimately, a community's political, social, and economic structures can wither under the pressure of daily dependency.

Yet the problem of the elephantine corporation in the community remains. While it is conceptually satisfying to urge that corporations concern themselves with economic markets while national, state, and local governments concern themselves with community needs, this conclusion alone will not do. For the market model will not soon work in Kannapolis, St. Marys, Centralia, or Delaware. Many corporations should not have such power over locales, but so long as they do, they must realize their special obligations as leading citizens. They must not abuse their unique sway to exploit the population and to discourage self-rule. Taken alone, this sentiment is inadequate to checkmate corporate depredations. But it does appropriately note that at some basic, noneconomic, nonlegal level, the issue becomes a moral one.

A plant closing is never painless, but its ill effects can be alleviated by an early announcement and vigorous efforts to relocate and retain the laid-off workers—as American Oil did in El Dorado, Arkansas, when it moved away. After a Swedish paper mill reduced the most obnoxious of its kraft mill pollution, its manager inexplicably spent a few hundred thousand dollars more to get rid of the nauseating odor; admitting there were no specific economic returns, he said that "it would attract people to the mill and the community." DuPont refusing to go along with a voluntary open housing ordinance, Ford not building low-income units in its new Dearborn complex, U.S. Steel abstaining on the issue of integration in its Birmingham mills in the early 1960s—in each case seeming neutrality, given the dominant position of the firm involved, had the effect of underwriting antisocial patterns. Yet even within market parameters, it is not impossible to be a good corporate citizen.

But this is more a plea than a proposal. Specific government mandates are needed to continue the fight against industrial pollution, to assure racial freedom, to encourage local investment, and to reduce corporate economic and political power. As for the corporation-community dilemma, beyond stressing the moral component of a dominant corporation's obligation to the community, a number of external rules could be attempted. If antitrust enforcement were more vigorous against conglomerate mergers—the Nixon Administration settled their anti-conglomerate cases before the Supreme Court could set precedent in this area—the extent of absentee control over communities would decline. Rather than wait for some future administration to take the plunge, new legislation should forbid any firm with over two hundred and fifty million dollars in assets from acquiring any other firm unless it spins off an equal amount of assets. This would arrest the trend toward increasing absentee ownership while permitting mergers motivated by real efficiencies rather than stock market manipulation or managerial empire-building.

Ultimately, however, reform of interstate and international corporations must occur at the federal level, where the jurisdiction equals the problem. That is why only a Corporate Democracy Act, described subsequently, can begin to make large corporations better citizens of their respective communities.

Hucksters in the Classroom—
A Review of Industry Propaganda in Schools

by Sheila Harty

In 1972, principals at 62,000 elementary schools around the country were sent a booklet by General Motors entitled "Professor Clean Asks . . . What is Air Pollution?" This booklet was designed to counteract what pollsters said were children's "negative" attitudes toward auto companies. In response to subsequent requests, General Motors estimates that 2.1 million copies of their air pollution comic were distributed to 8,000 schools in the 1972-73 academic year.

Throughout the booklet the cartoon characters "Charlie Carbon Monoxide" and "Harry Hydrocarbon" dispel any fear of the serious health hazards of air pollution. Professor Clean assures students that air pollution will "no longer be a problem" with the "addition of new devices in the near future"—devices to meet government emission standards which the auto industry has resisted.

With recent curricula innovations such as environmental science and consumer economics, corporations have stepped up production of supplementary classroom materials where standard texts and school budgets have failed to meet curricula needs. According to Educational Products Information Exchange in New York City, only 1% of school budgets is spent on instructional materials, although more than 90% of classroom time is spent using those materials. Requisitions for teaching aids must compete against salary demands and high maintenance overhead. On cue, industry has picked up the tab.

If sponsored materials are to meet the needs of the classroom teacher, should advertising be allowed as a return on the sponsors' investment? What minimum standards exist to restrain brand name or product promotion in sponsored teaching materials? Are any professional or administrative agencies helping teachers assess promotional bias in complex, controversial subjects?

A recent survey reveals that 64% of *Fortune*'s 500 industrials, 90% of major trade associations, and 90% of electric utilities send "informational" materials in response to teachers' requests. Of those materials sent, 29% of *Fortune*'s 500, 47% of the trade associations, and 53% of the utilities design their materials specifically for students' use—with full classroom sets, graded K-12, mimeograph stencils and teachers' guides included. And teachers are often willing buyers. With an overloaded class schedule in addition to administrative obligations, teachers have an overwhelming job. In this context, corporations with free multi-media can be successfully seductive. In a 1977 membership survey, the National Education Association found that 50% of the teachers responding admitted using industry materials, increasing that use slightly with their age and years on the job.

Certainly the problem of financing education and the budget constaints on curricula materials needs re-evaluation. But drawing on private monies to underwrite these materials should be considered contrary to the structure and principles of our tax-supported schools. Curricula materials, like teachers' salaries, should come from public monies. In their own defense, industry insists on the viability of "their point of view" as legitimate subject matter for a truly relevant curricula. The result: students in one elementary school actually spelled "relief", r-o-l-a-i-d-s.

Efforts in economic education by major corporate sponsors received their impetus in 1972 from the Powell Memorandum. Named after its author, now Supreme Court Justice Lewis F. Powell, this lengthy memorandum was written to the Education Chairman of the U.S. Chamber of Commerce. Entitled "Attack on the American Free Enterprise System," it exhorts the business community to defend itself against anti-profit sentiments from the Left, the Naders, and others who would "fatally weaken or destroy the system." The unpopularity of business is attributed to the public's ignorance of economics and the free enterprise system. Consequently, business members are encouraged to 1) evaluate textbooks; 2) get on school boards; 3) set up Speakers Bureaus; 4) produce economics education materials; and 5) establish faculty positions of private enterprise at universities. We have seen all of this occur.

But economic education efforts from corporations fail to address reasons for government intervention, such as welfare or the reduction of pollution; or to present differences from the classical system, such as oligopolies; or to discuss defects in the system, such as occupational disease, injury and price fixing; or alternative forms of organizing economic power, such as cooperatives and federal chartering of corporations. What is presented instead is what is consistent with existing market control.

Over 20 states now require some curriculum offerings in economics as a result of lobbying by business groups. But funds have not been adequately appropriated to finance this. Thus, business interests have assumed the task. Although individual companies and trade groups produce their own teaching materials in economics for the schools, those from the U.S. Chamber of Commerce appear to be the dominant influence.

The Chamber's two part audio-visual kit, entitled *Economics for Young Americans* (with two more segments planned), contains filmstrips, tapes, scripts, and teacher's guides, plus mimeo stencils. Rather than publicize these materials to the schools, the Chamber personalizes the process by contacting a local business to underwrite the purchase and distribute the kit personally. Thus, each economics program is assured a business person in the classroom for these initial contacts. The pressure of personality and community relations work their effects.

An issue arises whether or not these materials constitute grass roots lobbying—advertising to promote or defeat legislation—which, unlike product and image advertising, is not tax deductible. In sections of the Chamber's materials, students are advised specifically to "let your Senators and Congressmen and your state legislators know . . . you want FEWER GOVERNMENT SPENDING PROGRAMS," and, ". . . to OPPOSE legislation that increases the tax burden on business."

Although the Chamber is tax-exempt, contributions from taxable dues-paying members may deserve scrutiny, as well as the purchase of Chamber materials by individual corporations for distribution to the schools. That school children don't vote does not invalidate a charge of grass roots lobbying. Children are a segment of the general public for purposes of advertising and propaganda. Promotional efforts in the schools also affect teachers, administrators, and eventually parents as these discussions make their way to the dinner table.

Beyond ideological complaints, corporate-sponsored economic education efforts which are legitimately tax deductible may not be economically wise. When propagandistic efforts are launched without critical appraisal or counterbalance, they may not be used. In 1969, the Joint Council on Economic Education sponsored an evaluation of economic education materials from special interest groups. A committee of scholars found that only 40% of the 5,000 items examined were usable in the schools.

More than any industry group, the electric utilities provide extensive multi-media materials for classroom use. These education efforts notably target the elementary grades through the use of films, comic books, and entertaining assembly programs. This emphasis on the lower grades seems aimed at cultivating a future constituency in support of the electric power industry in general and nuclear power in particular.

Discussions on the economics, health, and safety issues relating to energy sources open up both science and social studies classes to instruction by the utilities. Yet the lack of candor on the economics of nuclear plant construction, decommissioning, the insurance availability, on the health effects of low level radiation on atomic workers and the public, as well as on the failure in safety standards and regulatory oversight, have certainly undermined the utilities' credibility.

A booklet from Westinghouse Electric Corporation, one of the major manufacturers of nuclear power systems, reveals the deceptive phrasing of "educational" materials motivated by public relations. Entitled *For A Mature Audience Only*, this booklet presents the safety, economics, and efficiency of nuclear power in elementary level graphics and phrasing. Under the heading, "Nuclear Energy is SAFE," we read:

No one has ever been injured or killed in a nuclear-related accident in any commercial nuclear power plant.

The catch phrases are "nuclear-related" and "commercial." There have been accidents from fire, mechanical failure, and human error which resulted in injury and death in Army-operated plants, weapons facilities, and experimental reactors. A similar catalog of contrary evidence could be made against the Westinghouse disclaimer "Nuclear Energy is ECONOMICAL."

Comic books are the most popular format for these messages. Some comics are publicized through order blanks sent with the monthly electric bills. Others come with a full color film and still others with reading tests and a teacher's copy with answers marked.

Comic books featuring Reddy Kilowatt, the registered trademark of the electric power industry, have been distributed to school system for years. This practice is growing more prevalent, especially in localities where a nuclear plant is planned. School-wide assembly programs frequently follow such campaigns making the message all the more palatable. As a private corporation serving a public purpose, utilities enjoy unquestioned access to schools, whereas a strictly private enterprise would be more thoroughly screened for promotional motives.

The question arises whether consumers should pay for the cost of educational efforts by local utilities through their monthly electric bills. Many state regulatory authorities have recently disallowed this kind of institutional advertising on ratepayers' accounts, such as the rate case settlement in 1972 against Consumers Power Company of Michigan. The state Public Service Commission agreed with the Attorney General that educational campaigns and goodwill advertising are more appropriately borne by stockholders. Oversight, however, is not always possible and some local utilities continue the practice.

Dr. Jean Mayer, noted nutritionist, suggests that the nutritional value of a food product varies inversely with the amount spent to advertise it. Yet most of the nutritional information provided to the schools comes from major food manufacturers who are of course major advertisers. Even though six of the ten leading causes of death in the United States are linked to our diet, these industry-sponsored materials promote foods contrary to the *Dietary Goals of the United States*—guidelines issued from the Senate Select Committee on Nutrition and Human Needs.

The National Dairy Council, for example, neglects to mention the detrimental effects from consuming high-fat dairy products and has opposed fat labeling. Indicative of such institutional disregard for health is the fact that in most states the price farmers receive for their milk is based primarily on its butterfat content. If, on the other hand, the consumption of low fat products was encouraged, the rate of coronary heart disease might decline.

Most food manufacturers address nutrition education through the "Four Food Groups" motif. From this perspective, any food product can be promoted as "part" of a balanced meal. The Kellogg Company describes the Dairy Group as "cereal with milk." Since milk is not the only component of the Dairy Group and cereal is a member of the Bread Group, this presentation is not only self-serving but confusing. The Four Food Groups approach to nutrition also fails to address the detrimental effects on sugar, salt, and additives in our highly processed foods. In addition, industry materials teach a "convenience mentality." Instead of learning to cook from scratch, home economics students learn to cook from cans. The basic white sauce in the casserole, for example, is replaced by Campbell's cheddar cheese soup.

Manufacturers also attempt to manipulate consumer buying habits by sponsoring school-wide collection drives. Campbell Soups, Post Cereals, Kool Aid, and Trident Gum offer "free" athletic and audio-visual equipment in exchange for a quota of labels gathered by students throughout their communities. The seduction of these promotional drives is aimed at the financial benefit for the school's budget; yet no one has determined how much the students have contributed to the companies in consequent sales.

The McDonald Corporation and Standard Brands (Planters Peanut products) have out-stretched others in providing teachers with booklets not only on Nutrition, but also on Ecology and Physical Education. McDonald's has an *Action Pack* on Economics as well. The *Mr. Peanut Guides* manage to mention peanuts here and there, ending with a page illustrating all Planters Peanut products. The mimeograph stencils which comprise McDonald's *Action Packs* include their "golden arches" trademark at the bottom.

Despite their long-standing policy of not directing advertising to children under 12, the Coca Cola Company responds to elementary teachers' requests for classroom materials by sending booklets on the history of the company with illustrations of its product. The company calls this "product information." However, it omits any mention, of the existence or effects, of caffeine in cola drinks—as does classroom material on coffee, tea, and chocolate from their respective companies. Such sins of omission are not mentioned to encourage unrealistic disclosures from profit-seeking corporations, but to prove that such sponsors cannot be considered reliable sources of educational material.

Finally the lack of extensive and effective standards within industry leaves corporate sponsored educational materials open to abuse. The lack of administrative guidelines or review procedures by federal, state or local educational authorities defers responsibility for evaluation to the classroom teacher—who already has too much to do.

Industry-education partnerships, disclosure labeling, debate formats, authorship or evaluation by educators, field testing, and other reforms are only concessions to an essentially unfair trade practice directed to a captive audience of minors. Corporate management should consider whether classroom materials prepared by such biased interests are in themselves inappropriate. The commercial exploitation of the curricula is reprehensible precisely because there is something for sale. The education of children should involve the delivery of ideas to students and not the delivery of students to markets.

Corporations and State Taxes: The Big Ones Get Away

by James Rosapepe

To the average taxpayer, battered for years with reports of tax dodging by the nation's biggest corporations and richest families, new revelations of tax avoidance by big interests tend to lack shock value. Nelson Rockefeller didn't pay a penny in federal income taxes in 1970. So what else is new?

But even the most cynical of us may be surprised by the estimate by some of the nation's top state tax officials that perhaps half the tax money legally owed state governments by the big corporations goes uncollected every year. "Avoidance of state tax liabilities by America's largest corporations has reached scandalous proportions," says Byron Dorgan, North Dakota's 32-year-old state tax commissioner. Lost revenue totals "hundreds of millions and perhaps billions of dollars," Dorgan estimates, and it is the result not of the legal forms of tax "avoidance" so characteristic of loophole-ridden state corporate tax laws, but of good old-fashioned, illegal, tax evasion. The reason they get away with it is simple: most states can't enforce the tax laws.

When Virginia changed its tax laws in 1972 from "straight line" depreciation to the much more generous "accelerated" depreciation allowed under federal law, state tax officials were surprised to find that most companies were not saving any money as a result of the change. After some inquiries, the officials discovered why: the companies had been using the "accelerated" depreciation schedules for years, in clear violation of Virginia law. But as the state's Deputy Tax Commissioner, Stuart Connock, explains, "The Department never checked, and the companies sure didn't volunteer the information."

A similar situation prevails in Illinois, which collected almost $235 million in corporate taxes in 1972. State Revenue Department official Harry Spellman told the *Chicago Tribune* last year that "if we spent $2 million [to improve the system], we could recover $50 million more." If the scale of evasion prevalent in Illinois is typical of that in the rest of the nation—and there is no reason to think it is not—non-payment of corporate taxes probably costs the 50 states over $700 million a year.

Corporate income taxes are not the only state taxes evaded on a large scale by businesses. For example, Albert Stoessel, former president of the Iowa Petroleum Association, estimates his state loses $50 million a year in uncollected diesel fuel taxes—a particularly hard area to enforce, since diesel fuel is chemically similar to non-taxed home heating fuel. Sales taxes are another area of undoubted abuse. Bill Brown of the Committee on State Taxation, a big-business group known as COST, claims, "There's a lot more sales tax revenue that they are not collecting than they have any idea. I say that on the basis of what the companies tell us in confidence." Illinois officials say they are losing around $25 million in cigarette tax revenue alone, and they won't even guess about total sales tax losses.

According to a 1974 report by New York State Comptroller Arthur Levitt, the state has been losing millions of dollars because the tax department has never collected from some 31,000 employers who have failed to turn over state taxes withheld from their employees' paychecks.

Over the last few years several states have toughened up their enforcement efforts. Their experience demonstrates that massive corporate tax evasion is no myth—and that it is surprisingly easy to control.

Until 1973, Virginia had never sent its auditors to out-of-state corporate headquarters to check corporate tax returns. In the first year it started doing so, the state collected more than $1 million from 54 of the 6,000 multistate corporations doing business in Virginia. "In a lot of cases it was just a matter of dropping by the corporate offices to pick up the check," one Virginia tax official said. "They knew they owed us the money, but we'd never asked for it before." Fifty-four down, only 5,946 to go.

In North Dakota, Commissioner Dorgan's aggressive enforcement efforts increased the state's corporate tax receipts by nearly 30 percent in two years. Since 1969 an average of 20 per cent of this revenue has been collected from audits, and Dorgan thinks he's just scratched the surface. Idaho, too, has collected 20 per cent of its recent corporate tax revenues through auditing, and the state's Chief Corporation Auditor, Frank L. Medlin, says improved enforcement efforts will soon yield even more "sizable tax recoveries."

But the best illustration of what a good auditor's division can do is in California. The state's Franchise Tax Board has 240 corporate auditors who collected an extra $51 million in 1972, including $35.8 million from field audits of 6,026 multistate corporations. To these substantial savings must be added the millions of dollars businesses paid voluntarily, aware that they were likely to be audited. Admitting in a *Wall Street Journal* interview that California has the toughest corporate tax enforcement around, U.S. Steel's Director, Arthur Hauser, said, "If we could get out of there, we would save a lot of money."

The most obvious difference between California's enforcement program and those in other states is its extensive network of trained auditors. In addition to its in-state staff, California has 200 field auditors located throughout the country, including those permanently based in offices in New York and Chicago. Idaho, by way of comparison, has six corporate auditors, all operating out of Boise. Even when the difference in the two states' population is taken into account, California clearly is devoting a greater effort to its program. You don't have to be a Wall Street tax lawyer to figure out which state ITT or GM is more likely to try to bilk at tax time.

Most other states resemble Idaho rather than California. Kentucky has 45 field auditors, who are responsible for auditing sales and personal income as well as corporate taxes, Vermont has 12. The deficiencies in Missouri's auditing operation are so great that U.S. District Court Judge William R. Collinson declared in a recent decision that "the enforcement of the tax laws in this state is notoriously lax and slipshod, apparently because the legislature will not appropriate the money to employ sufficient persons to even begin to adequately police the system."

"One of the facts of life is that most states are limited in resources," confesses Eugene Corrigan, executive director of the Multistate Tax Commission, a joint agency of

MTC is that it treats foreign source and dividend income just like any other income and requires conglomerates and multinationals to be taxed as a complete unit, the way the corner drugstore is. The ins and outs of this are too complicated to explain briefly, but enough money is at stake that the companies have mobilized for a real fight in Congress.

COST's major efforts in this session of Congress have been on behalf of S. 1245 (sponsored by liberal Senators Charles Mathias and Abraham Ribicoff). The key provision of S. 1245 would, in most cases, bar the states from taxing profits from foreign sources and dividends from corporate subsidiaries. Thus, by excluding foreign profits and other dividends, S. 1245 limits the taxable income of multinationals, like the oil companies, and of conglomerates with far-flung subsidiaries like ITT. Brown of COST points out that only two or three states, among them California, now tax these dividends, and he stresses that S. 1245 would guarantee "uniformity" by getting these states, as well as the MTC, in line.

Byron Dorgan denounces S. 1245 as "a massive tax giveaway program for the largest corporations," and so far he and his colleagues at the MTC have managed to keep the bill bottled up in the Senate Finance Committee.

But the fight continues at the state level as the big corporations try to undermine the MTC and its joint audit efforts. Earlier this year, when Missouri Revenue Director James Spradling asked the state legislature for permission to join the Commission's joint audit program, large corporate interests, including the Missouri Oil Council, led the opposition. In Indiana, the State Chamber of Commerce has announced that "efforts to end Indiana's participation in the Multistate Tax Compact" is one of its top lobbying priorities in the 1975 legislative session.

Given the widespread political popularity of taxing giant corporations, it is somewhat surprising that Dorgan is just about the only state official who has attempted to focus public attention on corporate tax evasion. One reason may be that he is the only elected tax commissioner in the nation. While California's corporate tax laws are supervised by the Franchise Tax Board, which is made up of two elected officials and one appointee, its chief administrative

21 state governments. "They just can't afford the major operation of auditing a giant corporation." Corrigan points out that it's the multistate, and often multinational, corporations with dozens of subsidiaries that are the source of most state enforcement problems.

"We don't have the resources or personnel to go to New York and audit the tax books of U.S. Steel, for example," admits Missouri's state revenue director, James R. Spradling. "It takes highly knowledgeable, highly trained people to audit giant companies like that," adds Corrigan, "and most states just don't have them."

To solve that problem, the Multi-state Tax Commission (MTC) was set up in 1967 to audit firms which operate nationwide. "These big corporations are not above telling different stories to each state—telling Illinois for example that certain income was produced in Indiana and telling Indiana the income came from Illinois," Corrigan explains. "What we are trying to do is joint audits for several states so a company can't do that." In the first nine months of the Commission's joint audit program, it recovered $2.5 million for the states from just ten corporations.

Meanwhile, the same corporations are prowling the halls of Congress, attempting to short circuit the MTC through federal legislation. Coordinating the fight is the pro-business COST, whose members include a number of the companies that are suing the MTC in court.

The principle which underlies the companies' various efforts, as explained by Bill Brown of COST, is as follows: "It's not a case of the states verses business, at all. Our view is simply within the law." Brown claims that corporate executives in his group do not object to joint audits in principle; rather "our members are concerned about the rules and regulations on auditing adopted by the MTC." While corporate spokesmen prefer to characterize their dispute with the MTC as "technical," Brown admits "the biggest problem is dividend and foreign source income."

This matter of "foreign" income is a complicated question, near the heart of the states' tax problems. Most states determine a multistate corporation's tax liability by calculating the firm's nationwide profits and then applying the state corporate tax rate to the state's proportional share of those profits. The big corporations' major objection to the

officer is appointed. And in the great majority of the other states, the position of tax director is appointive, similar to the Commissioner of the Internal Revenue Service at the federal level.

Like so many appointed officials at any level of government, many state tax directors tend to see as their constituency not the public but the big corporations they are supposed to audit. Or they may develop incestuous personal and professional relationships with the companies. Illinois Revenue Director Robert Allphin is on leave from his regular job as tax manager of Pittsburgh Plate Glass. Paul Dillingham started out with the Kentucky Revenue Department and now manages Coca Cola's tax business as a corporate vice president, while Arizona State Tax Commission Chairman John Hazelett previously handled state tax matters for an aircraft firm. A familiar story, but it helps explain why state tax officials are not beating down the doors of the daily press with exposés about corporate tax evasion.

This particular case of governmental surrender to corporate pressure would be discouraging if the solution were not so obvious: auditors, auditors, and more auditors. Experience in dozens of states shows that when the corporations are audited, they pay more taxes; when they are not audited, they pay less. For example, of the 13,736 corporations that California field audited in 1972, 44 per cent owed the state more money and only five per cent had been overtaxed.

Indeed, for a governor or state legislature trying to balance the state's budget, tax auditing is one of the few areas in which the state can save money by expanding the payroll. State auditing of large, multistate corporations normally returns to the states anywhere from $5 to $10 for each dollar spent on auditing. In its first year of corporate field audits, Virginia was earning a return of 12 to 1. Obviously the ratio will decrease as the state moves from detecting the most obvious evasion to more sophisticated and complex cases. But even California, with its highly developed audit operation, still produces nearly $9 in new revenue for every dollar spent on corporate field audits.

For years the federal government has known that the

best way to insure voluntary compliance with income tax laws is to have a staff of auditors ready to catch reluctant taxpayers. It's time for the states to apply the same principle to the corporations.